The least
you need to know
about
Windows 3.1

About the author

Steve Eckols has a Masters degree in Educational Technology and specializes in training and performance tools. He is also the author of ten books on mainframe computer subjects. To develop this book, Steve combined his educational and technical talents in a way that we think has led to something special.

About the cover

Luther Bertando is the creator of the photographic drawing on the cover. Although photography is the medium, he does a drawing like this in total darkness using light pens. As a result, he sees the resulting image for the first time only after he develops the film. He has developed this creative process during the last 12 years, although he continues to make his living as a computer programmer.

The least you need to know about Windows 3.1

Steve Eckols

Mike Murach & Associates
4697 West Jacquelyn Avenue, Fresno, California 93722-6427
(209) 275-3335

Production Team   Managing editor: Mike Murach
Editor: Cris Allen
Graphics designer: Steve Ehlers

Other books for *Windows* users

The Essential Guide to Lotus 1-2-3 for Windows, Release 4, by Anne Prince and Michael Farino

Books for DOS users

The Least You Need to Know About DOS, Second Edition, by Doug Lowe
The Only DOS Book You'll Ever Need, Second Edition, by Doug Lowe
The Least You Need to Know About Lotus 1-2-3 by Patrick Bultema
The Practical Guide to Lotus 1-2-3 by Patrick Bultema
The Least You Need to Know About WordPerfect 5.0 and 5.1 by Joel Murach
The Essential Guide to WordPerfect 6.0 by Joel Murach and Tom Murach

10 9 8 7 6 5 4 3 2 1

ISBN: 0-911625-74-7

Library of Congress Cataloging-in-Publication Data

Eckols, Steve.
  The least you need to know about Windows 3.1 / Steve Eckols.
    p. cm.
  Includes index.
  ISBN: 0-911625-74-7 (paper alkaline)
  1. Windows (Computer programs) 2. Microsoft Windows (Computer
file) I. Title.
QA76.76.W56E25 1993
005.4'3--dc20   93-28014
                                                           CIP

Contents

Preface   VI

Section 1   **PC concepts and terms for every *Windows* User**   1

      Chapter 1   Hardware concepts and terms for every *Windows* user   2

      Chapter 2   Software concepts and terms for every *Windows* user   16

Section 2   **A complete course in *Windows* in just a few hours**   33

      Chapter 3   How to use *Windows* and its Program Manager   34

      Chapter 4   How to use the standard features of *Windows* programs   90

      Chapter 5   How to use the File Manager to manage directories and files   132

Section 3   **Other essential *Windows* skills**   169

      Chapter 6   How to get the most from the Program Manager   170

      Chapter 7   How to get the most from the File Manager   194

      Chapter 8   How to work with printers and fonts   228

      Chapter 9   How to use the Control Panel to customize *Windows*   246

      Chapter 10 How to run your DOS programs under *Windows*   258

Section 4   **Additional perspective**   285

      Chapter 11 A survey of the other programs that come with *Windows*   286

      Chapter 12 Object Linking and Embedding   312

Fast reference   Keyboard alternatives and shortcuts   324

Index   329

Preface

Do you match one of these descriptions?

• Your department or company is upgrading from DOS to *Windows* so you're forced to convert to *Windows*. Unfortunately, you're extremely short on time so you want convert to *Windows* and regain your old levels of productivity as quickly as possible.

• You've just bought a new PC, and it came with *Windows* installed on it. Although you're not sure that you want to use *Windows*, you want to at least find out what it can do for you because you've heard so much about it.

• You want to use a high-powered program like a modern graphics or spreadsheet program, but all of the programs that meet your requirements are *Windows* programs. Although you don't really want to convert to *Windows*, you have to if you want to use the new application program.

• You've been using a Macintosh computer for years, but you've just joined a company that uses PCs and *Windows*. Although the graphical user interface is similar to what you've used on the Mac, you still haven't figured out how to do some basic functions that you could do with ease on the Mac.

These are descriptions of just a few of the people that this book is designed for. In short, if you need to learn *Windows*, this book is for you.

What this book does

If you look back at the table of contents, you can see that this book is divided into the four sections that are summarized in figure P-1. Sections 2 and 3 are the critical sections, while sections 1 and 4 provide additional information that will be useful to many readers.

The two chapters in section 1 present the hardware and software concepts and terms that you need to be familiar with before you start using *Windows*. If you've been using PCs and DOS for years, you probably don't need to read this section. But if you're relatively new to PCs and DOS, you should. As this section explains, *Windows* and DOS work together, so you use DOS conventions to identify files when you work with *Windows*. If you need to learn these conventions, chapter 2 explains them in detail.

Section	Chapters	Contents	Read these chapters	Prerequisite
1	1-2	PC concepts and terms for every *Windows* user	In sequence	None
2	3-5	A complete course in *Windows* 3.1 in six hours or less	In sequence	Section 1
3	6-10	Other essential *Windows* skills	In any order you like	Section 2
4	11-12	Additional perspective	In any order you like	Section 2

Figure P-1   How this book is organized

The three chapters in section 2 present a complete course in *Windows* that is designed to help you convert from DOS to *Windows* in six hours or less. In chapter 3, you'll learn how to use *Windows* to start your programs and how to switch from one to another. In chapter 4, you'll learn how to use the functions and features that are common to all *Windows* programs. These are the skills that will make it easier for you to learn how to use your *Windows* application programs. Then, in chapter 5, you'll learn how to manage directories and files from *Windows* so you won't ever have to use DOS commands or the DOS shell again. To make your learning as thorough and efficient as possible, the chapters in this section include guided exercises that you can do on your own PC.

When you complete the course in section 2, you will be a competent *Windows* user. In fact, this section may tell you everything you want to know about *Windows*. But if you have some special *Windows* requirements or you just want to know more about *Windows*, the chapters in section 3 present other *Windows* essentials. If, for example, you want to continue to run some of your DOS programs when you use *Windows*, chapter 10 shows you how to do that. Or if you want to install a new printer on your PC, chapter 8 shows you how to do that. To make this section as useful as possible, its chapters are independent of each other so you don't have to read them in sequence. That means you can learn whatever you want to learn whenever you have 10 or 15 minutes to spare.

The chapters in sections 2 and 3 tell you everything you need to know for using *Windows* with confidence and efficiency. But there's more to *Windows* than that. So the chapters in section 4 introduce you to the other programs and features that come with *Windows*. In chapter 11, for example, you can learn about the 13 accessory programs that come with *Windows*. In chapter 12, you can learn about the Object Linking and Embedding (OLE) feature of *Windows* that there's so much talk about.

Who this book is for

As I said at the start of this preface, this book is for anyone who needs to learn how to use *Windows*. Since most of the people in that category already have experience with PCs and DOS, this book builds on that knowledge and experience. The more experience you have, the more quickly you'll be able to master the essential *Windows* skills that are presented in chapters 3 through 5. If you have just a minimum of experience, you should be able to complete the course in those chapters in six hours or less. If you have a lot of experience, you may be able to complete the course in just three or four hours.

On the other hand, this book also works if you don't have any experience at all with PCs or DOS. In that case, you need to read chapters 1 and 2 to get the background you need for using *Windows*. Also, the course in section 2 may take you more than six hours. When you're first learning how to use a PC, there is so much to learn that the time you need for getting started varies widely from one person to the next. With this book, though, you can be sure that you're getting started right.

If you're in charge of PC training for your company or if you teach a *Windows* course, this book can help you teach *Windows* faster and more thoroughly than you probably think is possible. If you want to improve your existing course, just add this book to its resource materials. If you want to teach a self-instructional course, that's what this book is designed for. And if you want to use this book as the primary resource for a class, an *Instructor's Guide* is available for it that provides all the instructional materials that you need for a powerful first course in *Windows*.

How this book works for other versions of *Windows*

As the title of this book specifies, this book is about *Windows* version 3.1. However, if you're willing to tolerate some minor differences in details, you can use it with *Windows* 3.0, *Windows for Workgroups*, and *Windows NT*.

As you can tell from the version numbers, *Windows* 3.0 is the predecessor of version 3.1. However, most of the techniques for using programs and managing files are the same in versions 3.0 and 3.1. On the other hand, version 3.1 is a major improvement over 3.0 because it is more stable and offers a broader range of features. In fact, I recommend that you upgrade to version 3.1 as soon as you can.

Windows for Workgroups is a superset of *Windows* 3.1. Because it offers everything that version 3.1 does, you can use this book for teaching those functions and features. In addition, however, *Windows for Workgroups* offers networking capabilities and programs that take advantage of these networking capabilities. These capabilities are not covered in this book.

Windows NT uses the *Windows* 3.1 interface and some of the same conventions for interacting with the PC user. As a result, you can apply much of what you learn in this book to *Windows NT*. However, *NT* is a completely new operating system that replaces DOS and offers sophisticated features that go beyond DOS and *Windows* 3.1.

If you want to know more about DOS...

As chapter 2 explains, DOS and *Windows* work together to provide the functions of an operating system. In fact, some of the *Windows* functions are directly related to DOS commands. That's why a knowledge of DOS can help you use some of the *Windows* functions more effectively. Although chapter 2 of this book presents the absolute least you need to know about DOS for using *Windows*, there are other DOS skills that can help you use *Windows*.

So if you want to learn more about DOS, here are two book recommendations. The first book is called *The Only DOS Book You'll Ever Need*. It tells you everything you need to know about DOS, and it includes complete coverage of the DOS 6.0 utilities that you can use with *Windows*. We believe this is the ideal book for people who provide support to less technical PC users. As a result, we recommend it for every corporate help desk, for every PC support person, and for the lead technical person in every user department.

The second book is called *The Least You Need to Know About DOS*, and it is the DOS counterpart to this book on *Windows*. This DOS book assumes that your PC has been set up for you and that help is available to you for the technical functions that are rarely needed. As a result, this book doesn't teach you how to install DOS on your system, how to partition a hard disk, how to detect disk problems, and so on. But otherwise, this book teaches you everything you need to know about DOS to work smarter, faster, and with less outside help.

Conclusion

I hope you enjoy using this book, and I hope it helps you enjoy using *Windows*. If you have any comments, criticisms, or suggestions, I would be delighted to hear from you. For that purpose, you'll find a postage-paid comment form at the back of this book. Thanks for reading this book, and good luck with *Windows*.

Steve Eckols
Fresno, California
July, 1993

PC concepts and terms for every *Windows* user

Before you can use *Windows* effectively, you need to understand the concepts and terms that apply to the PC you're using. That's why the two chapters in this section provide you with this background. In chapter 1, you'll learn the hardware concepts and terms that every *Windows* user should know. In chapter 2, you'll learn the software concepts and terms that every *Windows* user should know.

If you're already familiar with PC hardware, you can probably skip chapter 1. But at the least, you may want to skim the chapter to see what the specific hardware requirements are for a *Windows* system. Similarly, if you're already familiar with application software, DOS, and *Windows*, you can probably skip chapter 2. But if you're not, you should definitely read the chapter to get the software background that you need for learning how to use *Windows*.

Hardware concepts and terms for every *Windows* user

An introduction to PCs
The physical components of a PC
    Systems unit
    Monitor
    Keyboard
    Mouse
    Printer

The primary components of the systems unit
    Hard disk drive
    Diskette drive
    Processor
    Internal memory
    Adapters and ports

Perspective
Summary

$\mathbf{D}$o you know what kind of processor your PC has? Do you know the difference between internal memory and disk storage? Do you know what computer equipment is required to run *Windows* and to run it well?

If you've answered "yes" to all of these questions, you can probably skip this chapter and go ahead with chapter 2. But if you've answered "no" to any of them, you need to improve your understanding of the computer equipment, or *hardware*, that you're using. That's why this chapter presents the hardware concepts and terms that every *Windows* user should know.

An introduction to PCs

Windows is used on *personal computers*, or *PCs*. IBM introduced the term *PC* as the name for its first personal computer. The original IBM PC was followed by the IBM PC/XT, the IBM PC/AT, then by IBM's Personal System/2 (PS/2) and Personal System/1 (PS/1) computers. Today, however, the term PC applies more generally to all personal computers, like those made by Compaq, Tandy, Dell, and dozens of other manufacturers. The PCs that aren't made by IBM are often called *clones* or *compatibles*. That means they work just like the PCs made by IBM.

This book is for people who want to use Microsoft *Windows* on their PCs. Today, many hardware manufacturers install *Windows* as a standard feature on the systems they sell. But you don't have to have a new computer to run *Windows* because many older PCs can run *Windows* too. In this chapter, I'll describe the hardware your PC needs to run *Windows*.

The physical components of a PC

Figure 1-1 shows a typical PC. As you can see, it consists of five physical components: a systems unit, a monitor, a keyboard, a mouse, and a printer. The PC in figure 1-1 is a *desktop PC*. In a typical desktop PC, these five components are separate pieces.

In contrast, a *laptop PC* is smaller and lighter than a desktop PC, and it's portable. Although a laptop PC looks different from the desktop PC in figure 1-1, it still has the same five main components. The difference is that in a laptop PC, the monitor, keyboard, and systems unit are combined into a single carrying case.

Whether you're using a desktop PC or a laptop PC, the concepts you need to understand about your PC's components are the same. Because you may already be familiar with these components, I'll describe them briefly.

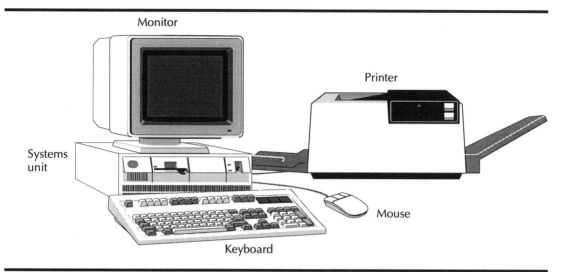

Figure 1-1   The physical components of a typical PC

Systems unit   The *systems unit* is the central component that all of the other components are connected to. This unit can also be referred to as the *electronics unit* or the *systems chassis*, but I'll use the term *systems unit* throughout this book. The systems unit contains the processor that controls the operations of the PC, the disk drives that store your programs and data, as well as other internal components.

I'll discuss the systems unit in more detail later in this chapter. But first, I want to describe the other main components of a PC. These components are either *input devices* (like the keyboard and mouse) or *output devices* (like the printer and monitor).

Monitor   Sometimes, the *monitor* is called the *display*, the *screen*, or the *CRT* (which stands for *cathode ray tube*). The monitor is your PC's primary output device. Monitors vary in how large their screens are, in the sharpness of the images they can display, and in the number of colors they can display.

Monochrome monitors can display only one color. It's usually green or amber on a dark background. *Color monitors* can display a variety of colors, and they're more expensive than comparable monochrome monitors. Even so, most people prefer color to monochrome. As a result, most new PCs are sold with color monitors.

A monitor uses dot patterns to display characters and images. Each dot is a *picture element*, or *pixel* for short. The more pixels a monitor can display, the higher its *resolution* and the sharper its image. Typically, monitors have screens that measure 14 inches diagonally. However, larger screens are becoming more and more common. As you'd guess, high-resolution monitors cost more than low-resolution monitors, and larger monitors cost more than smaller ones.

The image that appears on your monitor screen is controlled by an electronic module within the systems unit. This module is called the *display adapter*. An *adapter* is usually a separate electronic card that's mounted inside the systems unit. The number of colors your monitor can display and the resolution of the dots that make up its image depend on both the monitor and the display adapter.

Monitors and display adapters are designed to follow agreed-upon standards. Most new PCs follow the *VGA* (*Video Graphics Array*) standard. With VGA, a PC's display has a resolution of 640 x 480 pixels. Some systems use still newer standards like *SVGA* (*Super VGA*, with 800 x 600 resolution) or *XVGA* (*Extended VGA*, with 1024 x 768 resolution). All three of these video standards can support at least 16 colors simultaneously.

Windows supports other video standards as well. Among them are IBM's EGA (Enhanced Graphics Adapter, with 640 x 350 pixel resolution and 16 colors) and Hercules Monochrome (with 720 x 348 pixel resolution, but only 2 colors). However, the results you get from these less capable standards will not be as pleasing as those you get from VGA, SVGA, or XVGA.

Because *Windows* depends on high-quality graphic displays, your PC needs a high-resolution monitor to run it properly. In general, the more colors your screen can display, the larger your screen is, and the higher its resolution, the easier it will be for you to work with *Windows*.

Keyboard   The *keyboard* is the main input device of a PC. Although it resembles the keyboard of a typewriter, the PC keyboard has more keys. Several different keyboard layouts are common, but the most common is the 101-key keyboard.

The 101-key keyboard has several types of keys. First, it includes a full set of typewriter keys, with upper- and lowercase letters, numbers, and special characters. Second, the PC keyboard has a separate numeric keypad (on the right side) that has the same key arrangement as the ten keys on a calculator. Third, the keyboard has a row of 12 function keys, numbered F1 through F12. Finally, the keyboard has a number of control keys, such as Esc (Escape), Ctrl (Control), Alt (Alternate), Page-up, and Page-down.

When you use DOS programs, you often have to use an exact sequence of keystrokes to perform a specific function. When you use *Windows*, you can still use the keyboard to perform functions. However, *Windows* also lets you work with another kind of input device: the mouse.

Mouse   A *mouse* is a small hand-held input device that has two or three buttons, like the one attached to the system in figure 1-1. Basically, the mouse is a pointing device. When you push the mouse across your table top (or across a special *mouse pad* on your table top), a *pointer* on the screen moves in the same direction.

You can guide the pointer to an item on the screen that you want to work with, like a menu option or a block of text. Then, you can *click* on one of the mouse buttons to "select" the item. Or, you may be able to *double-click* on one of the mouse buttons to "open" the item. Or, you may be able to *drag* the item to move it from one spot to another on the screen.

When I introduce you to the basic features of *Windows* in chapter 3, you'll learn how to use the mouse in each of these ways. Although using the mouse may seem difficult at first, it will soon become second nature. Once you master the use of the mouse, you'll find that you can perform some functions faster with the mouse than with the keyboard.

Printer   The *printer* is one of your PC's output devices. Although various kinds of printers are in use, the most commonly used ones are matrix printers and laser printers. A *dot-matrix printer* works by striking small pins against an inked ribbon. The resulting dots form characters or graphic images on paper. Today, most dot-matrix printers are either 9-pin or 24-pin printers. As you might expect, 24-pin printers print better images than 9-pin printers.

In contrast to dot-matrix printers, *laser printers*, like the one in figure 1-1, work on the same principle as photocopiers. Laser printers print faster than dot-matrix printers, and they print higher quality images. Today, most laser printers print at 300 dpi (dots per inch), but higher resolution printers (600 dpi, 800 dpi, and more) are also available. Naturally, the quality of a laser printer's output depends on the number of dots per inch, and high-resolution laser printers cost more than low-resolution laser printers.

Because *Windows* users often require high-quality printed output, most PCs that run *Windows* have a laser printer available to it. This printer can be attached to the systems unit or available through a network.

The primary components of the systems unit

If you've ever opened up the systems unit of a PC, you know that it's full of electronic components. These components are attached to electronic cards that are inserted into the systems unit. Although you don't have to know how these components work, you should at least have a conceptual idea of what the primary components of the systems unit are and how they affect the way you work with *Windows*.

Figure 1-2 is a conceptual drawing of the components of a typical PC. As you can see, all of the input and output devices (the monitor, the keyboard, the mouse, and the printer) are connected to the systems unit. Within the systems unit, you can see five main components: the hard disk drive, the diskette drive, the processor, internal memory, and adapters and ports.

Hard disk drive   The *hard disk drive* stores the programs you run on your PC and the data you process with it. If you like, you can think of the hard disk as a large electronic filing cabinet. In fact, each of the items stored on a hard disk is stored in a unit called a *file*. The hard disk has enough room to store many program files and many data files. Plus, it can quickly retrieve any of the files it stores.

The files on the hard disk drive are recorded electronically on rigid metal disks that are coated with a magnetic material. While the disks spin at high speed inside the case, an access mechanism can move directly to any location on the disks to store (write) or to retrieve (read) information. That information can be a data file or a program file.

The capacity of a hard disk drive is measured in terms of how many *bytes* of information it can contain. For practical purposes, you can think of one byte of data as one character of data. Because the capacities of hard disk drives are so large, it's easier to measure them in a larger unit called a *megabyte* (abbreviated *MB*). One megabyte is approximately one million bytes. Today, few hard disk drives are sold with capacities of less than 80MB, and even higher capacity hard disk drives are common. My PC, for example, has a 200MB hard disk drive.

To put these numbers into perspective, think about how much data 80MB is. If a typical page of typewritten text contains about 2,000 characters, one megabyte of hard disk storage can store the equivalent of 500 pages of typewritten text. And 80MB of hard disk storage can store the equivalent of 40,000 pages of typewritten text.

Although the chances are slim that you'll need enough storage space for 40,000 pages of text, you do need enough space for both your data files and your program files. To start, *Windows* itself uses more than 9MB of storage space. In addition, each *Windows* program is likely to require several megabytes of storage space. On my PC, for example, my *Windows* programs alone take up 65MB of disk storage. That's why a *Windows* PC should have at least 80MB of disk storage, and you can't go wrong by having a lot more storage than that.

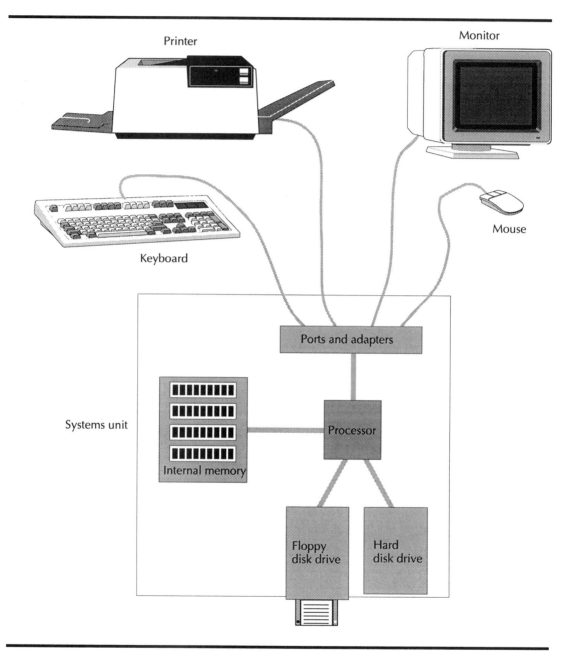

Figure 1-2   The internal components of the systems unit

The hard disk drive is almost always installed inside the systems unit. As a result, you usually can't see it unless you remove the cover of the systems unit. If you do look at it, you'll see that the disk drive is just a metal case with connectors for the cables that attach it to other components in the systems unit. Although most PCs have only one hard disk drive, some have two or more. As long as the systems unit has enough room for it, you can usually add a second hard disk drive to a PC without much trouble.

When hard disk drives are mounted permanently inside the systems unit, they're sometimes called *fixed disks*. Some PCs, however, have *removable hard disk drives*. For example, SyDOS manufactures a removable hard disk drive that uses a *disk cartridge* with a capacity of 88MB. With a SyDOS drive, you can remove the disk cartridge and replace it with another to access a different set of programs or data files. Although removable hard disk drives are convenient, they're also expensive so few PCs have them.

Diskette drive   A *diskette drive* reads and writes information on a *diskette*. Because you can remove a diskette and replace it with another one, diskettes are the most common medium for storing information off the hard disk drive and for transferring information between PCs.

A diskette consists of the recording medium where information is stored and a jacket that protects the recording medium. The recording medium is a disk-shaped piece of paper-thin plastic with a magnetic coating. Because the recording medium is flexible, diskettes are sometimes called *floppy disks*. But I'll use the term *diskette* throughout this book.

PC diskettes come in two sizes: *5.25-inch diskettes* and *3.5-inch diskettes*. Figure 1-3 shows both sizes. To read and write information on a diskette of a specific size, your PC must have a diskette drive of that size. Some PCs have two diskette drives, one of each size, so they can use both 5.25-inch and 3.5-inch diskettes. Other PCs have two diskette drives, but both are the same size. And still other PCs have just one diskette drive.

The 5.25-inch diskettes really are floppy diskettes. Because the jacket that protects the flexible recording medium is flexible too, you can bend them. In figure 1-3, you can see part of the recording medium through the oval shaped opening near the bottom of the 5.25-inch diskette. You can also see that the 5.25-inch diskette has a separate paper sleeve. When the diskette isn't in the diskette drive, you should store it in the paper sleeve to protect it.

Originally, all PCs used 5.25-inch diskettes. But when IBM introduced its PS/2 line of personal computers, it used the newer 3.5-inch diskette. Since then, 3.5-inch diskettes have become popular. Although the recording medium in a 3.5-inch diskette is still a floppy piece of plastic, the diskette jacket is rigid. As a result, 3.5-inch diskettes aren't as fragile as 5.25-inch diskettes. Also, a

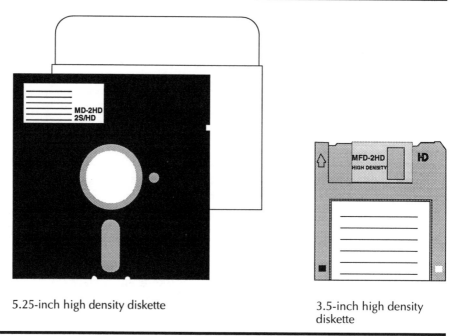

5.25-inch high density diskette

3.5-inch high density diskette

Figure 1-3   The two sizes of diskettes

spring-loaded metal shutter protects the recording medium in a 3.5-inch diskette when the diskette isn't in the diskette drive. That's why a 3.5-inch diskette doesn't need a paper sleeve like a 5.25-inch diskette does.

Like hard disk storage, the capacities of diskettes are measured in terms of how many bytes of data they can store. The larger capacities are measured in megabytes, which you've already been introduced to. The smaller capacities are measured in *kilobytes* (abbreviated *KB*), and one kilobyte is approximately one thousand bytes.

To complicate matters, both 5.25- and 3.5-inch diskettes are available in two different storage densities, or capacities. Figure 1-4 summarizes the capacities and labeling conventions for all four kinds. Today, the most common kinds of diskettes are *high density diskettes*, also called *HD diskettes*. The capacity of a 5.25-inch HD diskette is 1.2MB, and the capacity of a 3.5-inch HD diskette is 1.44MB. To use HD diskettes, you have to have a high density diskette drive on your PC, but all newer PCs come with this type of drive. In general, if a PC system is powerful enough to run *Windows*, it's going to be able to handle HD diskettes.

Size	Density	Capacity	Commonly labeled
5.25 inch	Double	360KB	Double-Sided, Double-Density (DSDD)
	High	1.2MB	Double-Sided, High-Density (DSHD)
3.5 inch	Double	720KB	Double-Sided, Double-Density (2DD)
	High	1.44MB	Double-Sided, High-Density (2HD)

Figure 1-4   A summary of diskette characteristics

The diskette drives on some older PCs aren't able to read and write HD diskettes. Instead, they're limited to lower density diskettes. These are often called *standard density diskettes*, even though HD diskettes are "standard" today. The technical name for these older diskettes is *double-sided, double-density diskettes* so you'll often see the abbreviations *DS/DD* or *2DD* on their labels. The capacity of a 5.25-inch DS/DD diskette is 360KB, and the capacity of a 3.5-inch 2DD diskette is 720KB.

Visually, you can't tell the difference between 5.25-inch diskettes of the two densities. However, you can distinguish between 720KB and 1.44MB 3.5-inch diskettes. As you can see in figure 1-3, a high density 3.5-inch diskette has two notches (one on each side of the label) and the HD logo. In contrast, a double-density 3.5-inch diskette has one notch and no logo.

When you use a diskette to transfer information from one PC to another, you must use the right kind of diskette. Not only must it be the right size for the diskette drive on the receiving PC, but it must also be the right capacity. Although a diskette drive that can read and write HD diskettes can also read and write DS/DD diskettes, a low capacity drive can't read and write HD diskettes. So if you're not sure what capacity of diskette to use, you should use a double-sided, double-density diskette instead of a high-density one. That way, you can be sure the receiving PC will be able to read the information on the diskette.

Processor   If you look back to figure 1-2, you can see that all of the components I've described so far are connected to the *processor*. The processor is an electronic chip. When a program is running, the processor controls all of the other components of the PC according to the instructions given by the program that's in control of the system. Other terms for a processor are *microprocessor, central processing unit*, and *CPU*, but I'll use the term *processor* throughout this book.

Processor name	Common abbreviation
8088	None
80286	286
80386SX	386SX
80386DX	386DX or just 386
80486SX	486SX
80486DX	486DX or just 486
80486DX2	486DX2

Figure 1-5   The names and abbreviations for Intel processors

Most PC processors are manufactured by Intel. Because Intel dominates the market, the names of its processors are widely used to describe all processors with similar capabilities. Figure 1-5 shows the names of the Intel chips and the abbreviations that are commonly used for them. As you can see, the shortened names of the chips are the 286, the 386SX, the 386, and so on.

The 8088, which was introduced in 1979, was the processor in the first IBM PC and in the IBM PC/XT. Today, the 8088 is old technology, and *Windows* won't run on a system with an 8088 processor. The oldest PC processor that *Windows* can run on is the 286. This processor is the one used in the IBM PC/AT (introduced in 1984) and in some PS/2 models. However, *Windows* works best on systems that are built around still newer processors: the 386, 386SX, 486, 486SX, and 486DX2. These processors are faster than the 286 processor, and they also offer more powerful features.

One measure of processor performance is *clock speed*. In general, the faster the processor's clock speed, the faster the computer operates. The clock speed of the original IBM PC was 4.77Mhz (*Mhz* stands for *megahertz*). Currently, some processors have clock speeds as high as 66Mhz.

You should realize, though, that clock speed isn't the only factor that determines your computer's performance. The processor chip your system is based on makes an even bigger difference. For example, the 386DX is inherently faster than the 286, and the 486DX is inherently faster than the 386DX.

Figure 1-6 compares the relative performance ratings of several typical PCs. For example, a system that uses a 286 running at 8Mhz is about four times faster than a system that uses an 8088 running at 4.77Mhz, even though its clock speed is less than twice as fast. And a 486 system running at 33Mhz is about 50 times faster than an 8088 running at 4.77Mhz, even though its clock speed is only about seven times faster.

Because the processor controls all of the operations of the PC, its performance has a major effect on how well *Windows* works. Today, most people agree that a 386SX is the slowest processor that is satisfactory for

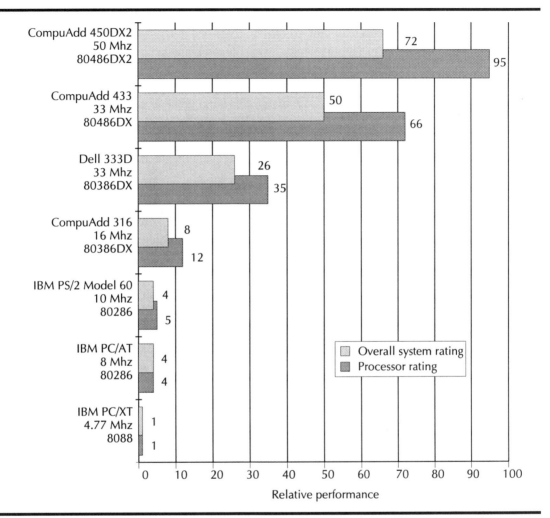

Figure 1-6   Performance ratings of several PC systems and their processors relative to the
IBM PC/XT and its 8088 processor

Windows use, and even that processor won't be satisfactory for the more
demanding *Windows* applications. In general, the faster your processor is, the
happier you're going to be with your PC's performance. On that basis, I
recommend a 486 processor for most *Windows* applications.

Internal memory   Before your PC can operate on the data that's stored on
a hard disk drive or a diskette, it must read that data into its *internal memory*.
Internal memory consists of chips that are attached to one or more of the circuit

boards inside the systems unit. This memory can also be called *internal storage* or *random access memory (RAM)*, but I'll always refer to it as *internal memory* in this book.

Internal memory is an "electronic workspace" for the processor. The processor uses internal memory to hold both data and programs. The contents of internal memory are maintained only as long as the computer system is on. Unlike the contents of disk storage, the contents of internal memory are lost when you turn your PC off. That's why you should "save" your work to hard disk or diskette storage before you turn off your PC.

Like diskette and hard disk storage, the capacity of internal memory is measured in kilobytes and megabytes. The first PCs were sold with 64KB, 128KB, or 256KB of internal memory. Before long, 640KB and 1MB became standards. Today, 4MB of internal memory is standard for new PCs.

Although you can run *Windows* on a PC with as little as 1MB of internal memory, that isn't enough workspace to use your programs effectively. To use *Windows* the way it was meant to be used, your PC needs at least 2MB of internal memory and 4MB or more is preferred. One reason why *Windows* requires so much memory is that it allows you to work on more than one program at the same time. So if you have enough internal memory to hold all of the programs that you're working with, *Windows* will run more efficiently.

Adapters and ports   Your PC's input and output devices communicate with the processor through adapters that are installed in the systems unit. For instance, I've already mentioned the display adapter that connects the processor to your PC's monitor. And if your PC is part of a network, it has a *network adapter* that handles communication with the network.

In addition to adapters, almost all PCs have standard outlets called *communication ports*. When you connect a device like a printer or a mouse to your systems unit, you do so through one of these ports. And if you use a *modem* for communicating over phone lines, it is connected to one of the ports.

Perspective

In this chapter, I've tried to present only the hardware terms that you're likely to encounter when you're using *Windows* or reading about it. Nevertheless, this chapter presents over 70 terms. What's worse, you're likely to hear most of these terms and more in a typical conversation with a PC salesperson or someone at your Help Desk.

The good news is that you don't have to remember all of the terms in this chapter just to use *Windows* effectively. You should be able to name the five physical components of a typical PC. And you should be able to name the five primary components of a systems unit. But once you can do that, you're ready for the next chapter.

Summary

- A typical *personal computer*, or *PC*, consists of five physical components: *systems unit*, *monitor*, *keyboard*, *mouse*, and *printer*.

- A systems unit contains five primary components: *hard disk drive*, *diskette drive*, *processor*, *internal memory*, and *adapters and ports*.

- The capacities of hard disk drives, diskettes, and internal memory are measured in *bytes*, *kilobytes* (*KB*), and *megabytes* (*MB*). A kilobyte is approximately one thousand bytes, and a megabyte is approximately one million bytes.

- Diskettes come in two sizes (5.25 and 3.5 inch) and two capacities (*high density* and *double-sided, double-density*). When you use a diskette to transfer data from one PC to another, you must use a diskette that has the right size and capacity for the receiving PC.

- Today, most printers are either *dot-matrix* or *laser* printers, and most *Windows* systems have access to laser printers.

- To run *Windows* effectively, a PC should have a high-resolution monitor, a hard disk with a capacity of 80MB or more, internal memory of at least 2MB with 4MB or more preferred, and a 386SX processor with a 486DX preferred.

Chapter 2

Software concepts and terms for every *Windows* user

The two types of programs every PC requires
Operating system programs
Application programs

How DOS and *Windows* work together to provide operating system functions
DOS is loaded into internal memory when you start your PC
DOS lets you start *Windows*
Windows lets you start your application programs
Windows provides multitasking
Windows provides I/O services for the keyboard, mouse, monitor, and printer
DOS provides I/O services for diskette and hard disk storage
Windows provides improved file management capabilities

How to identify a file using DOS conventions
Disk drive
Path
File name

Perspective
Summary

Do you know the difference between an operating system program and an application program? Do you know how DOS and *Windows* work together to provide the operating system functions? Do you know how to give a complete specification for a file that's used by a DOS or *Windows* program including drive, directory, and file name?

Unless you answered an unqualified "yes" to those questions, you should read this chapter before you go on to the next one. To use a PC effectively, you must have a basic understanding of what software does and how it works. The term *software* refers to the programs that direct the operations of your PC's hardware. *Windows* is software, and it interacts with the other software that's on your system. When you complete this chapter, you'll have the software background that every *Windows* user needs.

The two types of programs every PC requires

In broad terms, PC software can be divided into two types: *operating system programs* and *application programs*. To use your PC, you need both types of programs. Interestingly, *Windows* provides both operating system and application programs.

Operating system programs   An *operating system* is a set of programs that lets you use your application programs on your PC. For example, an operating system lets you load an application program into internal memory so you can use it. An operating system also provides functions that let your application programs read a file from a disk drive, print on a printer, and so on.

The concept of an operating system is elusive because much of what it does goes on without you knowing about it. For instance, when you save a word processing document to your hard disk, it's the operating system, not your word processing program, that actually saves the information. Without the operating system, your application programs wouldn't work.

The most widely used operating system on PCs is *DOS*. It's pronounced doss, and it's short for *Disk Operating System*. Without DOS, you can't run *Windows* 3.1. However, *Windows* 3.1 also provides operating system functions. In fact, Microsoft's documentation for *Windows* identifies it as the "Microsoft Windows Operating System." Some of the *Windows* functions duplicate or replace DOS functions, and others improve upon DOS functions. In a moment, I'll show you how DOS and *Windows* work together to provide the operating system functions.

Application programs   An *application program* lets you apply your PC to the jobs you want to do. For instance, a word processing application program like *WordPerfect* lets you apply your PC to tasks like writing letters, memos, and reports. Similarly, a spreadsheet application program like *Lotus 1-2-3* lets you apply your PC to tasks like creating budget analyses and cash flow studies. Other kinds of application programs, such as graphics, telecommunications, and data management programs, let you apply your PC to other kinds of work.

An application program that is designed to run in the *Windows* environment is called a *Windows application*. In contrast, a program that is designed to be run under DOS alone can be called a *DOS application program*, or just a *DOS application*. When you use *Windows*, you can run both *Windows* and DOS applications.

Figure 2-1 lists some common DOS and *Windows* applications. As you can see, *Windows* applications fall into two categories: programs that come with *Windows* and programs that are separate products. For instance, *Windows* comes with several application programs that you can use for basic tasks. These programs include a simple text editor (Notepad), a word processing program (Write), a graphics program (Paintbrush), a telecommunications program (Terminal), a simple data base program (Cardfile), and several others. In contrast, programs like *Word for Windows* and *Excel for Windows* are separate products.

Some people use the term *applets* for the application programs that come with *Windows* because these programs don't offer the full range of functions that separate application programs do. For instance, neither Notepad nor Write has all the functions that a word processing program like Microsoft *Word for Windows* or *WordPerfect for Windows* has. Even so, some of these applets are useful. So in chapter 11, I'll introduce you to all of the other applets.

One of the benefits of using *Windows* applications is that all of them are based on the same design conventions. These conventions specify how a *Windows* application should look on the monitor and how a user should be able to interact with the program. This makes it easier for a *Windows* user to learn how to use a new *Windows* application. In contrast, there were no design conventions for DOS programs. As a result, there is little or no continuity from one DOS program to another. That's why learning how to use a new DOS program is usually more difficult than learning how to use a new *Windows* application. In chapter 4, you'll be introduced to the conventions that are common to all *Windows* programs.

	DOS applications	***Windows* applications**	
		Supplied with *Windows* ("Applets")	**Not supplied with *Windows***
Word processing	Microsoft *Word*	Notepad	Microsoft *Word for Windows*
	WordPerfect	Write	*WordPerfect for Windows*
Spreadsheet	*Lotus 1-2-3*		*Excel*
	Quattro Pro		*Lotus 1-2-3 for Windows*
Graphics	*Freelance Plus*	Paintbrush	*CorelDRAW!*

Figure 2-1   Examples of DOS and *Windows* applications

How DOS and *Windows* work together to provide operating system functions

Figure 2-2 is a listing that shows how DOS and *Windows* work together to provide operating system functions. As you can see, DOS is in control when you first start your PC, and DOS lets you start *Windows*. Once *Windows* is running, DOS works in the background to help your application programs retrieve and store diskette and hard disk files, but *Windows* provides most of the other operating system functions.

DOS is loaded into internal memory when you start your PC   When your PC starts, a portion of DOS is loaded from disk storage into internal memory. This process is called *booting*. The part of DOS that's loaded when you boot the PC takes up a modest amount of internal memory, and it's available to provide DOS services as long as the PC is on.

Unlike DOS, *Windows* 3.1 can't be used in the booting process. As a result, *Windows* 3.1 isn't a complete operating system. You should know, however, that Microsoft recently released a new version of *Windows* that is able to boot the computer. It is called *Windows NT* (New Technology). Because *NT* is a complete operating system, you don't need DOS to run it. However, it requires an even more powerful PC than *Windows* 3.1 requires, and it provides functions that most PC users don't need. As a result, *Windows* 3.1 and DOS will continue to be widely used.

- DOS is loaded into internal memory when you start your PC.
- DOS lets you start *Windows.*
- *Windows* lets you start your application programs.
- *Windows* provides multitasking.
- *Windows* provides I/O services for the keyboard, mouse, monitor, and printer.
- DOS provides I/O services for diskette and hard disk storage.
- *Windows* provides improved file management capabilities.

Figure 2-2   How DOS and *Windows* work together to provide operating system functions

DOS lets you start *Windows*   After DOS is running, you can direct it to start an application program. One way to do this is to enter a command at a *DOS command prompt* like the one in part 1 of figure 2-3. When the command prompt is displayed, DOS is waiting for you to enter a command to tell it what to do next.

To start *WordPerfect* 5.1, for example, you type a command like the one shown in part 2 of figure 2-3 and press the Enter key. DOS then retrieves the *WordPerfect* program from the hard disk drive, loads it into internal memory, and passes control of the PC to it. When you exit from *WordPerfect*, control of the PC is passed back to DOS, and it displays the command prompt again.

When you use *Windows*, you normally start all of your application programs from *Windows*. As a result, the only program that you need to start from the command prompt is *Windows*. To do that, you enter the command shown in part 3 of figure 2-3. The command is simply the word *win*. When DOS runs this command, it starts *Windows*.

***Windows* lets you start your application programs**   Once it's running, *Windows* lets you start your application programs. But with *Windows*, you don't have to remember the command that starts a program, and you don't have to type it in at a prompt. Instead, a *Windows* program called the *Program Manager* displays small pictures called *icons* that represent the programs on your PC. This is illustrated in figure 2-4. Then, all you have to do to run a program is point at one of the pictures with the mouse pointer and double-click the mouse. To start the Write applet, for example, you point to its icon with the mouse as indicated in the figure and you double-click the left mouse button.

Windows provides many different ways to start applications. Some of these can be used when the Program Manager is active. Others can be used when

Part 1

A typical DOS
command prompt

Part 2

The command to
start *WordPerfect*
5.1

Part 3

The command to
start *Windows*

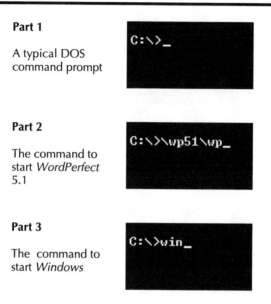

Figure 2-3   How to start programs from the DOS command prompt

another *Windows* component, the File Manager, is active. All of the methods can be used for starting DOS applications as well as *Windows* applications.

***Windows* provides multitasking**   When you start an application program from DOS, it retrieves the program from disk, loads it into memory, and lets the application program take control of your PC. From that point on, your program is in control of the computer, although it may call upon DOS for some services. DOS doesn't gets full control of the PC again until you end the application program.

In contrast, when you start an application program from *Windows*, it still runs and supervises what's happening. As a result, you can interrupt your application program, return to *Windows*, and start another program without leaving the first one. When you run more than one program at the same time, it is called *multitasking*. During multitasking, *Windows* manages the programs in internal memory and keeps them from conflicting with one another.

As I write this paragraph in Microsoft *Word for Windows*, for example, I can switch immediately to Paintbrush to work on an illustration. Then, I can switch to a third program to manage my files. All the time, *Word for Windows*

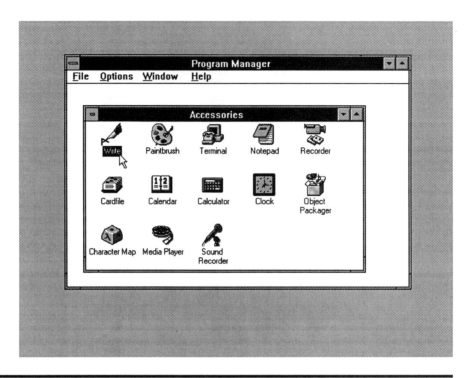

Figure 2-4   How the Program Manager uses icons to represent programs

and my document remain in internal memory. When I'm ready to return to them, *Windows* returns me to the same place in my document that I was before I switched to Paintbrush.

The advantages of multitasking go beyond switching between programs, though. Multitasking also lets two programs run at the same time and share the resources of your PC. For instance, I can run a telecommunications program to transfer a large document from another PC to my PC and still continue to work on my word processing document. In addition, I can display more than one of the programs I'm running on my screen at the same time. This makes it easy to cut and paste information between the programs.

The multitasking that *Windows* provides is different from the simple *task switching* that DOS versions 5.0 and later provide. Although DOS lets you switch from one program to another, it doesn't let you run more than one program at a time. As a result, it doesn't let you display more than one program at a time on your screen or let your programs share your PC's resources.

***Windows* provides I/O services for the keyboard, mouse, monitor, and printer** When an application program is running, it usually doesn't take direct control of your system's input and output devices. Instead, the operating system provides *input/output services*, or *I/O services*, that let a program receive information from an input device like the keyboard or mouse and send information to an output device like the monitor or printer. Fortunately, you don't have to worry about I/O services because they work automatically without you knowing about it.

Although both DOS and *Windows* provide I/O services, most of the services that *Windows* programs request are satisfied by *Windows* services, not by DOS services. In particular, *Windows* uses its own services for the keyboard, mouse, monitor, and printer. This means that once *Windows* is set up with the right *device drivers* for these devices, all of your *Windows* applications can use those devices. In contrast, you often need to install special device drivers for different DOS application programs.

DOS provides I/O services for diskette and hard disk storage Although *Windows* replaces the DOS I/O services for the keyboard, mouse, monitor, and printer, it still uses the DOS I/O services for accessing information on diskettes and hard disks. As a result, you still use DOS specifications for identifying your files. In a moment, I'll review the rules for creating those specifications.

***Windows* provides improved file management capabilities** If you're an experienced DOS user, you know that you can use *DOS commands* to manage the directories and files that are stored on your diskettes and hard disks. For instance, you can use the Make-directory (MD), Remove-directory (RD), and Change-directory (CD) commands to manage the *directories* on your hard disk. You can use the Directory (DIR) command to look at the contents of a directory. And you can use the Copy, Delete, and Rename commands to manage the *files* within a directory.

If you're using DOS release 4.0, 5.0, or 6.0, you can use the *DOS shell* to perform many of the same functions. This makes it considerably easier to perform these functions. For many functions, though, you still have to know some of the command details.

When you use *Windows,* you can use its File Manager to perform all of the functions that you need for managing directories and files. In part 1 of figure 2-5, for example, you can see that the File Manager uses small icons to represent files and directories. By using the mouse to select and drag icons, you

Part 1

The File Manager
displays a tree
that represents a
disk's directory
structure and the
files that are in
the selected
directory.

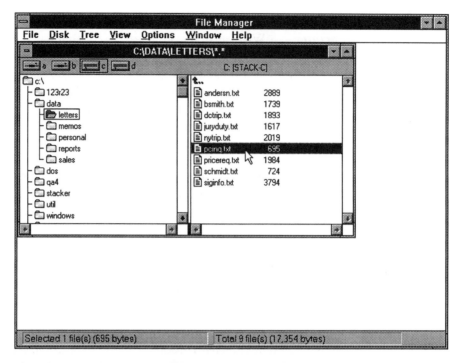

Part 2

The File Manager
also provides
menu commands
that perform the
same functions as
DOS commands.

Figure 2-5   How the File Manager displays directories, files, and the commands you use to
manage them

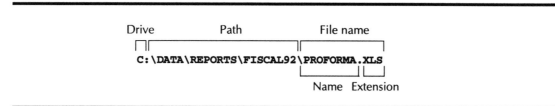

Figure 2-6   The parts of a file specification

can easily move and copy files from one directory to another. You can also pull down a menu as shown in part 2 of this figure to perform other operations on the files that you've selected. In chapter 5, you'll learn how to use the File Manager to perform common file and directory operations that are often difficult to perform when using DOS. Then, in chapter 7, you'll learn how to get the most from the File Manager by mastering all of its features.

How to identify a file using DOS conventions

Whether you're using a DOS application or a *Windows* application, you use DOS *file specifications* to identify the files that you want to work with. Although *Windows* often lets you identify a file just by clicking on a file specification in a list, you at least have to know what the right specification looks like.

A complete file specification consists of a disk drive identifier, a path, and a file name. To illustrate, figure 2-6 shows a complete file specification for a file on a hard disk drive. A file stored on a diskette is identified similarly, except it's seldom necessary to include a path for a file on diskette.

Disk drive   You identify your PC's disk drives with letters. Those letters are called *disk drive identifiers*. When you specify the disk drive identifier in a file specification, you always give the drive letter followed by a colon. In figure 2-6, you can see that the example identifies a file that is stored on the C drive.

Drive letters identify both diskette drives and hard disk drives. The first diskette drive on a PC is always drive A, and the second diskette drive, when there is one, is always drive B. The first hard disk drive on a PC is drive C, the second is drive D, the third is drive E, and so on.

Although it's common today for a PC to have more than one hard disk drive, it's even more common for a PC to have one physical hard disk drive that has been divided into two or more *logical drives*. Then, the computer seems to have two or more hard disk drives, even though the same hardware device provides the storage for each drive. When that's the case, each logical drive is assigned a different drive letter, just as though it were a separate physical drive.

If your PC is attached to a network, you can probably access disk drives that aren't a part of your PC. These are called *network drives,* and you identify them with letters just as you do for the drives on your own PC. However, network drive identifiers don't always fall in strict alphabetical order. For example, a PC may have access to network drives lettered J and M. If your system is part of a network, you can check with your supervisor or network administrator to find out what network drives you can use and what their drive letters are.

Path   When you use DOS or *Windows*, every file on a diskette or hard diskette drive must be stored in a *directory*. The 3,584 files on my PC, for example, are organized into 135 different directories. These directories are just special types of files that DOS and *Windows* use to keep track of the locations of the files on the disk.

When you create directories, you can organize them into a hierarchical structure. In other words, you can create directories that are subordinate to (or are "in" or are "owned by") other directories. When a directory is subordinate to a higher-level directory, it can be called a *subdirectory.* By using two or three directory levels, you can organize your files in a way that lets you keep track of them.

Figure 2-7 illustrates a directory structure for a hard disk drive on a typical system. This figure is from a screen displayed by the *Windows* File Manager. The File Manager shows the contents of a hard disk drive or diskette as a set of folders arranged hierarchically in a tree structure. The folder at the top of the tree represents the *root directory*. It's the one labeled C:\ in the figure.

In figure 2-7, the root directory contains references to eight level-1 directories. Two of these directories contain operating system files: DOS and WINDOWS. Three of these directories contain program files for DOS applications: 123R23 (for *Lotus 1-2-3* release 2.3), QA4 (for *Q&A* release 4), and WP51 (for *WordPerfect* release 5.1). Two others contain program files for DOS utilities: STACKER and UTIL. And the DATA directory contains data files.

In figure 2-7, you can see that the DATA directory has five directories that are subordinate to it: LETTERS, MEMOS, PERSONAL, REPORTS, and SALES. You can also see that the REPORTS subdirectory contains two lower-level subdirectories named FISCAL91 and FISCAL92. Regardless of their level in the hierarchy, though, subdirectories are often just called directories.

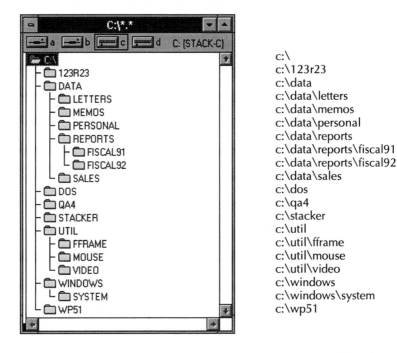

Figure 2-7   A typical directory structure and a list of the path names for each directory and subdirectory

The *path* is the part of a file specification that tells DOS how to get from the root directory of a disk drive or diskette to the directory that contains the file you want. In figure 2-6, for example, the path goes from the root directory for the C drive to the DATA directory, to its REPORTS subdirectory, then to its FISCAL92 subdirectory.

Next to the directory structure in figure 2-7, you can see the specifications for all of the 20 directories in the structure. The root directory is always specified by a backlash (\\). The level-1 directories are specified by a backslash for the root directory followed by the directory name as in these examples:

```
\DATA
\DOS
\WINDOWS
```

The level-2 directories are specified by a backslash for the root directory, the level-1 directory name, another backslash, and the level-2 directory name. For example,

`\WINDOWS\SYSTEM`

is the path for a file that resides in the SYSTEM subdirectory in the WINDOWS directory.

Similarly, the path to a level-3 directory consists of the backslash for the root directory, the level-1 directory name, another backslash, the level-2 directory name, a third backslash, and finally the level-3 directory name. For example,

`\DATA\REPORTS\FISCAL92`

is a valid path for one of the level-3 directories in figure 2-7.

Note, however, that \FISCAL92 by itself isn't a valid path. To be valid, it must be preceded by the names of all of the directories that it's subordinate to. As a result, you can use the same subdirectory name in more than one directory. For example, you can create subdirectories named FISCAL91 and FISCAL92 in the MEMOS directory, even though those names are already in use for subdirectories in the REPORTS directory.

File name   When you work with application programs under *Windows*, you need to create and use valid *file names* to identify the documents you process. If you look back to figure 2-6, you'll see that a valid file name has two parts that are separated by a period. The part that comes before the period is called the *name* portion of the file name, and it's always required. The part that comes after the period is called the *extension,* and it's optional.

Figure 2-8 gives the rules for forming valid file names. As you can see, you can use from one to eight characters for the name portion and from one to three characters for the extension. This figure also shows the characters you can't use in a file name, and it presents examples of valid and invalid names.

Although extensions are optional as far as DOS and *Windows* are concerned, many application programs use them to identify the files they create and process. For example, Microsoft *Word for Windows* uses the extension DOC as a default for its files, and Microsoft *PowerPoint* uses the extension PPT as a default. Although most programs let you override their default extensions when you create files, you shouldn't as a general rule. That's because *Windows* uses the extension of a file to associate the file with the application that created it. Then, if you double-click on the File Manager icon

What you can use

1. The file name can be from 1 to 8 characters in length.

2. The extension is optional, and it's separated from the file name by a period. It can be from 1 to 3 characters in length.

3. You can use letters (either upper- or lowercase) and numbers in the name or extension.

4. You can also use these special characters except as a *first* character:

> ! @ # $ % ^ & ( ) _ + - { } < > ' ~

What you can't use

1. You can't use a *space* or any of these special characters:

> . , [ ] / \ : ; | " =

2. You can't use these names because DOS reserves them for its own purposes:

COM1	COM2	COM3	COM 4
LPT1	LPT2	LPT3	
PRN	CON	AUX	NUL

Valid file names

> FEB92RPT
> feb92rpt
> 5-16-93.DOC
> LTR10-21
> win.ini

Invalid file names   **Reason**

Invalid file names	Reason
JOHNLETTER.DOS	The name is longer than 8 characters.
JAN:93.WK	The colon is an invalid character.
smith.lttr	The extension is more than 3 characters.
(SMITH).LTR	The left parenthesis is invalid as a first character.
CON.TXT	The name is a reserved name.

Figure 2-8   How to form valid file names

for a file, *Windows* automatically loads the document into internal memory along with the program that created it.

Perspective

Now that you've finished this chapter, you can start to see why *Windows* is becoming so popular. First, the multitasking feature of *Windows* lets you run two or more application programs at the same time. This lets you switch from one program to another whenever you need to, and it makes it easy for you to transfer data from one program to another. Second, *Windows* programs look and operate in consistent ways because they are based on the same design conventions. This makes it easier for you to learn how to use new *Windows* applications. Third, the *Windows* File Manager makes it easier for you to manage your files because you don't have to use DOS commands or the more cumbersome DOS shell.

Each of the chapters in the next section focuses on one of these three *Windows* features. In chapter 3, you'll learn how to start your application programs, switch from one to another, and work with the windows that your programs are displayed in. In chapter 4, you'll learn how to use the *Windows* conventions that are common to all *Windows* programs. And in chapter 5, you'll learn how to use the *Windows* File Manager. By the time you complete these chapters, you'll be a competent *Windows* user.

Summary

- An *operating system* is a set of programs that lets you use your application programs. DOS is the operating system that's used on most PCs, and *Windows* 3.1 also provides some operating system functions.

- An *application program* lets you apply your PC to the jobs you want to do. Application programs that are designed for *Windows* can be referred to as *Windows applications*, and those that are designed for DOS can be referred to as *DOS applications*. The *Windows* applications that come with *Windows* can be referred to as *applets*.

- Because all *Windows* applications follow the same design conventions, it's usually easier to learn how to use another *Windows* application than it is to learn another DOS application.

- You can't run *Windows* 3.1 without DOS. After DOS is loaded into internal memory when you start your PC, you can start *Windows* from DOS. After that, you can start your application programs from *Windows*.

- Unlike DOS, *Windows* provides *multitasking*. That means you can run more than one program at the same time. This makes it easy for you to switch from one program to another or to transfer data from one program to another.

- Although *Windows* provides the *I/O services* for the monitor, keyboard, mouse, and printer, DOS still provides the I/O services for diskettes and hard drives. That's why you still need to use DOS file specifications.

- The *Windows* File Manager provides file management capabilities that improve upon those provided by DOS commands or the *DOS shell*.

- A DOS *file specification* consists of a disk drive identifier, path, and file name. The *drive identifier* is a letter followed by a colon that identifies a disk drive. The *path* is one or more directory names separated by backslashes. And the *file name* is a name of from one to eight characters with or without an *extension* of from one to three characters. If a file name has an extension, a period must separate the extension from the name.

A complete course in *Windows* in just a few hours

If you're new to *Windows*, this section is for you. In chapter 3, you'll learn how to use *Windows* and its Program Manager. When you complete this chapter, you'll have a solid understanding of what *Windows* is and how it works. You'll also be able to start and end your application programs, to switch from one to another as you use them, and to work with the windows that the programs are in. Then, in chapter 4, you'll learn how to use the standard features of all *Windows* programs. This will make it easier for you to learn how to use any *Windows* program. Last, in chapter 5, you'll learn how to use the *Windows* File Manager to manage your directories and files.

As you read each chapter in this section, you'll come upon sets of practice exercises. These will give you the chance to practice the *Windows* skills that have been presented to that point in the chapter. These exercises will also help you check your understanding of the terms and concepts presented to that point. If you do all of the exercises for each of the chapters in this section, you should be able to complete this section in six hours or less. If you don't feel that you need to do all of the exercises, you can complete this section more quickly. When in doubt, though, please do the exercises. They're carefully designed to help you learn quickly and thoroughly.

When you complete the three chapters in this section, you'll be a competent *Windows* user. In fact, this section may teach you everything that you need or want to know about *Windows*. But if you do want to know more or if questions arise that aren't covered in this section, you can refer to the chapters in section 3 for additional information. For instance, chapter 8 gives you more information about managing your printers, and chapter 10 gives you more information about running DOS programs from *Windows*.

Chapter 3

How to use *Windows* and its Program Manager

An introduction to *Windows*
   How to start *Windows*
   Application and document windows
   How to end *Windows*

Basic mouse skills for working with windows
   The four basic mouse actions
   How to minimize, maximize, and restore windows
   How to move a window
   How to size a window
   How to scroll through the contents of a window

Exercise 3-1: Basic *Windows* skills

How to use the mouse to start and end a *Windows* application
   How to start a program by double-clicking on its icon
   How to end a program by double-clicking on its control-menu box

Four ways to switch from one *Windows* application to another
   Click on any part of an inactive application window
   Use Fast Alt+Tab Switching
   Use Alt+Esc Switching
   Minimize and restore application windows

Exercise 3-2: How to start your applications, switch between them, and end them

How to issue menu commands
How to issue a program menu command
How to issue a control menu command

How to use a dialog box
How to use the Program Manager's Run command to start a program
How to use the Options and Window menu commands for the Program Manager
The commands of the Options menu
The commands of the Window menu

How to use the commands of a control menu to work with windows
How to use a command to end a *Windows* application
From the control menu
From the program's File menu

Exercise 3-3: How to use menu commands

How to use the Task Manager
How to access the Task List dialog box
How to use the dialog box to switch from one program to another
How to use the dialog box to organize icons and windows
How to use the dialog box to end an application program

Exercise 3-4: How to use the Task Manager

Perspective
Summary

Ｏne of the primary *Windows* features is that it lets you run more than one program at the same time. This capability is called *multitasking*. For instance, do you use two or more of these programs?

- a word processing program to write memos and reports

- a spreadsheet program to prepare worksheets

- a presentation graphics program to create materials for a briefing

- a terminal emulation program to access your firm's on-line databases

- an electronic mail package to communicate with your co-workers

With *Windows*, you can have all of these programs, and more, available to you at the same time. This makes it easy for you to switch from one program to another and to transfer data from one to another.

In this chapter, you'll start by learning the basic skills for working with *Windows*. Next, you'll learn how to start your application programs from the *Windows* Program Manager, how to switch from one program to another, and how to end your programs. Then, you'll learn how to select and use menu commands. Last, you'll learn how to use the Task Manager for some common *Windows* functions.

As you read this chapter, you'll come upon sets of exercises. These will help you check your understanding of the concepts and terms presented to that point in the chapter. And they will let you practice the skills that you've read about. Because practice is an essential part of the learning process, I recommend that you do the exercises when you come to them. But if you prefer not to or if a PC isn't available to you while you're reading, you can do all of the exercises after you complete the entire chapter.

To get you started right, this chapter introduces you to several different *Windows* features and shows you their relationships. That way, you'll have a solid understanding of what *Windows* does and how *Windows* works by the time you complete this chapter. If you find that this is more information than you have the time or energy for in a single session, you can take a break after each set of exercises. In all, there are four sets of exercises in this chapter. As soon as you finish the second set, you'll know how to start your application programs, switch from one to another, and end them, so that's the best time for an extended break.

As you read this chapter, you'll discover that *Windows* often provides two or more ways for performing a task, even a simple task. That's why *Windows* is likely to be confusing when you first start using it. In this chapter, for example, you'll learn two ways to start your programs, two ways to end them, and five ways to switch from one to another. By the time you complete this chapter, though, you should realize that you don't have to use all of the methods for performing each task. Instead, you can use the ones that seem easiest or most appropriate for the jobs that you do.

An introduction to *Windows*

Before you can run your application programs under *Windows*, you need to know how to start *Windows*. You need to know the difference between an application window and a document window. And you may want to know how to end *Windows*.

How to start *Windows* If *Windows* is installed properly on your PC, all you have to do to start it is type *win* at the DOS command prompt and press the Enter key. Although you can specify some options when you use the *win* command, it's unlikely that you'll need to. That's because *Windows* inspects the configuration of your PC as it starts and adapts appropriately. On many PCs, the *win* command is already in the file that contains the start-up commands for your system (AUTOEXEC.BAT) so *Windows* starts automatically when you start your PC.

As *Windows* starts, it displays the logo screen in part 1 of figure 3-1. After a moment, the logo disappears and a blank screen appears. *Windows* displays an hourglass on this screen. The hourglass means that you should wait while the start-up process finishes.

During start-up, *Windows* always loads and executes at least one program called the *Windows shell*. The shell lets you start other programs. If you look at part 2 of figure 3-1, you can see the default shell program. It's called the *Program Manager*, and that's the shell that most *Windows* users prefer.

The distinguishing feature of *Windows* is its *windows*. These are just the rectangular workspaces that appear on the screen. In part 2 of figure 3-1, you can see two windows. One is labeled "Program Manager;" the other is labeled "Main." As you will soon see, you are by no means limited to two windows at a time.

When you start *Windows* right after you install it, the opening screen looks like the one in part 2 of figure 3-1. However, you're not going to find many PCs where *Windows* looks exactly like this. That's because the *Windows* display changes as you work with it. On some systems, for example, the starting *Windows* screen looks the way you left it at the end of your last work session. In addition, you can customize *Windows* so it looks the way you want it to.

Part 1

The logo screen that *Windows* displays immediately after start-up.

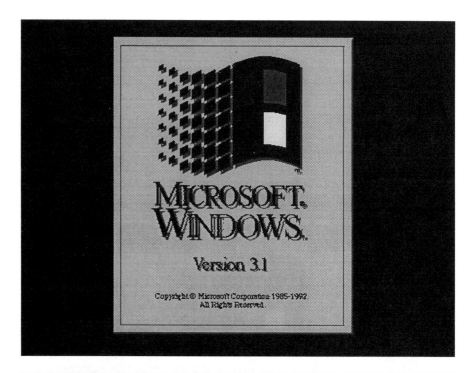

Part 2

Windows displays the Program Manager as the default shell program after start-up is complete.

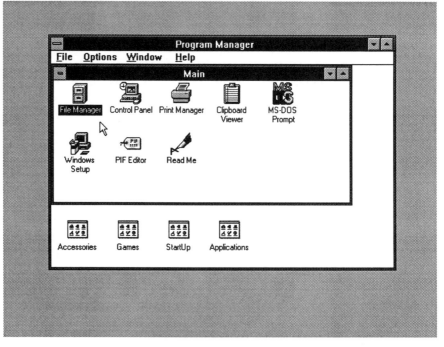

Figure 3-1   The logo screen and shell program that *Windows* displays by default

Figure 3-2 gives some examples of the types of starting screens you may encounter as you move from one PC to another. In example 1, you can see a Program Manager screen that's similar to the one in figure 3-1. In fact, the only difference is that this screen doesn't show a window labeled Main within the Program Manager window. Instead, the Main window has been reduced to an *icon*, which is just a small symbol that represents a program or a group of programs.

Example 2 shows you what the starting screen looks like when the File Manager is used as the shell program instead of the Program Manager. On the left inside the smaller window is a structure that shows the directories that are stored on one of the PC's disk or diskette drives. On the right is a list of all the files that are stored in the highlighted directory on the left. In chapter 5, you'll learn how to use the File Manager for managing your directories and files.

Example 3 shows what the starting screen can look like when more than one program is started when *Windows* starts. If you study this screen, you'll see windows entitled Clock, File Manager, Write, and Paintbrush. One program is running in each of these windows, and the windows are overlapped so only the Paintbrush window shows completely. Although few people would want to start all the programs in this example, don't be surprised if you see two or more applications running when you start *Windows*.

Example 4 in figure 3-2 shows one way to take control of a complicated *Windows* environment like the one in example 3. Here, the same programs that are running in example 3 are still running, but each program appears as an icon. Then, whenever you want to work with a program, you just restore it to full size with a simple mouse action. Later in this chapter, you'll learn how to minimize a window to an icon and how to restore it to a useful size.

Application and document windows   When *Windows* is running, the background is called the *desktop*. Then, when a program is started, *Windows* creates a workspace for it on the desktop called an *application window*. All of the activity of the application program takes place inside its application window. In figure 3-3, the gray area is the desktop, and the larger window is the application window for the Program Manager.

Within an application window, a typical program creates its own workspaces called *document windows*. These windows are always inside and subordinate to the application windows of the programs that created them. Although the name "document window" only makes sense for a program like a word processor that actually creates documents, all windows that are used by application programs are called document windows. In figure 3-3, for example, the Main window is a document window that's subordinate to the application window of the Program Manager. Instead of a document, though, this window

Example 1

Some *Windows*
systems display
the Program
Manager at start-
up with program
groups reduced to
icons.

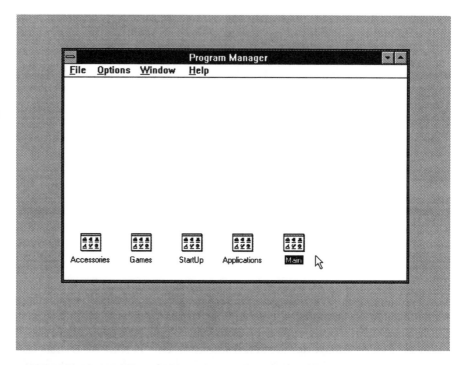

Example 2

Some *Windows*
systems display
the File Manager
as the shell
program at start-
up.

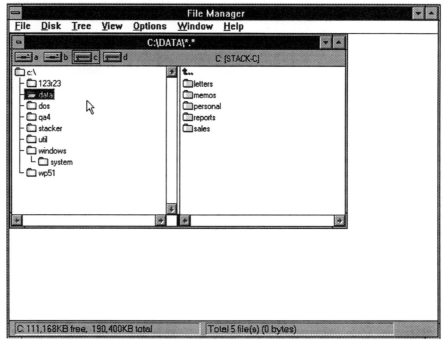

Figure 3-2   Four examples that show the variety of screens a *Windows* system can display after
start-up

Example 3

Some *Windows* systems launch two or more application programs at start-up.

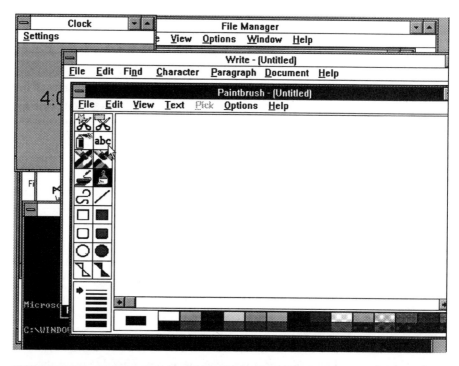

Example 4

Some *Windows* systems launch two or more application programs at start-up, but display them as icons.

Figure 3-2   Four examples that show the variety of screens a *Windows* system can display after start-up (continued)

displays the icons for programs that are in the Main group of *Windows* programs.

Nearly all windows have *title bars* at their tops as shown in figure 3-3. The title bar of an application window shows the name of the program that owns the window. The title bar of a document window depends on what the window contains. If the document window contains a document, like a word processing file or a spreadsheet, the title bar shows the name of the document. When you work with more than one window at a time, you'll come to depend on title bars because they help identify the windows.

On the left side of a window's title bar, you'll find a box that contains a horizontal line. This is the *control-menu box*, and you can access the window's *control menu* through it. The control menu provides commands that you can use for managing the window, and you'll learn how to use them in this chapter.

Beneath the title bar of an application window, you'll always find a *menu bar*. In figure 3-3, you can see the menu bar for the Program Manager. The menu bar lets you access *program menus* so you can issue the commands that the program provides. Usually, you can use the menu bar to help identify an application window because document windows don't have menu bars.

How to end *Windows*   Before I show you how to end *Windows*, you should know that most *Windows* users never need to leave the *Windows* environment. Once you end the application programs you've been using and return to the Program Manager, it's safe to turn your PC off with *Windows* still running. Since you can run your DOS programs while you're using *Windows*, you usually don't have to leave *Windows* for that reason. But in the unlikely event that you need to run a DOS application without *Windows* running, here's how to end *Windows*.

To exit from *Windows*, you just close the application window for the shell program you're using. Because most people use the Program Manager as their shell program, that means you'll probably end *Windows* by closing the window for the Program Manager. To close an application window, you can use several different methods. One of them is pressing the F4 key while you hold down the Alt key (Alt+F4). Later in this chapter, you'll learn other techniques for ending programs.

When you end the *Windows* shell program, *Windows* warns you that it's about to end and gives you a chance to change your mind by displaying a message like the one in figure 3-4. If you've changed any documents but haven't saved your work, *Windows* displays a different warning. Then, you can return to the application program and save your work. Or, you can choose to abandon the work you were doing and end *Windows*.

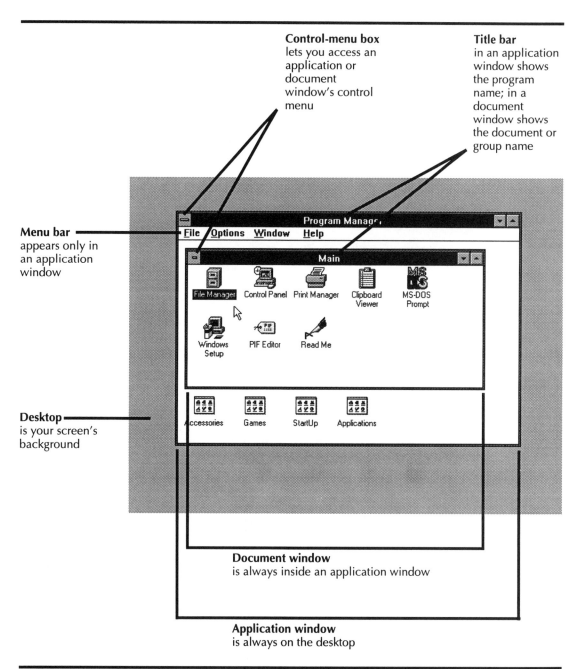

Control-menu box
lets you access an
application or
document
window's control
menu

Title bar
in an application
window shows
the program
name; in a
document
window shows
the document or
group name

Menu bar
appears only in
an application
window

Desktop
is your screen's
background

Document window
is always inside an application window

Application window
is always on the desktop

Figure 3-3   The two types of windows that you work with in *Windows*

When you quit
the shell program,
Windows displays
this message to
have you verify
that you really
want to quit
Windows.

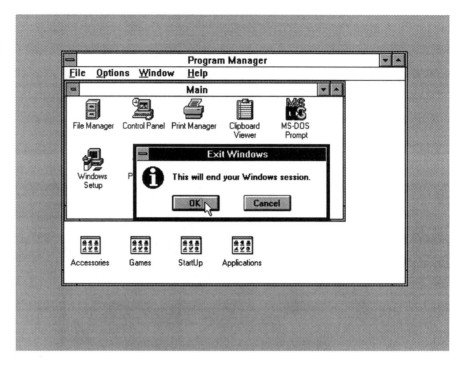

Figure 3-4   The message *Windows* displays before it ends

Basic mouse skills for working with windows

Windows was designed to be used with a mouse. That's why you can perform
many of the *Windows* functions more easily with a mouse than you can with
a keyboard. Once you learn the basic mouse actions, you can use the actions
to minimize, maximize, and restore windows; to move a window; to change the
size of a window; and to scroll through a window.

The four basic mouse actions   To use a mouse with *Windows*, you need
to know how to use four mouse actions. These are summarized in figure 3-5.
Although these mouse actions may seem a little difficult if you haven't used
a mouse before, you'll get plenty of practice with them if you do the exercises
in this chapter. Before long, I think you'll agree that using a mouse is a natural,
easy, and efficient way to work in the *Windows* environment.

The first mouse action is *point*. To *point* means to move the mouse so the
mouse pointer is on an object. You use pointing in combination with one of the
other three mouse actions.

Action	How to do it
Point	Move the mouse so the mouse pointer is positioned on the object or control that you're interested in.
Click	Without moving the mouse pointer off the object you're pointing to, press the left mouse button down, then release it.
Double-click	Without moving the mouse pointer off the object you're pointing to, press the left mouse button down, then release it, then press it down again, then release it again. Do this quickly, in less than a second.
Drag	After you point to an object, press and hold down the left mouse button, move the mouse pointer to a new location, then release the left mouse button.

Figure 3-5	The four basic mouse actions you use with *Windows*

After you point to an object, you *click* the mouse to tell *Windows*: "That's the one I want," or "I want to do that." To click, you just press the left mouse button down and release it. A click isn't completed, though, if you press the left mouse button down, but move the mouse pointer off the object you were pointing to before you release the button. This is an intentional part of the design of the *Windows* interface. If you have second thoughts about an operation, you can often cancel it by not completing a click while it's on an object.

To *double-click* means to click the mouse twice in quick succession, usually, in less than a second, without moving the mouse pointer off the object you've pointed to. Often, you click to select the object you've pointed to, and you double-click to activate a function. If, for example, you want to start, or *launch*, a program from an icon, you double-click on the icon. Often, a double-click is a shortcut for an operation that would require you to point at one object, click on it to select it, then point to another object, and click on it.

If you need to move an object from one place to another, you can use the mouse to *drag* it. To do this, you point to an object, press and hold down the left mouse button, move the mouse pointer to the new location while the object is dragged along with it, and release the mouse button. When you release the mouse button, the object is "dropped" at the new location. You can also use the drag action to select a menu command, as you'll soon see. And in most word processing programs, you can drag the mouse pointer across a block of text to select it for a subsequent action like copying, moving, or deleting.

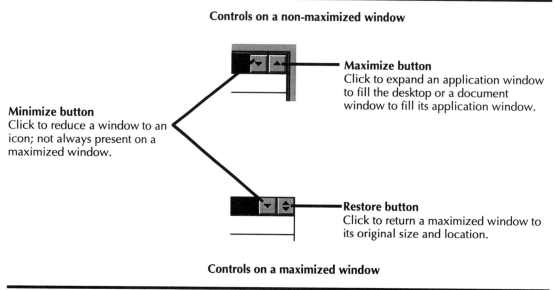

Controls on a non-maximized window

Maximize button
Click to expand an application window to fill the desktop or a document window to fill its application window.

Minimize button
Click to reduce a window to an icon; not always present on a maximized window.

Restore button
Click to return a maximized window to its original size and location.

Controls on a maximized window

Figure 3-6   The control buttons for minimizing, maximizing, and restoring windows

How to minimize, maximize, and restore windows   *Minimizing* a window means reducing it to an icon. *Maximizing* a window means expanding it so it uses all of the space available to it. And *restoring* a window means returning it to the size, shape, and location it had before it was minimized or maximized.

To perform one of these operations, you just click on one of the buttons shown in figure 3-6. These buttons are located in the upper right corner of a window, and both application and document windows usually have these buttons. The effect of clicking on one of the buttons is shown in figure 3-7. When you click on a *minimize button*, the window is reduced to an icon. When you maximize a window, its *maximize button* is replaced by another kind of button, one with a double-headed arrow that points up and down. This is the *restore button*. To restore a maximized window, you click on the restore button. To restore a minimized window from an icon, you double-click on the icon.

When you work with a document window, the maximize action is confined to the application window that owns the document window. Thus, the document window fills the entire area available in the application window as shown in the top screen in figure 3-7. When you work with an application window, minimized icons appear at the bottom of the desktop, and maximized windows fill the entire screen. You'll see examples of this later in this chapter.

Maximized document window
Click on the restore button to restore the window to its original size, shape, and position.

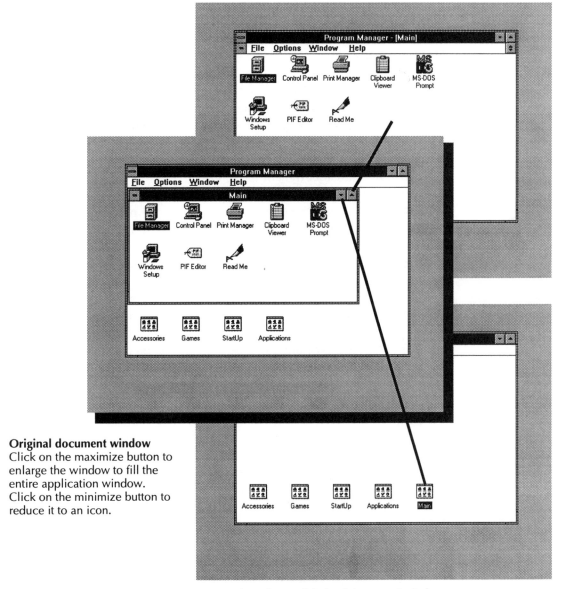

Original document window
Click on the maximize button to enlarge the window to fill the entire application window. Click on the minimize button to reduce it to an icon.

Icon for a minimized document window
Double-click on the icon to restore the window to its original size, shape, and position.

Figure 3-7   The effects of clicking on the minimize, maximize, and restore buttons

How to move a window   *Windows* lets you move an application window anywhere on the desktop. You can also move a document window, but only within the application window that owns it. The easiest way to move a window is to drag its title bar to a new location with a mouse. I'll show you an example of that in a moment.

How to size a window   To change the width or height of a window, you can use the mouse to drag the *border* or *corner* of a window to a new position. When you point to a border or corner, the mouse pointer changes. If you point to the top or bottom border of a window, the mouse pointer changes to a vertical bar with arrows on each end. Then, you can drag that border up or down to make the window taller or shorter. If you point to the left or right border of a window, the mouse pointer changes to a horizontal bar with arrows on each end. Then, you can drag that border right or left to make the window wider or narrower. And if you want to change both the vertical and horizontal dimensions of a window, you can point to a corner. When you do, the pointer changes into a diagonal bar with arrows on each end. Then, you can drag that corner to a new position.

Figure 3-8 illustrates the use of a mouse for moving and sizing a window. In parts 1 through 3, you can see how the mouse is used to move a window. In parts 4 and 5, you can see how the mouse is used to change the size of a window. Note in part 4 how the mouse pointer looks when it's on a corner. The key to using this technique for sizing a window is making sure that the mouse pointer changes to the right type of pointer before you start an operation.

How to scroll through the contents of a window   If a window is too small to show all of its contents, *scroll bars* are automatically added to it as illustrated in figure 3-9. Then, you can use the mouse to work with the *scroll arrows*, *scroll boxes,* and scroll bars to move the contents of a window up, down, right, and left. If you experiment with the mouse techniques that are summarized in this figure, you'll soon see how easy it is to work with scroll bars. And you can practice all of the mouse techniques you've just learned in the exercise that follows.

Part 1

To move a
window, position
the mouse pointer
on its title bar and
drag the window
to the new
location.

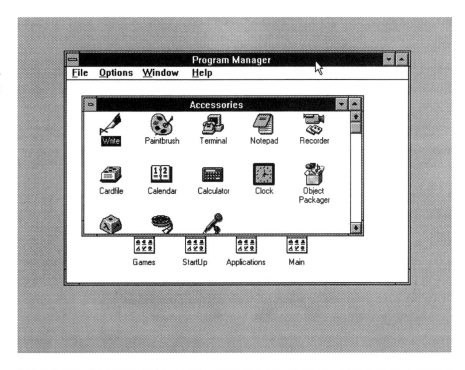

Part 2

As you drag a
window to
reposition it, a
"ghost" outline
follows the mouse
pointer to show
where the new
position will be if
you release the
mouse button.
When you release
the mouse button
to complete the
drag, the window
pops to the new
location as you
can see in Part 3.

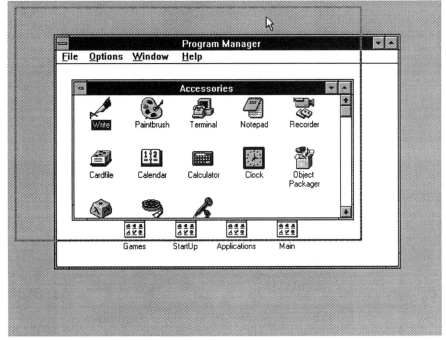

Figure 3-8   How to move and size windows

Part 3

To resize a
window, drag one
of its borders or,
as in this exam-
ple, one of its
corners.

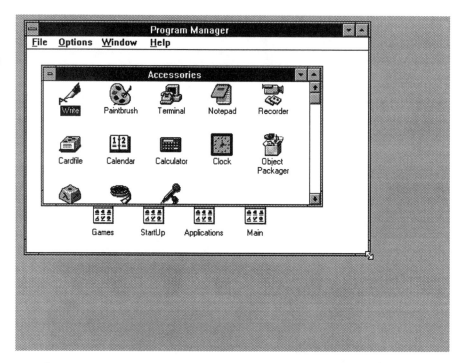

Part 4

As you drag the
corner, a "ghost"
image of the
window outline
follows the mouse
pointer to let you
decide when to
release the mouse
button and
complete the drag
operation.

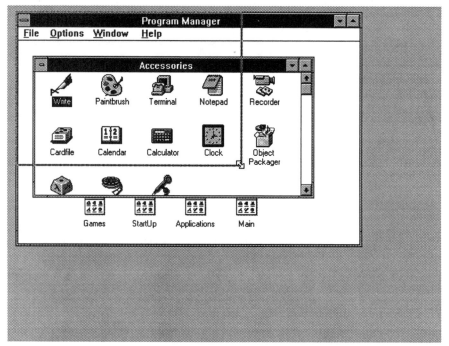

Figure 3-8   How to move and size windows (continued)

Part 5

When you release
the mouse button,
the window's size
is adjusted.

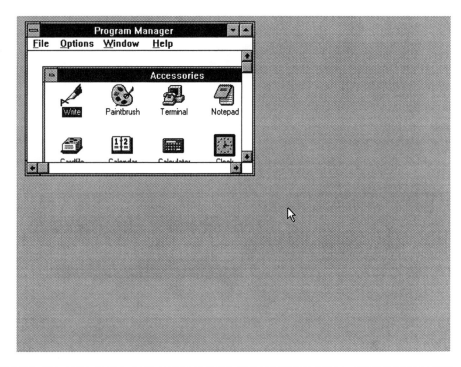

Figure 3-8   How to move and size windows (continued)

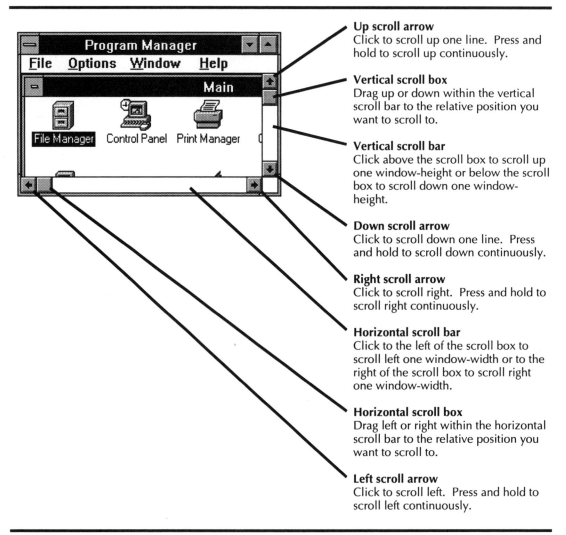

Up scroll arrow
Click to scroll up one line. Press and hold to scroll up continuously.

Vertical scroll box
Drag up or down within the vertical scroll bar to the relative position you want to scroll to.

Vertical scroll bar
Click above the scroll box to scroll up one window-height or below the scroll box to scroll down one window-height.

Down scroll arrow
Click to scroll down one line. Press and hold to scroll down continuously.

Right scroll arrow
Click to scroll right. Press and hold to scroll right continuously.

Horizontal scroll bar
Click to the left of the scroll box to scroll left one window-width or to the right of the scroll box to scroll right one window-width.

Horizontal scroll box
Drag left or right within the horizontal scroll bar to the relative position you want to scroll to.

Left scroll arrow
Click to scroll left. Press and hold to scroll left continuously.

Figure 3-9   How to scroll through the contents of a window

Exercise 3-1

Basic *Windows* skills

1. If it isn't already running, start *Windows* on your PC by typing *win* at the DOS command prompt and pressing the Enter key.

2. When *Windows* completes its start-up, count the application windows you can see. How many of them are there, and what programs are running in them?

3. Minimize each application window on your desktop by clicking on its minimize button. When you've finished, there shouldn't be any open windows. There should be an icon at the bottom of the desktop for each minimized application window. At the least, there should be an icon for the Program Manager.

4. Practice restoring, minimizing, and maximizing the Program Manager's application window:

    (a) Restore the window by double-clicking on its minimized icon.

    (b) Minimize the window again by clicking on its minimize button.

    (c) Restore the window by double-clicking on its icon.

    (d) Maximize the Program Manager's application window by clicking on its maximize button. Now, the window should fill the desktop.

    (e) Restore the window to its original size by clicking on its restore button.

5. Practice restoring, minimizing, and maximizing document windows:

    (a) If any document windows are open inside the Program Manager's application window, minimize each of them by clicking on its minimize button.

    (b) Restore the window for the Accessories program group by double-clicking on its minimized icon.

    (c) Maximize the Accessories group window by clicking on its maximize button. How does maximizing a document window differ from maximizing an application window?

    (d) Restore the Accessories group window to its original size by clicking on its restore button.

    (e) Minimize the Accessories group window by clicking on its minimize button.

    (f) Restore the Accessories group window by double-clicking on its minimized icon.

Continued on the next page...

Exercise 3-1 (*continued*)
Basic *Windows* skills

6. Practice moving an application window by dragging the Program Manager's application window to different positions on the desktop:

    (a) Drag the title bar of the Program Manager's application window a bit to move the window, then release the mouse button to complete the move. Notice that *Windows* uses a ghost outline as you drag the window to show where its new position will be.

    (b) Drag the window down so only the top of it is visible, then drag it back to its original position.

    (c) Drag the window far to the right so only its left side is visible, then drag it back to its original position.

    (d) Drag the window as far up as you can (notice that you can't move it so far up that you can't still point to the very bottom of its title bar), then drag the window back to its original position.

7. Practice moving a document window:

    (a) The Accessories document window should still be open inside the Program Manager's application window. If it isn't, double-click on the Accessories icon to restore the window.

    (b) Drag the title bar of the Accessories window to move it. Notice that you can't drag it outside the Program Manager's application window. A document window exists only inside the application window of the program that owns it.

    (c) Drag the title bar of the Accessories window to move it back to its original position.

8. Practice sizing the Program Manager's application window:

    (a) Drag the top or bottom border of the Program Manager window until it's roughly half its original height. Notice that the items that appeared at the bottom of the window are no longer visible. Also notice that *Windows* added a vertical scroll bar to the window.

    (b) Drag the top or bottom border of the window to make the window as short as possible.

    (c) Drag a border of the window to return it to its original size.

    (d) Drag the left or right border of the window to resize it so it's as narrow as possible. Notice that when you do this, *Windows* "stacks" the menu names so you can still see all of them.

    (e) Drag a border of the window to return it to its original size.

    (f) Drag one of the corners of the window to change its shape and size so the window is about half its starting width and height.

Continued on the next page...

Exercise 3-1 (*continued*)
Basic *Windows* skills

9. Practice with the scroll bars that are now part of the Program Manager's application window:

   (a) Use the mouse to operate the vertical scroll bar to scroll down so you can see the contents of the window that are no longer visible now that you have reduced its height.

   (b) Use the mouse to operate the horizontal scroll bar to scroll left and right so you can see the contents of the window that are no longer visible now that you have reduced its width.

   (c) Scroll so the upper-left corner of the window's contents appears.

10. Resize and move the Program Manager's application window so it's roughly its original size and in its original position.

11. To end *Windows,* press the F4 key while you hold down the Alt key (Alt+F4). Then, click on the OK button when *Windows* asks if you want to end your *Windows* session.

How to use the mouse to start and end a *Windows* application

In all, *Windows* provides seven different ways to start an application program and several ways to end a program. In practice, though, all you have to know is a simple mouse technique for starting any *Windows* application and another simple technique for ending any application.

How to start a program by double-clicking on its icon   The easiest way to start a program from the Program Manager is to double-click on its icon. However, the Program Manager uses two kinds of icons. One type of icon represents a specific program called a *program item*. You can refer to this type of item as a *program item icon*, or just as a *program icon*. The other type of icon represents a group of programs called a *program group*. You can refer to this type of item as a *program group icon*, or just as a *group icon*. To find the icon for a program item, you may have to *open* the program group that contains the program item.

To illustrate, figure 3-10 shows you how to start the Notepad program, which is in the Accessories program group. To open the group, you double-click on the Accessories icon as shown in part 1 of this figure. This opens the document window shown in part 2. Because this document window contains a group of programs, it can also be called a *group window*. As you can see, the Accessories window contains one icon for each of the 13 *Windows* accessory programs. These programs are sometimes referred to as *applets* instead of application programs, because they are simpler than the applications that are sold separately.

Once its group window is open, you can start Notepad by double-clicking on its icon as shown in part 2 of figure 3-10. Then, *Windows* retrieves the Notepad program file from the hard disk, loads it into internal memory, and starts it in a new application window as shown in part 3. At this point, you can start using the program.

Although you can't see it in part 3, the Program Manager is still running, and its application window is still on the desktop. You just can't see it because it's smaller than Notepad's application window, and Notepad's window is on top of it.

If you want to run a DOS program from the Program Manager, you can probably find an icon for it. That's because *Windows* automatically creates icons for most of the DOS programs that are on your PC as part of the *Windows* installation procedure. If you add a DOS program to your PC after you've installed *Windows*, though, you may not be able to find an icon for it. In that case, you can create an icon for it as explained in chapter 10.

Part 1

The icon for the
Notepad program
is in the Accesso-
ries group. Point
to the icon for the
program group
and double-click.

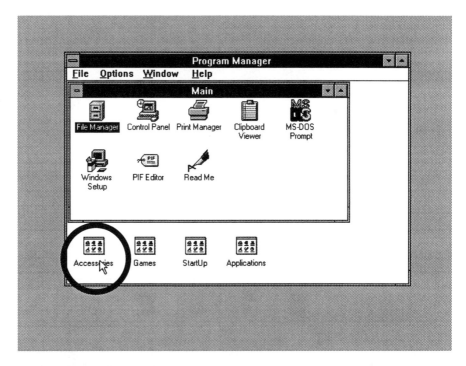

Part 2

With the Accesso-
ries document
window open,
double-click on
the Notepad icon
to start the
program.

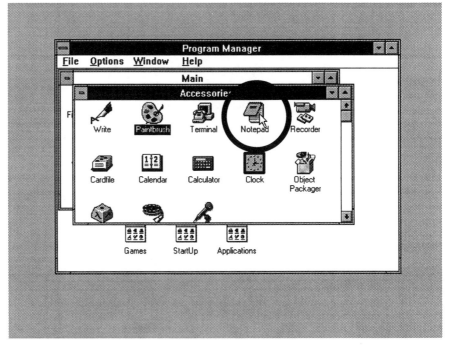

Figure 3-10   How to use the mouse to start and end an application program

Part 3

Windows
retrieves the
application
program associat-
ed with the icon
from the disk,
loads it into
internal memory,
and opens a new
application
window for it. To
end the program,
point to the
control-menu box
and double-click.

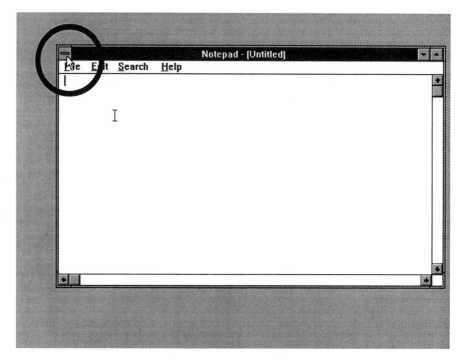

Figure 3-10   How to use the mouse to start and end an application program (continued)

How to end a program by double-clicking on its control-menu box   The
easiest way to end a program is to double-click on the control-menu box for the
program's application window. This is illustrated by part 3 of figure 3-10. If
you haven't saved your work when you end a program, a warning message
appears. Then, you can return to the program to save your work. Or, you can
go on to end the program.

Four ways to switch from one *Windows* application to another

Because *Windows* provides for multitasking, you can start two or more
programs at the same time. However, you can only work on one program at a
time. That program is called the *active program*, and it is running in the *active
application window*. If several application windows are displayed on the
desktop, the active window is always the one on top, and the title bar of the
active application window is always highlighted. In part 3 of figure 3-10, for
example, Notepad is the active program, and its application window is on top
of the Program Manager's

To switch from one program to another, *Windows* gives you several
methods. Each one is appropriate in some situations. Figure 3-11 lists the four

1.　Click on an inactive application window.

2.　Use Fast Alt+Tab Switching.

3.　Use Alt+Esc Switching.

4.　Minimize and restore application windows.

Figure 3-11　　　Four ways to switch between programs

methods that I'll cover next. And later in this chapter, I'll show you a fifth method.

Click on any part of an inactive application window　　　The most direct way to switch from one program to another is to click on any part of an inactive application window. When you do, *Windows* brings that application window to the top of the stack and makes it the active window. Of course, some part of the application window has to be visible in order to click on it.

　　I prefer this method because it's natural and easy for me. As a result, I often arrange the windows on my desktop so they overlap with a part of each window visible, much like example 3 in figure 3-2. Although a desktop with this many open windows looks cluttered, it can still be easy and efficient to use.

Use Fast Alt+Tab Switching　　　Another way to switch from one application to another is to use a *Windows* option called *Fast Alt+Tab Switching*. This feature lets you scan through the names of the programs that are running and switch to the one you want. To use this feature, you hold down the Alt key and press the Tab key repeatedly. Each time you press Tab, a panel like the one in figure 3-12 appears. Then, when the name of the program you want appears, you release the Alt key and that program becomes the active application.

　　Fast Alt+Tab Switching is simple and efficient. And you can use this method for switching between both DOS and *Windows* programs. But you should realize that it is an optional feature. Although this option is on by default, someone may have deactivated it on your PC. In that case, you can reactivate it by using the Control Panel as described in chapter 9.

Use Alt+Esc Switching　　　A third way to switch from one program to another is to use the Alt+Esc keystroke combination. Each time you press this combination, the next program in sequence becomes the active program. If just two programs are running, that's what you want. But if several programs are running, this can be inefficient. Unlike Fast Alt+Tab Switching, Alt+Esc Switching can't be turned off, so it's always available. And this method can be used for switching between both DOS and *Windows* applications.

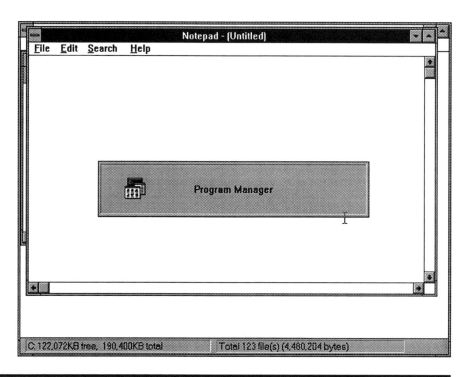

Figure 3-12   An example of the program-name panel that *Windows* displays when you use Fast Alt+Tab Switching

Minimize and restore application windows   The first three ways to switch from one program to another leave the application windows unchanged. In contrast, this fourth way uses the minimize and restore functions, which change the size of a window. When you want to switch to another program, you click on the minimize button for the current program. This reduces the active window to an icon that appears at the bottom of the desktop, but the program is still running. Then, to switch to another program, you double-click on its icon.

Figure 3-13 illustrates the use of this method. In parts 1 and 2, you can see what happens when you minimize the Notepad window. Because Notepad is reduced to an icon at the bottom of the screen, the Program Manager becomes visible, and it is the active program. Then, if you minimize the Program Manager too, your desktop looks like the one in part 3. At this point, you can start either program by double clicking on its icon. In part 4, you can see what happens when you double-click on the Notepad icon. And in part 5, you can see what happens when you maximize the Notepad program.

When you use this method for switching between programs, you usually start by minimizing all of the program windows. Then, when you activate a window, you maximize it so you can use the full screen while you work with it.

Part 1

You can click on an application window's minimize button to reduce the window to an icon.

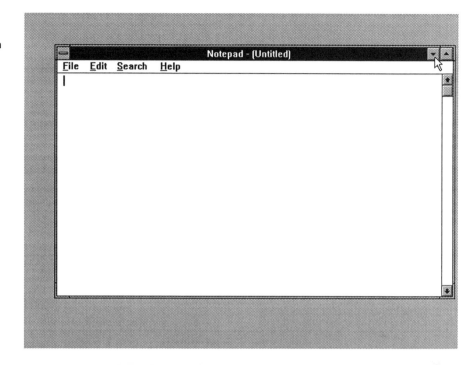

Part 2

After you minimize an application window, you can see other windows that it was covering so you can minimize them too.

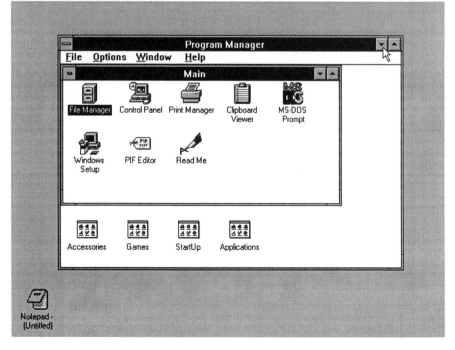

Figure 3-13   How to switch between programs by minimizing, maximizing, and restoring application windows

Part 3

Now, both of the
programs that are
running have
been reduced to
icons. To restore
a minimized
program, you
double-click on
its icon.

Part 4

When you restore
an application
window, it returns
to its original size,
shape, and
position. If you
want an application
window to fill the
entire screen, click
on its maximize
button, as in this
example.

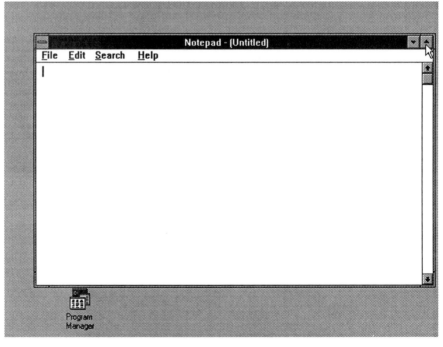

Figure 3-13   How to switch between programs by minimizing, maximizing, and restoring
application windows (continued)

Part 5

When you
maximize a
window, its
maximize button
is replaced with
the restore button.
If you click on the
restore button, the
Notepad applica-
tion window will
return to the size,
shape and
position it had in
part 4.

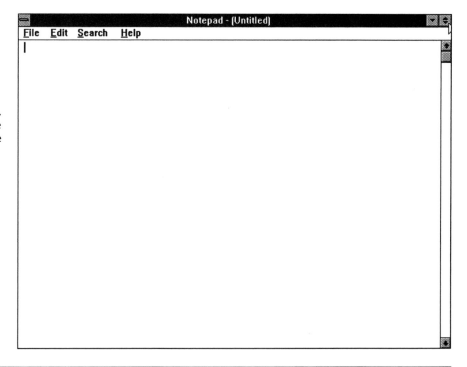

Figure 3-13   How to switch between programs by minimizing, maximizing, and restoring
application windows (continued)

Exercise 3-2

How to start your applications, switch between them, and end them

1. If it isn't already running, start *Windows* on your PC by entering *win* at the DOS command prompt.

2. When *Windows* completes its start-up, count the application windows you can see. How many of them are there, and what programs are running in them?

3. Minimize all of the application windows on your desktop, except the one for the Program Manager. To do so, click on the minimize button of each application window.

4. If any document windows are open inside the Program Manager's application window, click on their minimize buttons to close them.

5. Double-click on the icon for the Accessories group to open its document window.

6. Start the Clock accessory program:

   (a) Find the icon for the Clock program in the Accessories document window. You may not be able to see the icon if the window is too small to show all of its contents. If that's the case, click on different parts of the scroll bars on the window to display the contents of the window or enlarge the window.

   (b) Double-click on the icon for the Clock program to start it. Now, the Clock application window is the active window.

7. Switch back and forth between the Clock and the Program Manager:

   (a) The easiest way to switch from the Clock to the Program Manager is to click on the application window for the Program Manager. Try it. Does the Program Manager's application window cover the Clock application window? Remember, the Clock is still running whether you can see it or not.

   (b) Use Fast Alt+Tab Switching to switch from the Program Manager to the Clock.

   (c) Use Fast Alt+Tab Switching to switch from the Clock to the Program Manager.

   (d) Use Alt+Esc Switching to switch from the Program Manager to the Clock.

   (e) Use Alt+Esc Switching to switch back to the Program Manager.

   (f) Switch to the Clock; you decide how.

8. Minimize the Clock program's application window.

Continued on the next page...

Exercise 3-2 (continued)
How to start your applications, switch between them, and end them

9. Start the Calculator program by double-clicking on its icon in the Accessories group window. How many programs are running now? Where are their windows? At the least, three programs are running (Program Manager, Clock, and Calculator).

10. Minimize the Calculator program's application window. How many icons appear at the bottom of the desktop? How many windows appear on the desktop?

11. Start the Notepad program by double-clicking on its icon in the Accessories group window. How many programs are running now? Where are their windows? At the least, four programs are running (Program Manager, Clock, Calculator, and Notepad).

12. Minimize the Notepad program's application window. How many icons appear at the bottom of the desktop? How many windows appear on the desktop?

13. Minimize the Program Manager's application window. How many icons appear at the bottom of the desktop? How many windows appear on the desktop? There shouldn't be any.

14. Restore the application windows for the Clock, Calculator, and Notepad programs by double-clicking on their icons.

15. Use Fast Alt+Tab Switching to switch between these programs:
    (a) Switch to the Clock program. How many application windows can you see?
    (b) Switch from the Clock to the Calculator.
    (c) Switch from the Calculator to the Clock.
    (d) Switch from the Clock to the Notepad.
    (d) Switch from the Notepad to the Program Manager. Notice that *Windows* restored the application window for the Program Manager automatically when you chose it as you used Fast Alt+Tab Switching.

16. Repeat step 15, only use Alt+Esc to switch from one program to another. How does this differ from Fast Alt+Tab Switching?

17. Close the application windows for the Clock, Calculator, and Notepad programs, but not for the Program Manager. You'll have to switch from program to program to do this. Try the different techniques you've learned for ending a program: double-click on the application window control-menu box for one, and type Alt+F4 for another.

18. To end *Windows*, point to the control-menu box in the upper left corner of the Program Manager's application window, then double-click. Click on the OK button when *Windows* asks if you want to end your *Windows* session.

How to issue menu commands

Windows applications make all of their commands available to you through menus. A *program menu* (also called an *application menu*) presents a list of commands, called *menu commands*, that are grouped under a *menu name* that appears in the menu bar of an application window. The number of menus that a program offers depends on the program. If you look at the Notepad window in part 1 of figure 3-13, you can see that this program offers File, Edit, Search, and Help menus. In contrast, the Program Manager in part 2 of this figure offers File, Options, Window, and Help menus. Although most programs have more than four menus, some have fewer.

A *control menu* is also available with each application and document window. The commands that are available in the control menu for an application window are almost the same as those available in the control menu for a document window. In particular, both menus offer Minimize, Maximize, and Restore commands. Because it's usually easier to perform these functions by clicking on the buttons for these functions, you probably won't use the control menus much. Nevertheless, I'll introduce you to these commands later in this chapter.

Figure 3-14 summarizes the procedures that you can use to issue menu commands. As you can see, you can use either the mouse or the keyboard to issue a command. Although the techniques for accessing a menu are slightly different for program and control menus, the techniques for selecting a command from a menu are the same for either type of menu.

How to issue a program menu command   To issue a command from a program menu with the mouse, you can use either of the two methods shown in figure 3-14. In step 1 of the first method, you pull down the menu that you want by pointing to it and clicking the mouse. In step 2, you issue a command by pointing to it and clicking. Because the menu appears to drop down from the menu bar, menus like these are often called *drop-down menus* or *pull-down menus*.

In the second method in figure 3-14, you use the mouse to point to the menu name. Then, you just drag the highlight down to the command you want to issue and release the mouse button. If you change your mind, you can drag the highlight off the menu before releasing the mouse button. This cancels the command.

To issue a program command with the keyboard, you can use either of the two methods that are summarized in figure 3-14. The first method is more efficient because it only requires three keystrokes to issue any command. In step 1, you press the Alt key. In step 2, you press the underlined letter of the

---

How to use the mouse to issue a command from a program menu

Method 1   1. Point to the name of the menu that contains the command you want to issue, and click on it to pull the menu down.

                  2. Point to the name of the command you want to issue and click on it.

Method 2   Drag the highlight from the menu name to the command you want to issue; then, release the mouse button.

How to use the keyboard to issue a command from a program menu

Method 1   1. Press the Alt key.

                  2. Press the underlined letter of the menu that you want to pull down.

                  3. Press the underlined letter of the command that you want to issue.

Method 2   1. Press the Alt key.

                  2. Use the left or right arrow key to move the highlight to the name of the menu that you want, and press the Enter key.

                  3. Use the up or down arrow key to move the highlight to the command that you want to issue, and press the Enter key.

How to use the mouse to issue a command from a control menu

                  Use the same techniques that you use for a program menu, but point to the control-menu box for the type of window that you want to work with. If you click once on a minimized application icon, the control menu pops up from the icon.

How to use the keyboard to pull down a control menu

Window type	Keystroke combination
For an application window	Alt, Spacebar
For a document window	Alt, Hyphen

Figure 3-14   How to issue a menu command

menu that you want to pull down. In step 3, you press the underlined letter of the command you want to issue.

In the second keyboard method, you use the arrow keys to move to the menu you want to pull down or the command you want to issue. Then, when the highlight is on the right menu or command, you press the Enter key. Since this takes more keystrokes, you probably won't use it unless you want to carefully review the menus and commands.

To issue a command to a *Windows* program, you pull down a menu and issue a menu command. In this example, the File menu of the Program Manager is pulled down, and the Run command is selected.

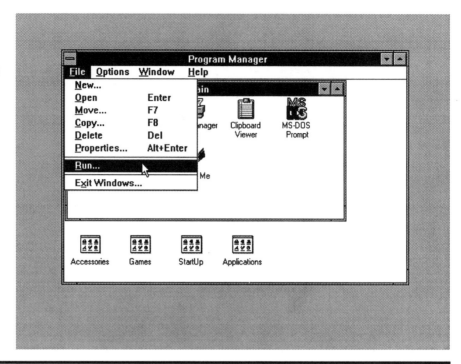

Figure 3-15   An example of a typical pull-down menu

Figure 3-15 shows a typical program menu. In this example, the File menu for the Program Manager is pulled down, and the Run command is highlighted. To issue this command from the keyboard, you just type Alt, *f*, and *r* since the letter F is underlined in File and the letter R is underlined in Run.

To the right of the commands in the menu in figure 3-15, you can see various keystroke combinations. For instance, Enter appears to the right of the Open command; F7 appears to the right of the Move command; and Alt+Enter appears to the right of the Properties command. These combinations represent *keyboard shortcuts*. If you want to start a command without using the menus, you can use the shortcut that's shown for the command.

Note also that the Run command in the menu in figure 3-10 is followed by three dots. This means that *Windows* won't execute the command right after you issue it. Instead, it prompts you for the information it needs for completing the command.

How to issue a control menu command   Although you probably won't use control menus much, figure 3-14 also summarizes what you need to know for using them. To pull down a control menu with the mouse, you just click on the control-menu box for the type of window that you want to work with. If you click on an icon for a minimized application, its control menu pops up. Once the menu is displayed, you use the mouse to select the command just as you do with a program menu.

To pull down a control menu with the keyboard, you use the Alt key followed by the Spacebar for an application window and the Alt key followed by the Hyphen for a document window. Then, you issue the command with the keyboard just as you do for a program menu.

If you press the Alt key followed by the right arrow key, the highlight moves from the first program menu name to the next one. If you continue to press the right arrow key, the highlight will move through all of the program menu names, then on to the control-menu box for the application window, and then on to the control-menu boxes for the document windows. When the highlight is on a control-menu box, you can press the Enter key to pull down the control menu.

How to use a dialog box

When a *Windows* program needs information before it can complete a command, it displays a *dialog box*. *Windows* also uses dialog boxes to display warning messages. The *Windows* standards provide for several types of dialog boxes that are appropriate for different circumstances, and you'll see most of them in this book.

To illustrate, figure 3-16 shows the dialog box for the Run command. As you can see, it contains a *text box*, *check box*, and four *command buttons*. To compete the command, you type the name of the program you want to run in the text box. If you want to start the program in minimized form, you also click on the check box to put a check (X) in the box. Then, when the dialog box looks the way you want it, you click on the OK command button to start the command.

Figure 3-17 shows the controls that you're likely to find in a dialog box. Only the first three are illustrated in this chapter, but you shouldn't have much trouble using any of them. The most complex controls are the drop-down list box and the combo box, and you'll see these illustrated in detail in the next chapter.

The easiest way to respond to a dialog box is with the mouse, but you can also use your keyboard. When you do, you have to be sure that the keystrokes you enter affect the proper control. The control that has the dialog box's *focus* is the one that most keystrokes will affect. In most cases, *Windows* marks the control that has the focus with a light dotted outline.

To move the focus forward from one control to another, press the Tab key. To move the focus backward, press Shift+Tab. If you press the Tab key when the focus is on the last control in a dialog box, the focus wraps around to the first control.

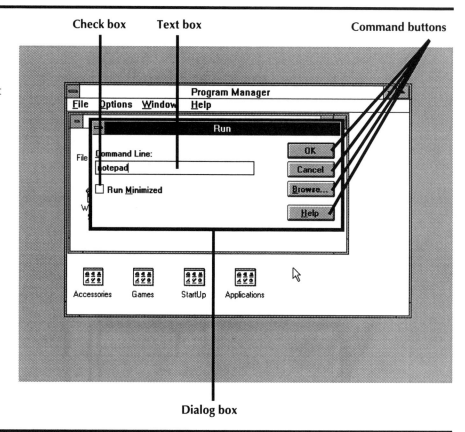

This dialog box appears in response to the Run command. It asks for the command line to run a program. This dialog box uses common types of dialog box controls: command buttons, a text box, and a check box.

Figure 3-16   An example of a typical dialog box

The keyboard technique that you use to change the setting of a control depends on the type of control. When the focus is on a text box, you type a new value through the keyboard. When the focus is on an option button, you can use the left and right arrow keys to change the setting. When the focus is on a check box, you can turn the option on or off by pressing the Spacebar. And when the focus is on a command button, you can activate it by pressing the Enter key.

In most dialog boxes, one command button responds to the Enter key whether or not the focus is on it, as long as the focus isn't on another command button. This means that you don't have to move the focus to it before you press the Enter key. *Windows* displays this default button with a dark outline around it as illustrated by the OK command button in the dialog box in figure 3-16. The default command button is usually the one you're most likely to use or the one that will have the least serious consequences if you choose it accidentally.

How to use dialog box controls	Before	After
Command button Click on the button to issue a command.	Cancel	The dialog box disappears or is replaced by another.
Text box Click in the text box, then type a value.	Command Line: [ ]	Command Line: notepad
Check box Click on a check box to switch an option on or off.	Run Minimized	☒ Run Minimized
Option button Click on one option button in an array to select it. That cancels the other options in the array.	Measurements: ⦿ inch ○ cm	Measurements: ○ inch ⦿ cm
Slider Click on the arrows to move the scroll box to the desired point in a continuous range.	Slow Fast	Slow Fast
Spin box Type a specific value in the text box component, or click on the up or down arrow to display available values.	Delay: 2 Minutes	Delay: 5 Minutes
Drop-down list box Click on the arrow on the right side of the box to display available options. Click on one of the options in the drop-down list box to select it.	Drives: c: stack-c	Drives: c: stack-c a: b: c: stack-c d: real-c
Combo box Type a value directly into the text box, or scroll the list and select an item from it. When you select a list item, it appears in the text box.	File Name: leaves.bmp egypt.bmp flock.bmp honey.bmp leaves.bmp marble.bmp redbrick.bmp rivets.bmp squares.bmp	File Name: rivets.bmp egypt.bmp flock.bmp honey.bmp leaves.bmp marble.bmp redbrick.bmp rivets.bmp squares.bmp

Figure 3-17 How to use common dialog box controls

How to use the Program Manager's Run command to start a program

If you look back to figures 3-15 and 3-16, you can see how the Run command can be used to start a program. After you issue the command, you type the command line that's required to start the program in the Run dialog box. In figure 3-16, *notepad* is typed in the text box so *Windows* will to try to start the program with that name. Since no path is given with the command in the text box, *Windows* will look for the program in its *Windows* directory. Because the Notepad applet is in this directory, this command will start the same program that's shown in part 3 of figure 3-13.

Usually, you won't use the Run command if there's an icon for a program because it's easier to double-click on the icon. However, the Run command is useful when you want to run a program that doesn't have an icon. Perhaps the most common use of this command is for starting the installation programs for new applications. But it can also be used for running a DOS program that doesn't have an icon. You probably won't ever need this command for running *Windows* programs, though, because icons are created for them when you install them.

If you want to run a program that isn't stored in the *Windows* directory, you may need to include the path with the program name. If, for example, you want to run a program named INSTALL from a diskette in the B drive, you can type B:INSTALL in the text box. If you know how to use DOS commands, you shouldn't have any trouble using the Run command because the command in the text box is simply a DOS command.

How to use the Options and Window menu commands for the Program Manager

Figure 3-18 presents the Options and Window menus for the Program Manager. Some of the commands in these menus can help you improve your efficiency as you work with windows.

The commands of the Options menu   The Options menu offers three options that can be turned on or off by selecting the option from the menu. A check by an option means that the option is on, so the first and third options in the menu in figure 3-18 are on. Once you turn one of the options on or off, it stays that way until you change it.

When the Auto Arrange option is on, *Windows* automatically maintains the arrangement of the program icons in a group window. When the Save Settings on Exit option is on, the layout of the Program Manager's windows is saved

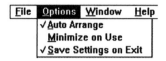

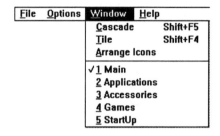

Figure 3-18   The Program Manager's Options and Window menus

when you end the Program Manager. Then, when you restart *Windows* and its Program Manager, its windows look the way they were when you last used them. Both of these options can help you work more efficiently, so you will probably want to keep them on.

The third option is Minimize on Use. If this option is on, the Program Manager is reduced to an icon whenever you start a program from it. This option can be useful if you frequently use the minimize and restore technique for switching from one program to another. Otherwise, you will probably want to keep it off.

The commands of the Window menu   The first two commands in the Window menu in figure 3-18 are the Cascade and Tile commands. When you issue either one of these commands, the Program Manager organizes all of the open group windows as shown in the two examples in figure 3-19. As you can see, the Cascade command overlaps the open windows; the Tile command moves and resizes all of the open group windows so they're roughly the same size and do not overlap. Because the Tile command often results in windows that are too small to be used effectively, the Cascade command is usually more helpful.

You can use the Arrange Icons command to put the program group icons that appear in the Program Manager's application window in order. To do that,

Group windows
arranged by the
Cascade com-
mand

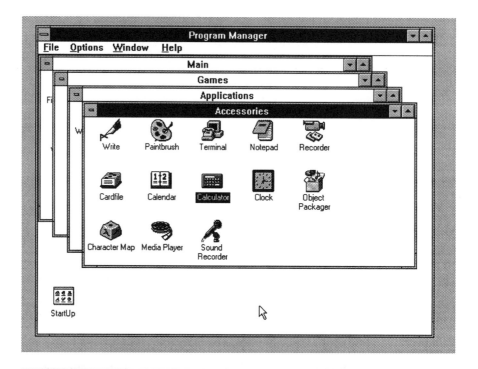

Group windows
arranged by the
Tile command

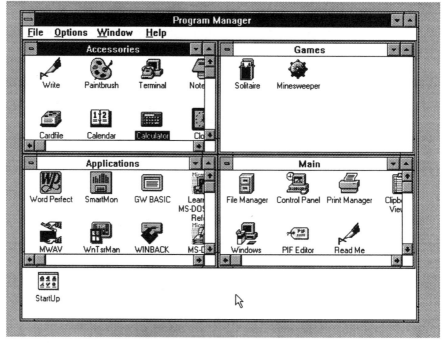

Figure 3-19   The effect of the Program Manager's Cascade and Tile commands on group windows

you must first select one of the program group icons. Then, you issue the Arrange Icons command from the Window menu. This causes the Program Manager to move all of the program group icons into their default positions at the bottom of its application window, evenly spaced, in as many rows are necessary to insure that all of them (or as many as possible) are visible at the same time. This is helpful after you've reduced the size of the Program Manager's application window so some or all of the program group icons seem to have disappeared. If you don't issue this command, you'll have to scroll to get to the icons that aren't visible.

If a program group icon isn't selected, the Arrange Icons command applies to the program icons in the active group window. But if the Arrange Icons option of the Options menu is on, you won't need to use the Arrange Icons command of the Window menu. Instead, the program item icons will be aligned automatically.

The last selections on the Window menu are the names of the group windows that the Program Manager offers. If you select one of these names, its group window becomes the active window. And if the group window isn't open, the Program Manager opens it. Using this method for switching from one group window to another is useful when you have several open group windows and you want to access one that's buried under the others.

How to use the commands of a control menu to work with windows

If you refer back to figure 3-14, you can see that you click on the control-menu box for a window to pull down its control menu. If you click on the icon for a minimized application, the control menu pops up from it. With the keyboard, you press Alt followed by the Spacebar to access the control menu for an application window, and Alt followed by the Hyphen to access the control menu for a document window.

Figure 3-20 presents the control menus for application and document windows. The first five commands in either window let you perform functions that I've already shown you how to do with the mouse. Since you can usually do them more easily with the mouse, you probably won't ever want to perform these functions from the control menu.

The sixth command in each control menu is the Close command. When you issue this command, the window is closed. As you can see in this figure, the shortcut keys are Alt+F4 for closing an application window, and Ctrl+F4 for closing a document window. The mouse shortcut for closing a window is to double-click on the control-menu box for the window.

Control menu from an
application window

Control menu from a
document window

Figure 3-20   Control menus from application and document windows

The last commands in the control menus in figure 3-20 are different. For an application window, the last command is the Switch To command. When you issue this command, a Task List dialog box is displayed that you can use for switching from one program to another. I'll show you how to use this dialog box in a moment. For a document window, the last command is the Next command. When you issue this command, the next document window becomes the active document window.

Because you can perform all of the commands in the control menus in another way, you don't ever have to use them. However, you at least need to know what control menus are because you sometimes display them accidentally by single clicking on a control-menu box or on a minimized application icon when you mean to double-click. Also, if you prefer the keyboard over the mouse, the control menus let you perform basic *Windows* functions without using the mouse.

How to use a command to end a *Windows* application

Ending a program and closing an application window have the same effect. When you end a program, its application window disappears. Similarly, when you close an application window, *Windows* ends the program that's running in it. Now that you've seen examples of control menus and program menus, you should be able to end a program from either a control menu or a program's File menu.

From the control menu   The easiest way to end a program is to double-click on the control-menu box in the program's application window. That's a mouse shortcut for issuing the Close command from the control menu. The keyboard shortcut is to use the Alt+F4 keystroke combination as shown in the control menu in figure 3-20.

From the program's File menu   The other way to end a program is to exit from the program itself. To do that, you can issue the Exit command from the program's File menu. When you issue it, the program ends, and its application window closes. You can issue this command with either the mouse or the keyboard techniques you learned earlier in this chapter.

If you look back to the File menu for the Program Manager in figure 3-15, you can see that its Exit command is named the Exit Windows command. That's because the Program Manager is the *Windows* shell program. When you exit from the shell program, you also exit from *Windows*. For other *Windows* programs, though, this command is just the Exit command.

Exercise 3-3

How to use menu commands

1. If it isn't already running, start *Windows* on your PC by entering *win* at the DOS command prompt.

2. Minimize all of the application windows on your desktop by clicking on the minimize button of each application window.

3. Use control menu commands with the keyboard to practice restoring, minimizing, and maximizing the Program Manager's application window:

   (a) Click once on the minimized icon for the Program Manager to cause its control menu to pop up.

   (b) Notice that the highlight is already on the Restore command. Use the up and down arrow keys to move the highlight from one command to another, and stop when the highlight is on the Maximize command.

   (c) Press the Enter key to issue the Maximize command.

   (d) Access the control menu of the Program Manager's application window with the keyboard: Press Alt, then press the right arrow key repeatedly until the highlight is on the application window's control-menu box. When it is, press Enter to cause the menu to drop down.

   (e) Press Esc twice to dismiss the menu.

   (f) Use Alt followed by the Spacebar to access the menu again.

   (g) Restore the Program Manager's application window to its starting size by issuing the Restore command. Because the highlight is already on the Restore command, all you have to do is press the Enter key.

4. Use Program Manager commands with the keyboard to access your group windows:

   (a) If any group windows are open, use the keyboard to minimize them: Press Alt, then press the right arrow key repeatedly until the highlight is on the active group window's control-menu box. When it is, press Enter to cause the menu to drop down, then type *n* to issue the Minimize command. Do this for each open group window. When you're done, no group windows should be open.

Continued on the next page...

Exercise 3-3 (continued)
How to use menu commands

4. (continued)

(b) Arrange the group icons in the Program Manager's application window by issuing the Arrange Icons command from the Window menu: Type Alt, *w, a.* If any icons were out of place, this command will align them.

(c) Open the first five group windows through the Window menu:

Type Alt, *w, 1* to access the first one in the list;

Type Alt, *w, 2* to access the second one in the list; and so on.

5. Use the mouse to issue Program Manager menu commands to organize your group windows:

(a) Use the mouse to issue the Tile command from the Window menu. You can either (1) drag the menu down to Tile, then release the mouse button or (2) click once on the Window menu name, then click once on the Tile command name. Notice how the tiled windows are arranged. Most will be too small to use.

(b) Use the mouse to issue the Cascade command from the Window menu.

(c) Use the mouse to switch from one group window to another through the Window menu. Choose the entry for the first window to make it the active document window. Do the same for the second entry, then the third, and so on.

6. Use the Program Manager's Run command to start the Clock accessory program. The steps that follow let you practice mouse techniques:

(a) Drag the File menu down to the Run command to issue it.

(b) Click in the Command Line text box and type *clock.* You don't need to specify a path because the program file for the Clock accessory is in the *Windows* directory.

(c) Click on the OK command button. The Clock will start in its own application window.

(d) Drag the Clock program's control menu down to the Minimize command, then issue the command.

Continued on the next page...

Exercise 3-3 (continued)
How to use menu commands

7. Use the Program Manager's Run command to start the Notepad accessory program. The steps that follow let you practice keyboard techniques:

    (a) Type Alt, *f, r* to issue the Run command.

    (b) The control in the Run dialog box that has the focus will be the Command Line text box, so you can type the value you want without moving the focus to it first. Type *notepad*. You don't need to specify a path because the program file for the Notepad accessory is in the *Windows* directory.

    (c) Notice that the OK command button has a dark border. That indicates that it's the default button that will respond to the Enter key, unless you've moved the focus to another command button. Press Enter to activate the OK command button.

    (d) Access the control menu for the Notepad program's application window by typing Alt, Spacebar.

    (e) Issue the Maximize command to expand Notepad's window to fill the desktop by typing *x*.

8. Use the keyboard to access and issue the Exit command to end the Notepad program: Type Alt, *f, x*.

9. Restore the application window for the Clock program. You decide which technique you want to use.

10. Use the keyboard to access and issue the Close command from the control menu of the Clock program's application window. Type Alt, Spacebar, *c*.

11. Use the keyboard to access and issue the Close command from the control menu of the Program Manager's application window. Type Alt, Spacebar, *c*.

12. Press Enter to activate the OK command button (the default button, marked with a dark border) in the dialog box that warns you *Windows* is about to end.

How to use the Task Manager

A key component of *Windows* that usually works behind the scenes is the *Task Manager*. It controls the switching from one program to another. To request Task Manager functions, you access its *Task List* dialog box. Then, you can use this box to perform a couple of useful functions.

How to access the Task List dialog box Figure 3-21 lists three ways to access the Task List dialog box. First, you can double-click on any unoccupied part of the desktop. Second, you can use the Ctrl+Esc keystroke combination. Third, you can issue the Switch To command from the control menu of any application window. When you issue it, the Task List dialog box appears. In part 1 of figure 3-22, you can see how the control menu can be used to access the Task List dialog box. In part 2, you can see the dialog box.

How to use the dialog box to switch from one program to another One of the primary uses of the Task List dialog box is switching from one program to another as illustrated by parts 2 and 3 of figure 3-22. To switch to the Program Manager, as shown in this example, all you have to do is double-click on its name. Alternatively, you can use a two-step process to switch to another program in the dialog box. First, click on the program name in the task list to select it. Then, click on the Switch To button at the bottom of the dialog box.

How to use the dialog box to organize icons and windows If you study the Task List dialog box in figure 3-23, you can see that the last three command buttons are Cascade, Tile, and Arrange Icons. By clicking on these buttons, you can perform commands that are analogous to those in the Window menu of the Program Manager. However, the Program Manager commands apply to document windows, while the Task Manager functions apply to application windows. As figure 3-23 shows, the Cascade command overlaps the windows of all of the applications that are running, and the Tile command arranges the windows so they don't overlap. (Although both commands change the size of most application windows, some programs specify a window with a fixed size; this is illustrated by the Calculator program in this figure.) If you click on the Arrange Icons button, the Task Manager arranges the icons for all minimized applications into a row along the bottom of the screen.

How to use the dialog box to end an application program If you want to end an application program, the Task List dialog box provides another way for doing so. Just select the entry for the program, and click on the End Task command button. If the program has any unsaved work, *Windows* displays a warning and gives you a chance to save your work before it ends the program.

1. Double-click on an unoccupied portion of the desktop.
2. Type Ctrl+Esc.
3. Issue the Switch To command from the control menu of an application window.

Figure 3-21   Three ways to access the Task Manager

Part 1

To access the Task Manager, you can use the Switch To command from the Control menu of the active application window.

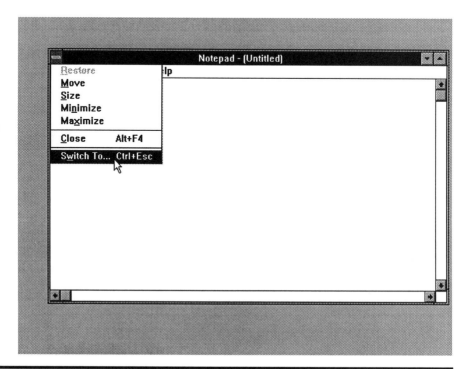

Figure 3-22   How to use the Task Manager

Part 2

Then, the Task List dialog box is displayed. To switch to one of the programs listed in the box, click on the name of the program, then click on the Switch To button. Or, simply double-click on the name of the program.

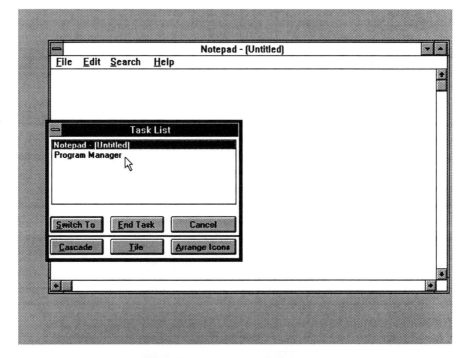

Part 3

When you choose a program from the task list, *Windows* makes it the active window.

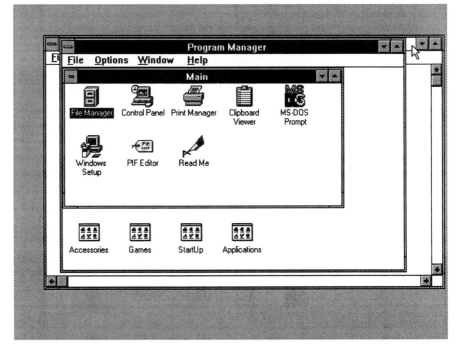

Figure 3-22   How to use the Task Manager (continued)

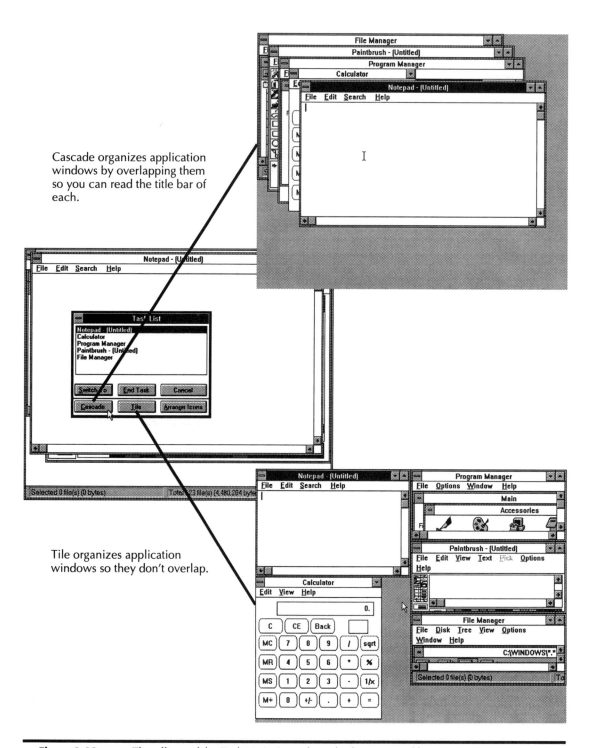

Cascade organizes application windows by overlapping them so you can read the title bar of each.

Tile organizes application windows so they don't overlap.

Figure 3-23   The effects of the Task List's Cascade and Tile command buttons

Exercise 3-4

How to use the Task Manager

1. If it isn't already running, start *Windows* on your PC by entering *win* at the DOS command prompt.

2. Access the Program Manager.

3. Open the Accessories group window.

4. Start the Clock, Calculator, Notepad, and Paintbrush programs. You'll need to switch back to the Program Manager after you start each program to start the next one.

5. How many programs are running on your PC now? Check to find out if your count is correct by accessing the Task Manager's Task List dialog box. To do that, double-click on any unoccupied area on the desktop. Were you right?

6. Close the Task List dialog box by clicking on the Cancel command button.

7. Access the Task List by using Ctrl+Esc.

8. Close the Task List by pressing Esc.

9. Access the control menu of the current application window. Issue the Switch To command. This is yet another way to reach the Task List.

10 Double-click on the entry for the Clock program to switch to it and make it the active program.

11. Access the Task List; use the technique you prefer.

12 Click on the entry for the Paintbrush program to select it, then click on the Switch To command button to make it the active program. Are the application windows on your desktop organized in a way that lets you use them effectively? Probably not, because some overlap others.

13. Access the Task List.

14. Click on the Tile command button to arrange the application windows so they don't overlap. Are they organized so you can use them effectively now? Again, probably not because most of them are too small.

15. Access the Task List.

Continued on the next page...

Exercise 3-4 (continued)
How to use the Task Manager

16. Click on the Cascade command button to arrange the application windows in another way. Are they organized so you can use them effectively now? This may be the best way to organize the desktop automatically. However, most of the windows are still too small to use.

17. Use the Task List to end the four accessory programs. For each:

    (a) Access the Task List.

    (b) Click on the entry for the accessory program you want to end.

    (c) Click on the End Task command button.

18. Use the Task List to end *Windows*:

    (a) Access the Task List.

    (b) Click on the entry for the Program Manager.

    (c) Click on the End Task command button.

    (d) Click on the OK command button in the confirmation dialog box *Windows* displays.

Two ways to start a program from the Program Manager

1. Double-click on a program item icon.

2. Use the Run command in the File menu of the Program Manager.

Five ways to switch from one program to another

1. Click on an inactive application window.

2. Use Fast Alt+Tab Switching.

3. Use Alt+Esc Switching.

4. Minimize and restore application windows.

5. Use the Switch To function in the Task List dialog box of the Task Manager.

Three ways to end a program

1. Double-click on the control-menu box for the program's application window. That's a shortcut for using the Close command in the window's control menu.

2. Use the Exit command in the File menu for the program.

3. Use the End Task function in the Task List dialog box of the Task Manager.

Figure 3-24   *Windows* often provides more than one way to perform a simple function

Perspective

As I said at the start of this chapter, *Windows* can be confusing when you first start using it because it often provides two or more ways for performing functions, even simple functions. For instance, you've already learned two ways to start a program, five ways to switch from one program to another, and three ways to end a program. These are summarized in figure 3-24. Beyond that, *Windows* provides both mouse and keyboard techniques for moving windows, sizing windows, and so on.

Now that you've been introduced to this variety of techniques, you can decide which ones are best for you. You may decide, for example, that you'll start your programs by double clicking on program icons, that you'll always switch between them by using Fast Alt+Tab Switching, that you'll use mouse techniques for moving and sizing windows, and that you'll end your programs by double-clicking on the control-menu box for the program's application window. Later, if you decide that one of the other techniques is appropriate for your work, you can refer back to this chapter to refresh your memory about how to use it. What's important now is that you understand that *Windows* provides these alternatives and that you see the relationships between them.

If your system is already set up the way you want it, this chapter may have presented all that you need to know or want to know about the Program Manager. If not, chapter 6 shows you how to get the most from the Program Manager. There, you can learn two more ways to start a program from the Program Manager; how to use all of the Program Manager's menu commands; and how to create, change, and delete program groups and program icons.

Summary

- You can start *Windows* from the DOS command prompt by entering *win*. On many PCs, this command is in the AUTOEXEC.BAT file, so *Windows* starts automatically when the system starts.

- When it starts, *Windows* can load more than one application program, but one of them will always be the *Windows shell*. The default shell is the *Program Manager*, and it lets you start application programs.

- When you start an application program, *Windows* creates a workspace on the *desktop* for it called an *application window*. Inside its application window, a typical program can create its own workspaces called *document windows*.

- You can use the *keyboard* or *mouse* to perform any *Windows* function. To use the mouse, you only need to know four basic mouse actions: *point, click, double-click, and drag*.

- Nearly every application and document window has a *title bar* across the top that identifies its contents, a *control-menu box* that lets you access the *control menu*, *borders* and *corners* that let you resize the window, and some combination of *minimize, maximize*, and *restore buttons*. When a window is too small to show all of its contents at the same time, *scroll bars* are added to it. You can use the mouse to minimize, maximize, restore, move, and size a window and to scroll through a window by working with the buttons, borders, corners, and bars in a window.

- The Program Manager organizes your programs into *program groups*, which can be displayed in document windows called *group windows*. When a group window isn't open, it appears as a *group icon*. When a group window is open, the programs within in it are displayed as *program icons*.

- To *open* a group window, you double-click on a group icon. To start a program, you double-click on its program icon. To end a program, you double-click on the control-menu box for the program's application window.

- *Windows* provides five methods for switching from one application window (or program) to another. One of the easiest is to click on any part of an inactive window. Another is to use Fast Alt+Tab Switching.

- Application windows have *menu bars* that let you access a program's *commands*. The commands appear in lists called *menus* that *drop down* under the *menu names* in the menu bar. *Control menus* drop down from the control-menu box for a window. You can use either mouse or keyboard techniques to access menus and issue commands from the menus.

- *Windows* uses *dialog boxes* to get more information about a command and to display warning messages. Dialog boxes have a variety of controls including *command buttons*, *text boxes*, *drop-down list boxes*, *option buttons*, and *check boxes*.

- You can use the Run command in the File menu of the Program Manager to start a program. You can use the Close command in a control menu for an application window or the Exit command in a program's File menu to end a program. And you can use the commands of the Options and Window menus of the Program Manager to arrange its icons and document windows.

- You can use the commands of an application or document window's control menu to maximize, minimize, restore, move, or size a window. However, you can do these functions more easily by using mouse techniques.

- The Task List dialog box of the Task Manager provides yet another way to switch from one program to another and to end a program. It also provides commands that let you arrange icons and application windows on the desktop.

Chapter 4

How to use the standard features of *Windows* programs

An introduction to the standard menus and commands in a *Windows* program
How to use the standard File menu commands in a *Windows* program
    How to open an existing document
    How to open a new document
    How to save a document
    How to close a document
    How to print a document
    How to exit from a program

Exercise 4-1: How to use standard File menu commands

How to enter and edit text in a *Windows* program
    How to move the insertion point
    How to insert text
    How to delete text
    How to use the mouse to select a block of text
    How to copy or move text using the clipboard
    How to cancel your last editing action

Exercise 4-2: How to enter text, edit text, and use the clipboard

How to use the standard Help feature in a *Windows* program
How to access the Help feature
How to navigate through the Help information
How to print Help information
The limitations of the Help feature

Exercise 4-3: How to use the *Windows* Help feature

Perspective
Summary

Unlike DOS applications, *Windows* applications are consistent. Even different kinds of *Windows* programs, like word processing and graphics programs, have similar menus for standard program functions such as opening, printing, and saving files. In addition, *Windows* applications use similar conventions for basic tasks such as entering and editing text. That means once you learn how to use one *Windows* program, you'll have skills that will help you learn how to use other *Windows* programs.

In this chapter, you'll learn the *Windows* conventions that are common to *Windows* applications. First, you'll be introduced to the menus that are common to most *Windows* programs. Next, you'll learn how to use the standard File menu commands for functions like retrieving, saving, and printing files. Then, you'll learn the standard methods for entering and editing text. Last, you'll learn how to use the *Windows* Help feature.

An introduction to the standard menus and commands in a *Windows* program

Windows programs are more consistent than DOS programs because they follow the same guidelines. These guidelines include dozens of recommendations for how programs should look and operate. Among the recommendations are: (1) the standard menus that every *Windows* program should have, (2) the basic commands that standard menus should have (like Open and Print commands for the File menu), and (3) how the basic menu commands should interact with the user.

To understand how this consistency helps you use programs more easily, consider figure 4-1. It shows application windows for three programs: Notepad, Write, and Microsoft *Word for Windows*. Although all three programs are word processing programs, they differ widely in the number of features they offer and in the complexity of those features. Nevertheless, they have three menus in common: a File menu, an Edit menu, and a Help menu.

If you look at the commands in the File, Edit, and Help menus for these programs as shown in figure 4-2, you can see that these menus provide standard commands. Although *Word for Windows* offers more commands than Write, and Write offers more commands than Notepad, the same basic commands are available in the same menus in each program. For instance, the File menu for each of these programs includes New, Open, Save, Print, and Exit commands. And the Edit menu for each program includes Undo, Cut, Copy, and Paste commands.

Notepad
offers a limited set of menu items. Each menu includes only fundamental text-processing commands.

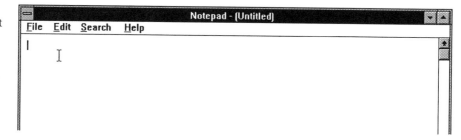

Write
offers a larger set of menu items and has a more complete set of word-processing commands under each.

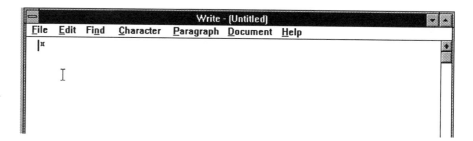

Microsoft *Word* for Windows
offers a comprehensive set of menus and word-processing commands.

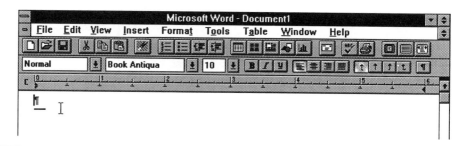

Figure 4-1   *Windows* programs offer three standard menus: File, Edit, and Help

Figure 4-3 summarizes the standard commands that most *Windows* applications offer in their File and Edit menus. If you learn how to use these commands in one program, you can use the same commands in the same way in almost every other *Windows* program.

	Notepad	Write	*Word for Windows*
File menu	**File** New Open... Save Save As... Print Page Setup... Print Setup... Exit	**File** New Open... Save Save As... Print... Print Setup... Repaginate... Exit	**File** New... Open... Ctrl+F12 Close Save Shift+F12 Save As... F12 Save All Find File... Summary Info... Template... Print Preview Print... Ctrl+Shift+F12 Print Merge... Print Setup... Exit Alt+F4 1 \MISCDOCS\PERSONAL\MEMO.DOC 2 SECTION2\NEWC3\F3.DOC 3 SECTION2\NEWC3\C3PLAN.DOC 4 SECTION2\E3.DOC
Edit menu	**Edit** Undo Ctrl+Z Cut Ctrl+X Copy Ctrl+C Paste Ctrl+V Delete Del Select All Time/Date F5 Word Wrap	**Edit** Undo Typing Ctrl+Z Cut Ctrl+X Copy Ctrl+C Paste Ctrl+V Paste Special... Paste Link Links... Object Insert Object... Move Picture Size Picture	**Edit** Undo Typing Ctrl+Z Repeat Typing F4 Cut Ctrl+X Copy Ctrl+C Paste Ctrl+V Paste Special... Select All Ctrl+NumPad 5 Find... Replace... Go To... F5 Glossary... Links... Object...
Help menu	**Help** Contents Search for Help on... How to Use Help About Notepad...	**Help** Contents Search for Help on... How to Use Help About Write...	**Help** Help Index Getting Started Learning Word WordPerfect Help About...

Figure 4-2   The standard *Windows* menus offer the same basic commands

Menu	Command	Description
File	New	Creates a new document. If the program supports multiple document windows, a new document window will open. If it doesn't, any contents of the application workspace are deleted after you confirm the deletion through a dialog box.
	Open	Retrieves an existing document file that you specify through a dialog box.
	Close	Closes the active document window, but leaves others open. If the active document window contains unsaved work, a dialog box alerts you. Programs that don't support multiple document windows typically don't offer the Close command.
	Save	Saves the contents of the active window in an existing data file that's already associated with the window. If the contents of the active window aren't associated with a data file, the Save As dialog box appears. In it, you specify the drive, path, and file name for the file.
	Save As	Saves the contents of the active window in a file you specify in the Save As dialog box. In it, you specify the drive, path, and file name for the file. You use the Save As command to save a new document for the first time, or to save an existing document under a new name.
	Print	Prints the contents of the active window on the current printer. Often, a Print dialog box appears to let you specify print options like a different printer or the number of copies you want.
	Print Setup	Displays the Print Setup dialog box to let you change the current printer or set printer options.
	Exit	Ends the current application program and closes the application window and any document windows it contains. If any of the windows contains unsaved work, a dialog box alerts you. Then, you can return to the program and save your work, or you can end the program and abandon the work.
Edit	Undo	Reverses the last editing change you made to your document.
	Cut	Stores the selection on the clipboard and deletes the selection from the active window.
	Copy	Stores the selection on the clipboard and leaves it in place in the active window.
	Paste	Inserts the contents of the clipboard in the active window at the insertion point. If any data is selected in the active window, the pasted data replaces it.

Figure 4-3   The basic File and Edit menu commands that most *Windows* programs offer

How to use the standard File menu commands in a *Windows* program

A standard File menu includes commands for opening a file, saving a file, and closing a file. That makes sense since all of these commands have to do with files. In addition, a standard File menu includes commands for setting up a printer and for printing a file. It also includes an Exit command for ending the program.

How to open an existing document   To retrieve a document file, you issue the Open command in the File menu. Then, your program displays a dialog box that prompts you for the information that's required in a file specification. To illustrate, figure 4-4 shows the Open command and the resulting dialog boxes for three programs: Notepad, Write, and *Word for Windows*. Notice that these dialog boxes are almost identical.

For a complete file specification, you need to supply the drive, path, and file name. The standard dialog box for the Open command provides controls that let you specify each of these components. Figure 4-5 shows you how to use these controls.

Figure 4-6 shows you how to use Notepad to open the CONFIG.SYS file that's stored in the root directory on the C drive. As you go through this example, remember that this works the same in most *Windows* programs. In part 1, you issue the Open command from the File menu. Then, the dialog box in part 2 appears. Here you can simply click in the text box under File Name and type C:\CONFIG.SYS over the default value (*.TXT). However, it's often more efficient to use the other controls in the dialog box to "build" the file specification. This is particularly true if you want to open a file that has a more complicated path or if you can't quite remember the path.

To build a file specification, you first select the appropriate drive. In part 2 of figure 4-6, you can see that the current drive (drive C) is already the appropriate drive so you don't have to select a different one from the Drives list box. But if you do need to change the current drive, you use the same technique that you use for any drop-down list box. First, you click on the arrow in the box; then, you click on the appropriate drive in the list.

Once the drive has been selected, the next step is to build the path. Because the current path is C:\WINDOWS, not the root directory, you need to change it. To do that, you put the mouse pointer on C:\ in the Directories list box and double-click. You can see the results in part 3 of figure 4-6.

If you want to specify a path other than the root directory, you build it one level at a time by double-clicking on a directory at each subsequent directory

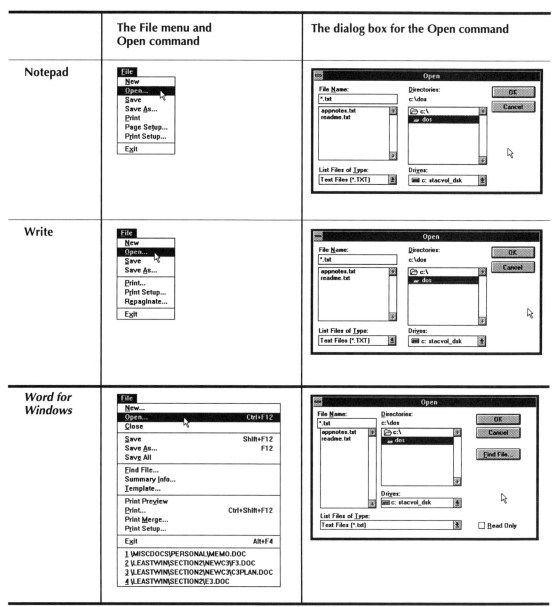

Figure 4-4 The Open commands in Notepad, Write, and *Word for Windows* display similar dialog boxes

File Name text box
(1) Type the appropriate file specification for the file you want to retrieve or (2) let *Windows* supply the specification based on selections you make in the other four boxes.

File Name list box
Click on a file name in this box to transfer it to the File Name text box. It lists eligible files from the selected drive and directory with extensions that match the selection in the List Files of Type drop-down list box.

List Files of Type drop-down list box
Select an extension option from this drop-down list box to restrict the kinds of files that appear in the File Name list box.

Directories list box
Select the directory that contains the file you're interested in. Double-click on a directory icon to display its contents in the File Name list box. To see another path, double-click on the icon for the root directory, then on the icon for the top-level directory, then on the icon for the appropriate subdirectory, and so on.

Drives drop-down list box
Select the drive to use as the current drive from the list that appears when you click on the arrow on the right side of the box.

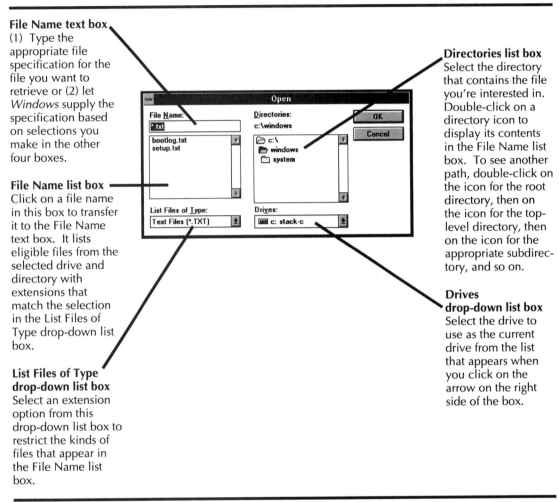

Figure 4-5   How to use the controls on typical Open, Save, and Save As dialog boxes

level until the path is complete. If, for example, you want to open a file in the C:\DATA directory, you double-click on DATA in the Directories list that's shown in part 3. This causes its subdirectories to appear in the Directories list. Then, if you want to continue the path, you double-click on the appropriate directory at the next level, and so on, until the path is complete.

Once you've got the drive and path right, you need to specify the file name. By default, Notepad displays files that have the extension TXT. But since there

Part 1

To retrieve a file
into Notepad's
workspace, issue
the Open
command.

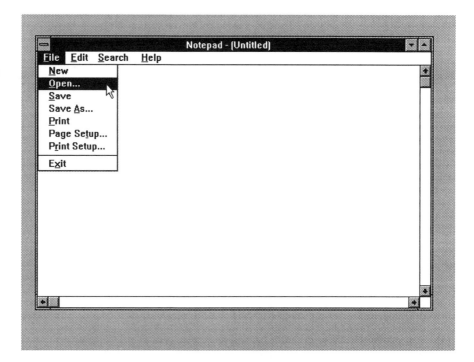

Part 2

Notepad then
displays the Open
dialog box. To
change the
current directory,
you can double-
click on an entry
in the Directories
list box.

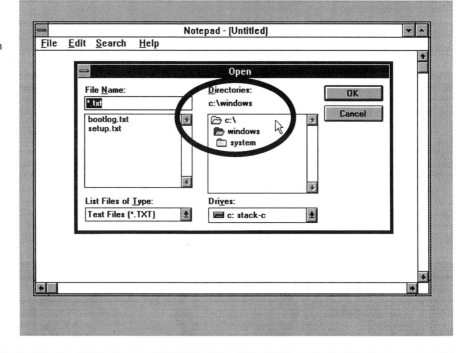

Figure 4-6   How to open a document

Part 3

If no files meet the default specification of *.txt, you can click on the arrow in the List Files of Type drop-down box to see alternative extensions. Then, click on one of the options.

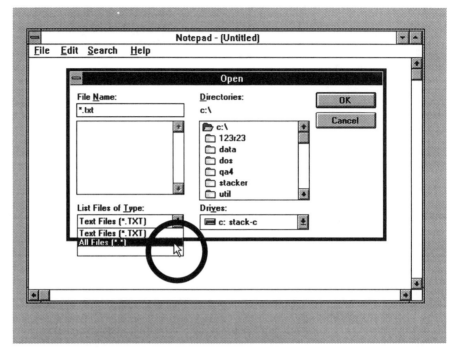

Part 4

The file names in the File Name list reflect the selection you make in part 3. Then, to select a file from the list (like config.sys), you can click on its name.

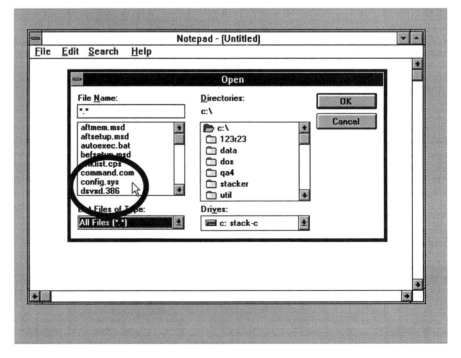

Figure 4-6   How to open a document (continued)

Part 5

When you click on the name for a file in the File Name list box, Notepad transfers the name into the File Name text box. Then, you can click on the OK button to verify that this is the file you want.

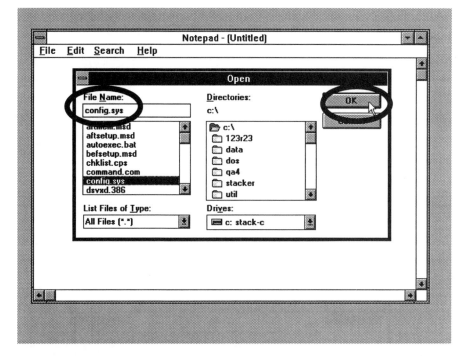

Part 6

The Notepad program reads the file and displays it in its workspace.

```
Notepad - CONFIG.SYS
File   Edit   Search   Help
DEVICE=C:\DOS\SETVER.EXE
LASTDRIVE=Z
files = 30
buffers = 30
INSTALL=C:\DOS\SHARE.EXE
DEVICE=C:\DOS\HIMEM.SYS
STACKS=9,256
SHELL=C:\DOS\COMMAND.COM C:\DOS\   /p
DOS=HIGH
DEVICE=C:\STACKER\STACKER.COM C:\STACVOL.DSK
DEVICE=C:\STACKER\SSWAP.COM C:\STACVOL.DSK /SYNC
DEVICE=C:\DOS\SMARTDRV.EXE /DOUBLE_BUFFER
```

Figure 4-6   How to open a document (continued)

are no files with that extension in the root directory, the File Name list box in part 3 of figure 4-6 is empty. To change that extension, you use the List Files of Type list box. When you click on the arrow for this box, a list like the one in part 3 appears. Then, to display all of the files in a directory, you can click on the All Files (*.*) item. This causes all the files in the current directory to be displayed in the File Name list box as shown in part 4 of this figure.

If you want to be more restrictive about the files that appear in the File Name list box, you can use wildcards in the File Name text box. If, for example, you want to see only those file names that begin with the letter *c*, you can change the file specification from *.* to c*.*. Similarly, if you want to list only files with the extension DOC, you can change the file specification to *.doc. If you're familiar with the use of wildcards, you shouldn't have any trouble doing this. If you're not, you can easily get by without using this technique.

To select a file from the File Name list box, you click on it. This causes the file name to be displayed in the File Name text box as shown in part 5 of figure 4-6. At this point, the file specification is complete so you can finish the command by clicking on the OK button in the dialog box. If you want to save a step, you can just double-click on the file name when it's in the File Name list box; then, you don't have to click on the OK button. Either way, when you finish the command, Notepad opens the file in its application window as shown in part 6 of this figure.

The more advanced *Windows* applications let you open more than one file at a time. For each file, a new document window is opened. Then, you can switch from one document to another whenever you need to. In contrast, simple programs like the Write and Notepad applets don't let you open more than one file at a time. They require that you work on one file at a time.

How to open a new document   When you start a *Windows* application, the program displays a blank workspace that you can start a new document in. Later, if you want to start work on another new document, you can use the New command of the File menu. For the more advanced *Windows* applications, this command opens another document window for the new document.

When you're using *Windows* applications that don't let you work on more than one document at a time, though, the New command works somewhat differently. If, for example, you've finished working on one Notepad document and you want to start another, you issue the New command. Notepad then erases the contents of its workspace, which means that the document that you've been working on is erased. If you've made changes to the old document that haven't been saved, however, the program warns you by displaying a dialog box. This gives you a chance to save your work before the program starts a new document.

How to save a document   *Windows* applications usually have two commands for saving a document: Save and Save As. You use the Save command to save changes to an existing document. When you issue this command, the document is saved immediately, and you continue with your work. You use the Save As command to: (1) save a new document for the first time, or (2) to save an existing document with a new name. When you issue the Save As command, you have to give a file specification through a dialog box just as you do when you open an existing file.

Figure 4-7 shows you how to use Notepad's Save As command to save a file with a new name on a diskette. Part 1 shows the selection of the Save As command, and part 2 shows the resulting dialog box. As you can see, the dialog box for saving a Notepad file is the same as the one for opening a file, and you use it to build a file specification in the same way that you do when opening a file. In parts 2 and 3, drive B is selected using the Drives list box. Because the file is going to be saved on diskette, there's no need to specify a directory. So in part 4, you just specify the file name by typing it in the File Name text box. In this example, CONFIG.TXT replaces CONFIG.SYS as the file name. To complete the operation, you click on the OK button.

How to close a document   If you look back to the menus in figure 4-2, you can see that *Word for Windows* has a Close command in its File menu, but the other two programs don't. That's because *Word for Windows* lets you open more than one document window at a time, but the other two programs don't. When you issue the Close command, it closes the active document window. If you haven't saved your most recent changes to the document in the window when you issue this command, a dialog box is displayed that lets you save the changes. Otherwise, the window is closed immediately.

How to print a document   Most *Windows* application programs have at least two printing commands in their File menus: Print and Print Setup. Figure 4-8 shows how you use these commands to print the CONFIG.SYS file in figure 4-6 from Notepad.

Part 1 of figure 4-8 shows the selection of the Print Setup command, and part 2 shows its resulting dialog box. As you can see, this command lets you specify the printer to be used and some printer settings. If you have only one printer on your PC and you don't use network printers, you won't ever have to change the printer. However, you may want to change the paper orientation, size, or source settings. Once you get the settings the way you want them, you click on the OK button.

Part 1

To save a file with
a new name you
can issue the Save
As command. If
you issue the Save
command, the
contents of the
original document
will be overwrit-
ten.

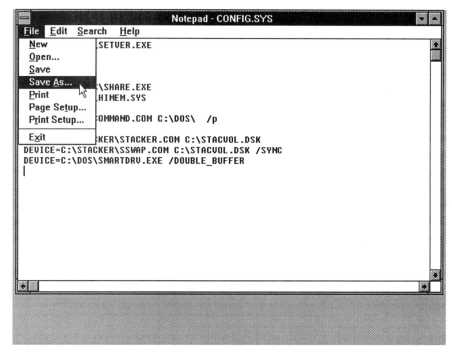

Part 2

You can click on
the arrow on the
right side of the
Drives drop-down
list box to display
the drives
available to you
to save the file.

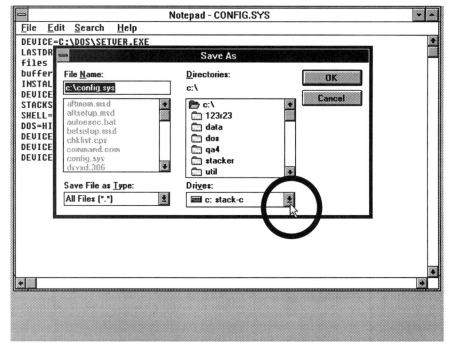

Figure 4-7   How to save a document

Part 3

For example, to save the file on a diskette in your PC's B drive, you can select it from the drop-down list.

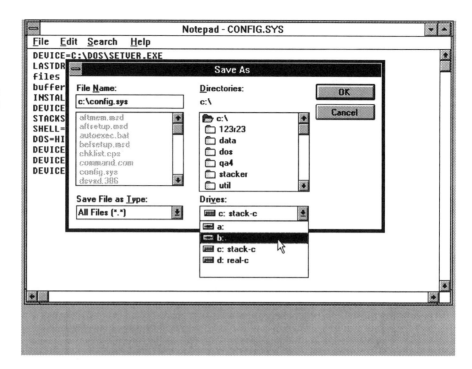

Part 4

After you've specified the directory and drive, you type the name for the new file in the File Name text box and click on the OK button.

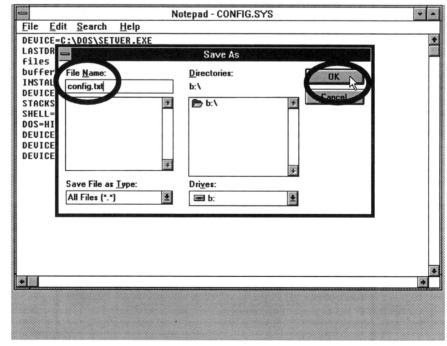

Figure 4-7   How to save a document (continued)

To print a document, you issue the Print command from the File menu as shown in part 3 of figure 4-8. When you issue the command from Notepad, the printing operation starts right away as shown in part 4. In contrast, some applications display a dialog box when you issue the Print command. This box lets you specify options such as the number of copies you want to print, which pages you want to print, and so on.

When a *Windows* application prints, it usually doesn't control the printing operation. Instead, *Windows* intercepts the information required to print the document, stores it temporarily, and starts another *Windows* program called *Print Manager*. Then, Print Manager, not the application program, controls the printing. Because Print Manager operates in the background, you can go on with other tasks while your document prints.

Although this is just a brief introduction to the printing commands of a typical *Windows* program, this is all that you need to know for printing most documents from most programs. If you want to know more about printing, though, you can refer to chapter 8. This chapter shows you how to do advanced printing functions such as setting advanced options, selecting the most efficient fonts, and using Print Manager.

How to exit from a program   When you issue the Exit command, the program ends. This is the same as double-clicking on the control menu box in the upper left corner of the application window. If you haven't saved the last changes you made to your work, a dialog box appears that gives you a chance to save the changes. Otherwise, you are returned immediately to the program that you started your application from (usually, the Program Manager).

Part 1

You can use the Print Setup command to verify or change the printer.

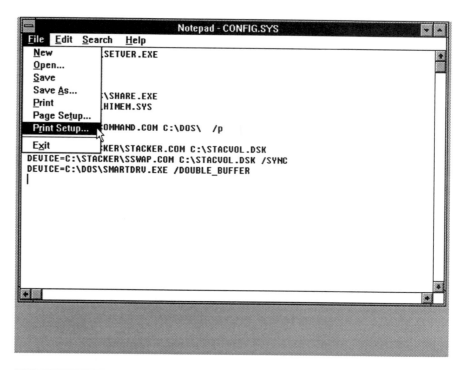

Part 2

In addition to changing the current printer, you can set some printing options through the Print Setup dialog box.

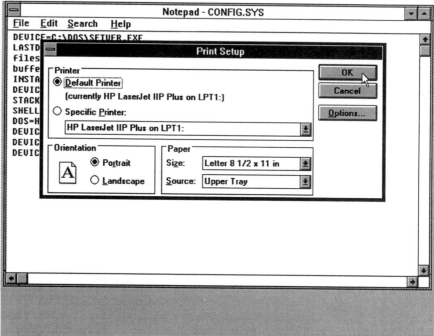

Figure 4-8   How to print a document

Part 3

After you've made setup changes, you use the Print command to actually print a document.

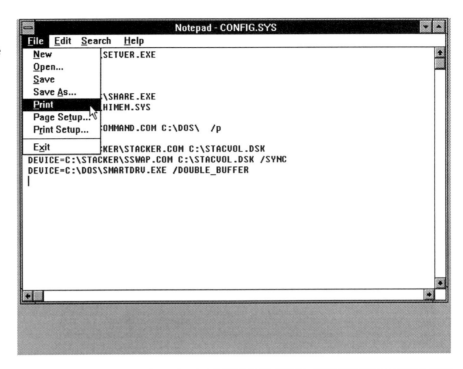

Part 4

Notepad displays a progress dialog box while the print job is sent to the Print Manager.

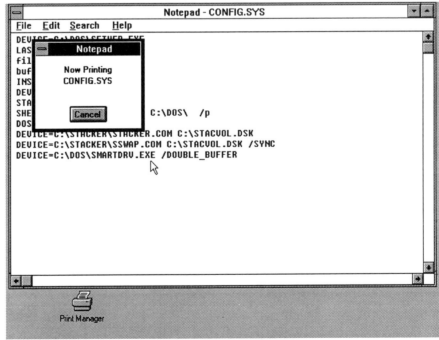

Figure 4-8   How to print a document (continued)

Exercise 4-1

How to use standard File menu commands

1. If it isn't already running, start *Windows* on your PC. Then, start the Notepad program.

2. From Notepad, open the CONFIG.SYS file in the root directory of your C drive. You'll need to change the current directory and the extension to see CONFIG.SYS in the File Names list box in the Open dialog box.

3. Issue the Save As command to create a copy of the document in a file called EXPER.TXT. This file should be saved on a diskette in one of your diskette drives.

4. Issue the Print Setup command to verify the print settings or to change the printer. Then, issue the Print command to print a copy of EXPER.TXT.

5. Issue the New command under Notepad's File menu to start a new Notepad document. This erases the EXPER.TXT document from Notepad's application window.

6. Open the EXPER.TXT file in the blank window. This shows how easy it is to retrieve a document that you've created in a *Windows* application.

7. Exit from the Notepad program. Because you haven't made any changes to EXPER.TXT, Notepad ends without displaying a dialog box that warns you to save your work.

8. Start the Write program.

9. Issue the Open command to retrieve the EXPER.TXT file using the Write program. Then, click on the No Conversion button in the dialog box that appears. Note how easy it is to access a file of a common data type, like plain text, from two different programs.

10. Exit from the Write program.

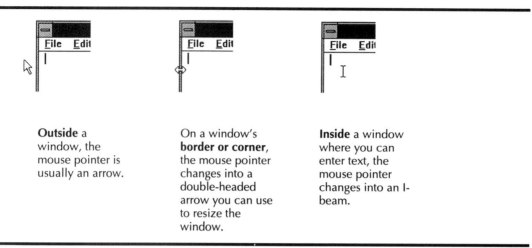

Outside a window, the mouse pointer is usually an arrow.	On a window's **border or corner**, the mouse pointer changes into a double-headed arrow you can use to resize the window.	**Inside** a window where you can enter text, the mouse pointer changes into an I-beam.

Figure 4-9   How the mouse pointer changes into an I-beam when you move it into a text area

How to enter and edit text in a *Windows* program

Just as the menus and menu commands are consistent from one *Windows* application to another, so are the techniques for entering and editing text. As you go from one *Windows* program to another, you'll always be able to use the skills that follow as you enter and edit text.

How to move the insertion point   In most of the screen examples that I've shown you so far, the mouse pointer has been shaped like an arrow. That's the case when the mouse pointer is located on the *Windows* desktop, inside the windows for many programs (like the Program Manager), and on many dialog-box controls. However, when you move the mouse pointer into an area where you can enter text, it changes into an *I-beam*. Figure 4-9 shows how the mouse pointer changes as you move it into a text area.

The *insertion point* in a text area is the point at which your keystrokes will be inserted into the area. This point is marked by a *cursor* that is usually a vertical bar. To move the insertion point with the mouse, you just move the I-beam where you want it and click the mouse. The cursor then jumps to the new insertion point.

If you prefer, you can also use the keyboard to move the cursor that marks the insertion point. Although this varies somewhat from one *Windows* program to another, the arrow keys move the cursor one character at a time. The Home key usually moves the cursor to the start of a line, and the End key usually moves it to the end of the line. The Page-Up and Page-Down keys usually move the cursor either one screen or one page up or down. And if you hold down the Ctrl key while you press the right or left arrow key, the cursor usually moves one word to the right or left.

How to insert text   Figure 4-10 illustrates how easy it is to insert text into a document. In part 1, you move the I-beam to the proper insertion point and click the mouse. Here, the insertion point is located immediately before the first character in the first line. Then, when you start typing, the characters appear at the cursor, and the text after the cursor moves forward one position with each character you type.

If you study figure 4-10, you can see that both an I-beam and a cursor are displayed on the screen. Although the I-beam represents the location of the mouse pointer, the cursor is the active insertion point. So when you're typing, only the location of the cursor matters.

How to delete text   You can use the Backspace key or the Delete key to delete one character of text at a time. The Backspace key deletes the character immediately to the left of the cursor, and the Delete key deletes the character immediately to the right. If you want to delete more than one character at a time, you can block the portion of the text that you want to delete using the techniques that follow. Then, you can press the Delete key to delete that portion of text.

How to use the mouse to select a block of text   If you want to perform an editing operation on a block of text, you start by selecting it. Usually, the easiest way to do that is by using the first mouse operation summarized in figure 4-11. That is, you drag the mouse pointer over the block of text that you want to select. Then, when you release the mouse pointer, the block is highlighted. If you want to select just one word, you can double-click on the word. And if you want to extend a selection, you can use the third procedure in figure 4-11.

Figure 4-12 shows you how you can select and delete blocks of text. In this example, I wanted to delete all of the lines from the CONFIG.TXT file that aren't DEVICE commands. So in part 1, I set the insertion point just before the first character in the first line that isn't a DEVICE command. Then, to select the block of lines that I wanted to delete, I held the Shift key down, pointed to the start of the second DEVICE command, and clicked the mouse again. This is the third technique that's summarized in figure 4-11. As you can see in part 2, four lines were selected by that action. Then, when I pressed the Delete key, the entire block was removed from the document as shown in part 3. After that, I used the first technique in figure 4-11 to select the other three lines that aren't DEVICE commands, and I pressed the Delete key again. This left the document as shown in part 4.

Part 1

Move the I-beam
to the point where
you want to start
editing and click
the mouse.

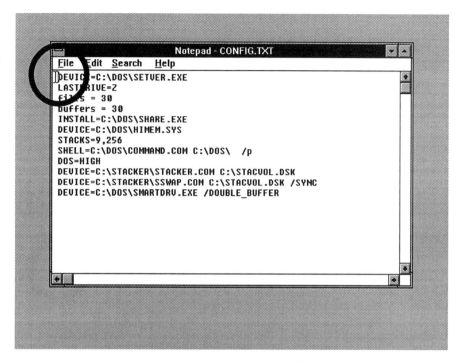

Part 2

The text you type
is inserted at the
cursor.

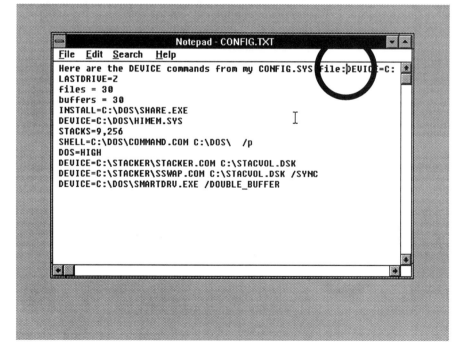

Figure 4-10   How to enter text at the insertion point

How to	Follow these steps
Select a block of text	1. Point to the location immediately before the first character in the block you want to select.
	2. Hold down the left mouse button and drag the selection highlight through the last character in the block.
	3. Release the mouse button.
Select a single word and the space that follows it	1. Point to the word.
	2. Double-click.
Extend a selection	1. Hold the Shift key down.
	2. Move the mouse pointer to just past the last character to be included in the selection.
	3. Click to extend the selection through the current location of the mouse pointer.
	4. Release the Shift key to complete the selection.

Figure 4-11   How to use the mouse to select text for a subsequent operation

How to copy or move text using the clipboard   As you edit, you'll often need to move or copy text from one location to another. To make this easy, *Windows* provides a feature called the *clipboard*. This is a temporary storage area that you can use to transfer information within a single document or from one document to another within a single program. You can also use the clipboard to transfer information from a document in one program to a document in another program.

To put text on the clipboard, you first select it. Then, you use either the Copy or Cut command in the Edit menu to put the current selection on the clipboard. This selection replaces whatever was on the clipboard before. The difference between these commands is that the Copy command leaves the selection in place in the source document, while the Cut command deletes it from the source document.

To retrieve the contents of the clipboard, you use the Paste command of the Edit menu. This command inserts the contents of the clipboard into your document at the insertion point. However, the contents of the clipboard remain there. As a result, you can paste the contents of the clipboard more than once. The contents of the clipboard change only when you use the Cut or Copy command to place a new selection on the clipboard.

Part 1

Move the insertion point to just before the first line you want to select.

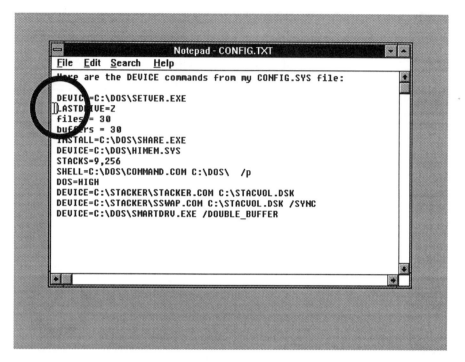

Part 2

To select the block, hold down the Shift key, point to the start of the next Device command, and click the mouse. Then, press the Delete key.

Figure 4-12   How to select and delete text

Part 3

To select the next block, you can use a different technique: Point to the first character in the STACKS command and drag the selection highlight down and across three lines.

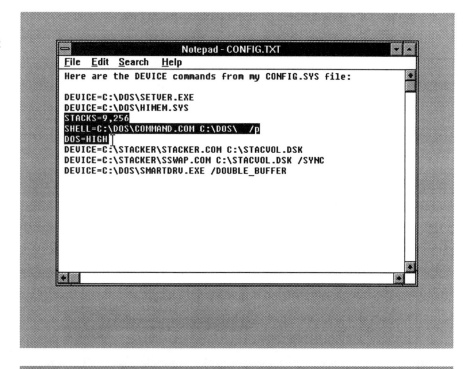

Part 4

After you press the Delete key, the selection will be deleted from the document. All that remains are the DEVICE commands.

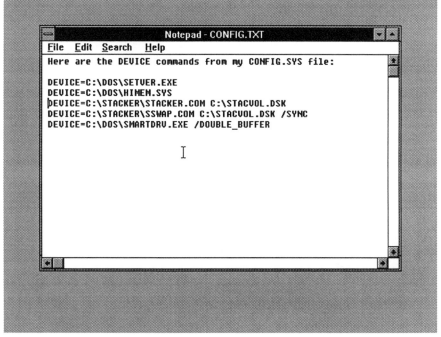

Figure 4-12 How to select and delete text (continued)

If you select a block of text before you issue the Paste command, the contents of the clipboard replace the selected text. Although this can be useful when you intend to replace the text, it can be an unpleasant surprise if you do it accidentally. In that case, though, you can use the Undo command to restore your document. I'll show you how to use that command in a moment.

Figure 4-13 illustrates how you can use the clipboard to move data from one program to another. In part 1, I selected the DEVICE command lines from the CONFIG.TXT document in the Notepad program. In part 2, I issued the Copy command. This caused the selection to remain in place in the source document while a copy of it was stored on the clipboard. In part 3, I'm moving the Notepad window down to reveal the Program Manager window so I can start the Write program as shown in part 4. In part 5, I issued the Paste command to insert the contents of the clipboard into the new Write document. Part 6 shows the result of the paste operation. The DEVICE command lines are now stored in three places: the new Write document, the original Notepad document, and the clipboard.

To make it easier for you to perform cutting, copying, and pasting operations, *Windows* provides three keyboard shortcuts that you can use instead of the commands. You can use Ctrl+X for the Cut command; Ctrl+C for the Copy command; and Ctrl+V for the Paste command. To help you remember these keystroke combinations, you can think of the letter X as a scissors, which represents cutting; the letter C as the first letter in Copy; and the letter V as the editor's caret mark for inserting text.

How to cancel your last editing action   Sometimes, you'll accidentally make an editing change you didn't mean to make. In that case, you can use the Undo command of the Edit menu. This command lets you cancel the last editing change you made. Because the Undo command applies to only your most recent editing change, though, you must issue it immediately after you make a mistake. If you do any additional editing, the Undo command will undo that editing, not the mistake.

Part 1

To copy the block of text that contains the five DEVICE commands from the Notepad document to a new Write document, you position the mouse pointer at the start of the first line. Then, you select the text.

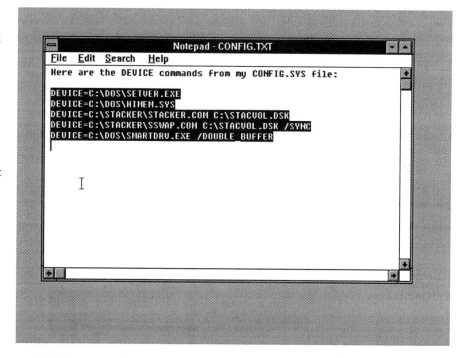

Part 2

To copy the selection to the clipboard, issue the Copy command from the Edit menu.

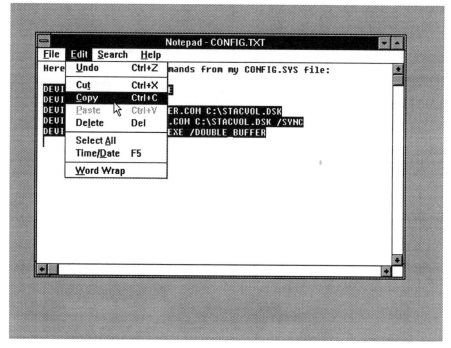

Figure 4-13   How to use the clipboard to copy and paste selected text

Part 3

The Copy command leaves the selected text in place and copies an image of it to the clipboard. Then, to start the Write program, you can drag the Notepad window down and to the left to uncover the Program Manager window.

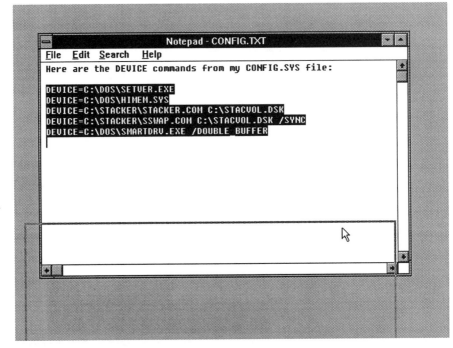

Part 4

Start the Write program by double-clicking on its icon in the Program Manager.

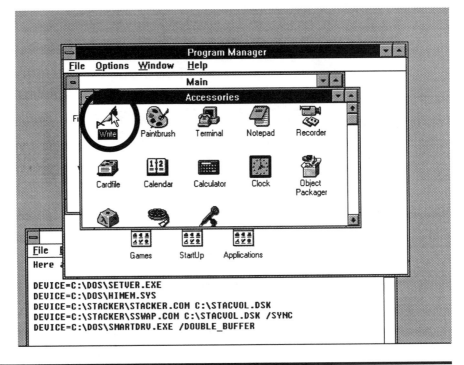

Figure 4-13   How to use the clipboard to copy and paste selected text (continued)

Part 5

Issue the Paste command from the Edit menu in the Write program to insert the contents of the clipboard into the new Write document.

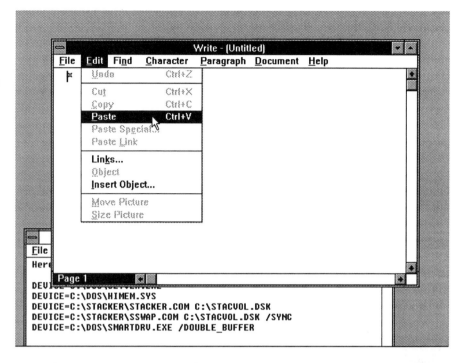

Part 6

The result of the paste operation is a new Write document that contains the DEVICE commands.

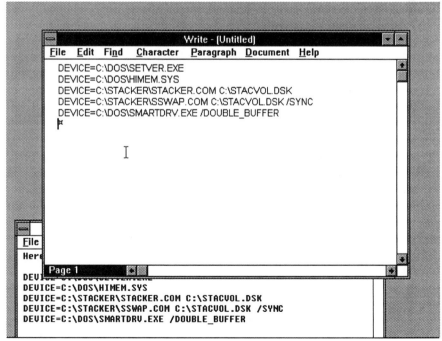

Figure 4-13   How to use the clipboard to copy and paste selected text (continued)

Exercise 4-2

How to enter text, edit text, and use the clipboard

1. If it isn't already running, start *Windows* on your PC. Then, start the Write program.

2. Switch to the Program Manager and start the Notepad program.

3. Enter this name and address as it would appear on a mailing label:

   John R. Smith
   500 8th Street
   San Francisco, CA 94107

4. Edit the name and address: (1) delete John's middle initial, (2) add a comma and the title "President" after his name, (3) add the company name "ABC Marketing, Inc." in a new line below his name, (4) spell the street name, and (5) spell the state name. Your label should look like this:

   John Smith, President
   ABC Marketing, Inc.
   500 Eighth Street
   San Francisco, California 94107

5. Select the entire name and address by dragging the selection highlight from the "J" in John through the end of the zip code. Then, issue the Cut command from the Edit menu. This removes the selection from the current document, but places an image of it on the clipboard.

6. Switch to the Write program. Then, issue the Paste command from the Write program's Edit menu. This pastes the contents of the clipboard (the name and address from the Notepad document) into the Write document. Because nothing else has been cut or copied to the clipboard, the name and address remain in the clipboard.

7. Switch back to the Notepad program. Then, enter your name and address in the same format as you entered John's. If you make any errors, correct them.

8. Issue the Paste command from the Notepad program's Edit menu. As you can see, the contents of the clipboard (John's name and address) are added to the Notepad document.

9. Select your name and address by dragging the selection highlight through it. Then, issue the Copy command from the Edit menu. This leaves the selection in the current document, and places an image of it on the clipboard.

Continued on the next page...

Exercise 4-2 (continued)
How to enter text, edit text, and use the clipboard

10. Switch back to the Write program. Then, move the insertion point immediately before the name and address that is already in the Write document. Next, issue the Paste command from the Write program's Edit menu. The contents of the clipboard (your name and address) are now in the Write document. And because nothing else has been cut or copied to the clipboard, your name and address are still there too.

11. Switch to the Notepad program. Then, start a new Notepad document by issuing the New command from the File menu. Click on the No button to reply to the dialog box that asks if you want to save your changes. This is one way to clear the Notepad work area. The contents of the previous document disappear.

12. Issue the Exit command from the File menu to end the Notepad program.

13. Switch back to the Write program, if you're not already there. Then, issue the Paste command from the Write program's Edit menu. Notice that the contents of the clipboard were maintained, even though the Notepad program ended.

14. Issue the Exit command from the File menu to end the Write program. Click on the No button to reply to the dialog box that asks if you want to save your changes.

1. Use the Help menu.
2. Press the F1 key.
3. Use the Help button in a dialog box.

Figure 4-14   How to access the Help feature of a program

How to use the standard Help feature in a *Windows* program

One of the standard features of a *Windows* program is its Help feature. Although the quality of the Help information varies from one program to another, the methods for accessing this feature are standard and the methods for navigating through the Help information are standard.

How to access the Help feature   Figure 4-14 lists three ways for accessing the Help feature for a program. First, you can use the Help menu, which is one of the standard menus for a *Windows* program. Second, you can press the F1 key. Third, you can use the Help button that's provided in some dialog boxes for some programs.

If you look back to the Help menus in figure 4-2, you can see that the commands in these menus vary from one program to another. Usually, though, you'll find a command like the Contents command that lets you access a table of contents for the Help information. You'll also find a command like the Search for Help On command that lets you access Help information by index name. For the more advanced *Windows* applications, you may find commands that provide different types of information for different types of users. For instance, the Help menu for *Word for Windows* provides a WordPerfect Help command for people who are converting from *WordPerfect* to *Word for Windows*.

If you use the F1 key to access Help information, some *Windows* programs provide *context-sensitive information*. Then, the Help information that's displayed applies to the function or feature that you were using when you pressed F1. If context-sensitive information isn't available when you press the F1 key, the Help information usually starts with a table of contents. When you use a Help button in a dialog box to access the Help feature, the information should always be context sensitive.

No matter how you access the Help feature, a window opens for the Help information. This window is actually an application window for a separate program that provides the Help information. As a result, you can minimize, maximize, restore, move, and size the window. However, when you end the application program that you're using, its Help program also ends.

How to navigate through the Help information   Once you access the Help feature for a program, you'll find that it's easy to navigate through the help information that's available for the program. This is illustrated by figure 4-15, which shows you how to use the Help feature of a spreadsheet program called *Excel*. In part 1 of this figure, I issued the Contents command from the Help menu to get the screen shown in part 2. This screen shows the first page of the Help feature's table of contents. Here, you can pick a topic by clicking on it. Sometimes, this leads directly to the information you want; other times, it leads to a list of subtopics that you can choose from.

When I scrolled through the contents, I didn't find the topic I wanted so I clicked on the Search button as shown in part 2 of figure 4-15. With this function, you can request information through the dialog box shown in part 3. This dialog box also appears if you issue the Search for Help On command directly from the Help menu. Since I wanted information about *Excel*'s Payment function, I typed "payments" in the text box, and clicked on the Show Topics button as shown in part 3. The topics shown in part 4 were then displayed. Here, I clicked on PMT() because that was the function I was interested in. Then, when I clicked on the Go To button, the Help screen in part 5 was displayed. This screen describes the PMT() function, and also refers me to related topics under "See Also."

When I clicked on one of the related topics in part 5, the screen in part 6 was displayed. This screen is a list of *Excel*'s financial functions. On your monitor, these functions are displayed in green type. To get more information on a function, all I have to do is click on it. Whenever you see green items in a Help window, you can click on them to jump directly to their information.

The Back and History buttons provide two more ways for navigating through Help information. When you click on the Back button, it takes you back to the screen or topic just previous to the one you're currently using. When you click on the History button, it presents you with a list of the topics that you've used in the current help session. Then, you can return to any one of these topics by double-clicking on the topic in the list.

How to print Help information   If you want to keep a permanent copy of the information you find through the Help feature, you have a couple of options. First, you can print a copy of the current topic by issuing the Print Topic command from the File menu of Help's application window. This is useful if you want a copy of a single page of Help information.

If you want a more extensive printed reference document, you can use a second approach. To create a customized reference document, you have to work with both the Help window for your application and a word processing program like Write. Then, you piece together the information for the reference document in the word processing program, but you get each piece from the Help window by using the Copy command under the Edit menu. When you issue the Copy command in a Help application window, a special dialog box appears that displays the text for the current topic. This dialog box lets you select the block you're interested in and copy it to the clipboard. After that, you switch to the word processing program and paste the text from the Help window. After you've assembled all of the information you need in the word processing document, you can print it.

The limitations of the Help feature   Unfortunately, the quality of the Help information varies from one program to another. Some programs provide extensive information; some provide sketchy information. But even when a program provides extensive information, a Help feature has its limitations.

In general, Help information is most useful when you already know how to use a function or feature, but you just can't remember some detail. If, for example, you need to look up the syntax for *Excel*'s PMT function, as in figure 14-15, using the Help feature is probably more efficient than using any other reference. This kind of information is even more useful when it's provided as context-sensitive information.

In contrast, Help information is least useful when you're learning how to use a new feature or function. If, for example, you're trying to figure out how to use the Tables feature of a word processing program, the Help information is likely to send you to several topics, waste your time, and confuse you. That's when a book like this one is likely to be far more valuable than the Help information that you can get from the program.

Part 1

To access
Windows Help
from *Excel*, you
pull down the
Help menu. The
Contents com-
mand will display
a table of
contents.

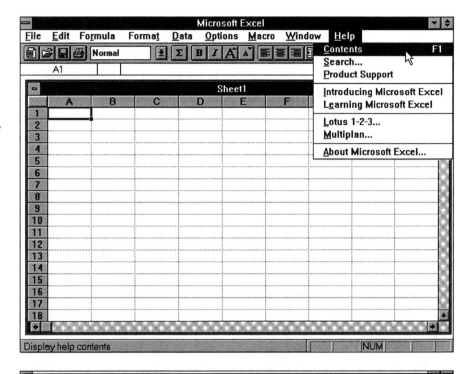

Part 2

Windows Help
lets you select
from subjects
related to the
program you're
running or the
specific task
you're trying to
perform. You can
read the table of
contents or click
on the Search
button.

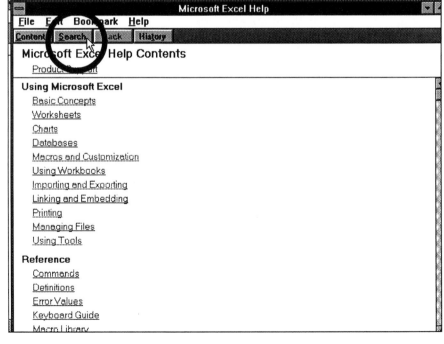

Figure 4-15   How to use the Help feature for *Excel*

Part 3

In the Search dialog box, you type the topic you're interested in, such as *payments*. As you enter the topic, the list of available topics automatically scrolls to entries that begin with the letters you entered. At any point, you can select a topic from the scrolling list box, then click on the Show Topics command button.

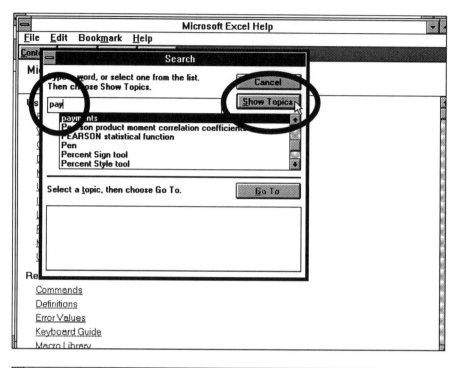

Part 4

After you click on the Show Topics command button, related topics appear in the list at the bottom of the dialog box. To select one, such as PMT(), click on it, then click on the Go To command button.

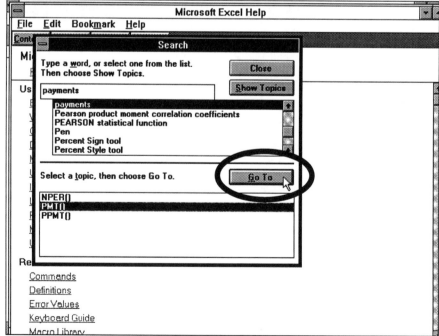

Figure 4-15   How to use the Help feature for *Excel* (continued)

Part 5

Help immediately displays the entry for the topic you selected. Often, related subjects appear, and you can navigate directly to one of them by clicking on it.

Part 6

You can click on any of the help items to jump directly to entries for specific information.

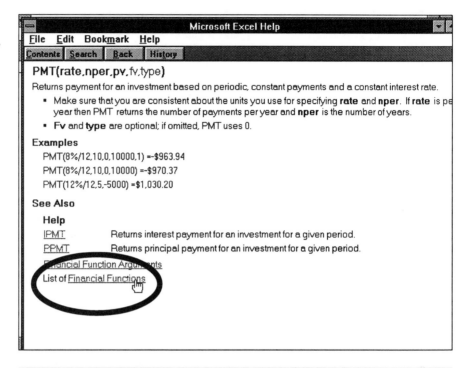

Figure 4-15   How to use the Help feature for *Excel* (continued)

Exercise 4-3

How to use the *Windows* Help feature

1. If it isn't already running, start *Windows* on your PC. Then, start the Write program.

2. Issue the Contents command from Write's Help menu. Then, to learn additional ways you can select text in a Write document, find out what Write's *selection area* is. You can scroll through the contents, or you can click on the Search button and use the dialog box that appears.

3. Close the Help window by double-clicking on its control menu box.

4. Switch from Write to the Program Manager. Then, start the Notepad program.

5. Issue the Search for Help On command from Notepad's Help menu. Then, search for information on formatting text. How many ways does Notepad provide to let you "format" text?

6. Close the Help windows that you've opened.

7. Switch from Notepad back to Write.

8. Issue the Search for Help On command from Write's Help menu. Then, search for information on formatting text. Look for related topics like fonts, characters, paragraphs, and styles. How do the text formatting capabilities of Write and Notepad compare?

9. Close the Help windows that you've opened.

10. Exit from Write, then switch to Notepad (if necessary) and exit from it too.

Perspective

With the skills you've learned in this chapter, you should be able to start using most *Windows* applications. If, for example, you've used a DOS word processing program before, you should be able to use *Word for Windows* for simple word processing functions. And if you've used a DOS spreadsheet program, you should be able to use *Excel for Windows* for simple spreadsheet functions. Of course, there's much more to learn about any advanced *Windows* program. But the standard *Windows* features will get you started.

Summary

- Almost all *Windows* applications provide three standard menus: File, Edit, and Help, and each of these menus provides standard commands. The File menu usually provides New, Open, Save, Save As, Print, and Exit commands. The Edit menu provides Undo, Cut, Copy, and Paste commands. And the Help menu usually provides Contents, Search for Help on, or Help Index commands.

- The dialog box for a file handling command like an Open or Save As command requires the use of a DOS file specification that includes drive, path, and file name. However, the controls in the dialog box let you build a specification instead of typing the specification.

- Printing commands like Print Setup and Print let you select a printer, set the options for a printing job, and print a document. The printing isn't done by the application program, though. It's done in the background by the Print Manager so you can continue working with your application program.

- Most *Windows* applications let you enter and edit text in the same way. This includes the techniques for moving the insertion point, selecting a block of text, moving and copying text, and undoing an editing mistake.

- To move or copy text, you use the Cut, Copy, and Paste commands of the Edit menu. To undo a mistake, you use the Undo command. For efficiency, you can use keyboard shortcuts for the Cut, Copy, and Paste commands: Ctrl+X, Ctrl+C, and Ctrl+V.

- When you cut or copy a selected block of text, the selection replaces whatever was on the *clipboard*. When you paste from the clipboard, the selection remains on the clipboard. You can use the clipboard to copy text from one document to another within the same program or from one program to another.

- The Help feature of a *Windows* program runs in a separate application window. You can access this feature from the program's Help menu or by pressing the F1 key. When you use the F1 key, some programs provide *context-sensitive information*. Once you access the Help feature, you can use standard techniques for navigating through the information.

Chapter 5

How to use the File Manager to manage directories and files

How to start the File Manager and work with its directory windows
How to interpret the contents of a directory window
What the icons represent
How to work with directories
How to work with more than one directory window

Exercise 5-1: How to work with directories and directory windows

How to manage files and directories
How to select files and directories
How to delete a directory, a file, or more than one file
How to copy or move a directory, a file, or more than one file
How to rename a directory, a file, or more than one file
How to create a directory

Exercise 5-2: How to manage files and directories

How to work with diskettes
How to format a diskette
How to copy a diskette

Exercise 5-3: How to format and copy diskettes

Perspective
Summary

The *Windows* File Manager program lets you manage your directories and files. Although you can perform the same functions by using DOS commands or the DOS shell, the File Manager lets you perform most of these functions more efficiently. That's why many *Windows* users use the File Manager for all of their file management activities.

In this chapter, you'll learn how to use the File Manager for most file management jobs. First, you'll learn how to work with the directory windows of the File Manager. Then, you'll learn how to use the File Manager to manage files and directories. Last, you'll learn how to use the File Manager to format and copy diskettes. When you complete this chapter, you probably won't ever want to use DOS again for managing your directories and files.

How to start the File Manager and work with its directory windows

By default, the program icon for the File Manager is in the Program Manager's Main group. To start the File Manager, you open the group and double-click on the icon that looks like a filing cabinet, as shown in part 1 of figure 5-1. The File Manager's application window is then displayed as shown in part 2. As you can see, this application window is similar to those for other programs. It has a control-menu box, minimize and maximize buttons, and several menu items.

How to interpret the contents of a directory window   The File Manager's application window always contains at least one document window. Because this document window shows information about a directory, it can also be called a *directory window*. The title bar of a directory window shows the name of the directory that's displayed in the window. In part 2 of figure 5-1, you can see that the C:\WINDOWS directory is the one that's displayed. That's the directory that contains the files that come with *Windows*.

Although the example in figure 5-1 shows only one directory window, the File Manager can display several directory windows at one time. Then, you can work with the contents of more than one directory at a time. To make these windows easier to work with, you can size or move them just as you can with Program Manager windows.

Beneath the title bar in the directory window, you see an icon for each disk and diskette drive on your PC. The drive that's marked with an outline is the current drive. In part 2 of figure 5-1, the C drive is the current drive. In a moment, you'll learn how to change the current drive.

Unless you've customized the File Manager, a directory window will have two *panes*: a *tree pane* and a *directory pane* as shown in part 2 of figure 5-1. The tree pane is on the left side of a directory window. It displays a *directory tree* to show where the selected directory is located within the structure of directories on the current drive. In figure 5-1, the WINDOWS directory is highlighted to show that it's the selected directory in the tree. You can also see in the tree pane that the WINDOWS directory has one subdirectory named SYSTEM.

The *directory pane* appears on the right side of a directory window. It displays the files and subdirectories that reside in the selected directory. You can see in the directory pane in figure 5-1 that the WINDOWS directory contains many files. Also, notice that an icon for the SYSTEM subdirectory appears in the directory pane as well as in the tree pane. In the directory pane, subdirectories always appear before files.

What the icons represent   The File Manager uses icons to represent different kinds of directories and files. These icons are summarized in figure 5-2. In the tree pane, the File Manager uses an icon shaped like a file folder for a directory. The selected directory shows up as an open folder, and all others appear as closed folders.

By default, the File Manager doesn't indicate which directories in the tree have subdirectories. In part 2 of figure 5-1, for example, the WINDOWS directory is open, or *expanded*, so you can see that it has a subdirectory. But you can't tell that other directories, like the DATA directory, also have subdirectories because their subdirectories are closed, or *collapsed*. In just a moment, I'll show you how to change the default setting so the icon for a directory has a plus or minus sign that tells you whether or not it has subdirectories.

In the directory pane, the icons for directories look like file folders just as they do in the tree pane. The four other icons that can be used in a directory pane are used to identify four types of files as summarized in figure 5-2. The File Manager uses one type of icon to identify program files, such as the CLOCK.EXE and CALC.EXE files that you can see in figure 5-1. These are the program files for the Clock and Calculator accessory programs. The other three icons are used to identify (1) files that are associated with an application program, (2) files that aren't associated with an application program, and (3) hidden or system files.

Part 1

To start the File Manager, you double-click on its icon in the Main program group.

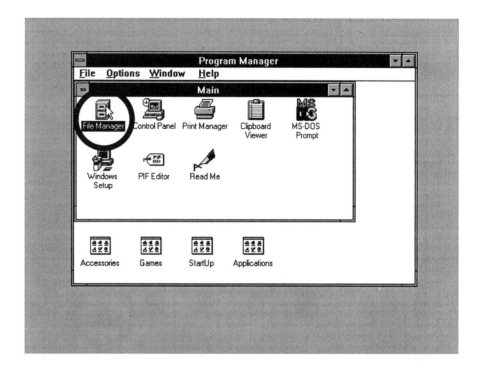

Part 2

The application window for the File Manager opens with one directory window.

Directory window

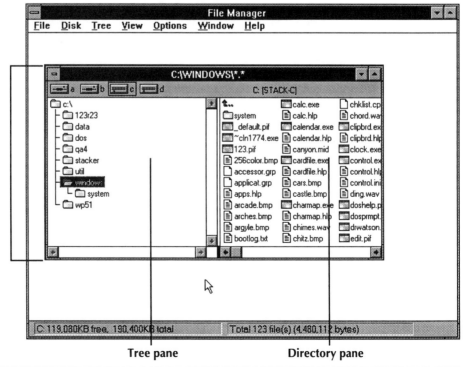

Tree pane　　　　　**Directory pane**

Figure 5-1　　　How to start the File Manager

Icons that appear in the tree pane	Icons that appear in the directory pane
Directory or subdirectory	Subdirectory to the current directory
Current directory	Program (EXE or COM), batch (BAT), or Program Information (PIF) file
Directory with (+) or without (-) expandable branches	File with an extension that's associated with a specific application program
Current directory with (+) or without (-) expandable branches	File with an extension that isn't associated with a specfic application program
	Hidden or system file

Figure 5-2   The icons that the File Manager uses to identify directories and files

How to work with directories   You can use the directory tree to display the contents of any of the directories on any of your disk or diskette drives. Figure 5-3 summarizes the methods you can use to work with directories. It shows you how to change the drive that's displayed, how to change the directory, how to expand or collapse the directory tree, and so on. As you can see, you can perform many of the functions by clicking or double-clicking the mouse on an icon. For some functions, though, you have to issue a command from one of the menus.

Figure 5-4 illustrates the use of many of the functions in figure 5-3. Usually, you will want the File Manager to indicate which directories have subdirectories. If so, you issue the Indicate Expandable Branches command from the Tree menu as shown in part 1 of figure 5-4. Then, the File Manager displays plus and minus signs on the icons in the tree pane. You can see the change in the tree pane in parts 2 and 3. A plus sign means the directory has subdirectories that aren't displayed in the tree. That's the case with the DATA and UTIL directories. A minus sign means that a directory has subdirectories, and they are displayed. That's the case with the WINDOWS directory and the root directory.

To change the directory, click on the icon for the new directory in the tree pane. As soon as you do, the File Manager displays the contents of the new directory in the directory pane. For example, WINDOWS is the selected directory in part 2 of figure 5-4. Then, to change to the DATA directory, you click on its icon. This causes the display shown in part 3 of the figure. As you

Basic functions	How to do it
Select a drive, directory, or file	Click on its icon. Or, press Tab to move the highlight to the drive icons, the tree pane, or the directory pane. Then, use the arrow keys to move the highlight to its icon and press Enter.
Change to another directory on the same drive in the current directory window	Select the directory in the tree pane using one of the methods given above.
Change to another drive in the current directory window	Select the drive using one of the methods given above. Or, press Ctrl+*drive letter*.
Refresh the contents of a directory window for a diskette drive	Issue the Refresh command in the Window menu. Or, press F5.

Expanding/collapsing the tree	How to do it
Expand the tree one level under a closed directory	Double-click on the icon for the closed directory. Or, select the directory icon. Then, press Enter, or type +, or issue the Expand One Level command in the Tree menu.
Collapse the tree under a directory	Double-click on the icon for the open directory. Or, select the directory icon. Then, press Enter, or type -, or issue the Collapse Branch command in the Tree menu.
Expand the selected directory completely	Select the directory icon. Then, type * or issue the Expand Branch command in the Tree menu.
Expand all of the directories on a disk drive	Press Ctrl+*. Or, issue the Expand All command in the Tree menu.
Use a plus or minus sign to indicate expandable branches	Issue the Indicate Expandable Branches command in the Tree menu.

Using multiple directory windows	How to do it
Open another directory window	Double-click on a drive icon. Or, issue the New Window command in the Window menu.
Switch from one directory window to another	Click on any part of the inactive window. Or, select the window's title in the Window menu.
Arrange directory windows	Issue the Cascade or Tile command in the Window menu.

Figure 5-3   How to work with directory windows

Part 1

To display plus
signs and minus
signs on the icons
for directories that
have branches,
issue the Indicate
Expandable
Branches
command from
the Tree menu.

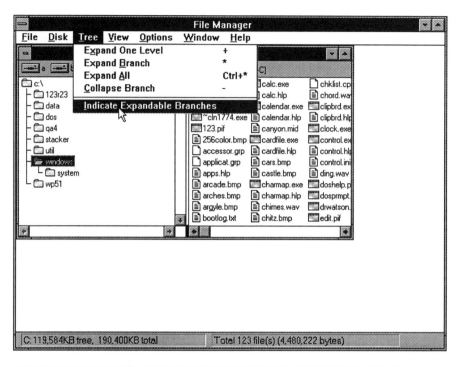

Part 2

WINDOWS is the
current directory,
and its contents
appear in the
directory pane.
To switch to
another directory,
such as DATA,
click on it.

Figure 5-4   How to expand, collapse, and select directories in the tree pane

Part 3

The name of the current directory appears in the title bar of the directory window, and its contents appear in the directory pane. To expand a branch of a tree one level, you double-click on its directory icon in the tree pane.

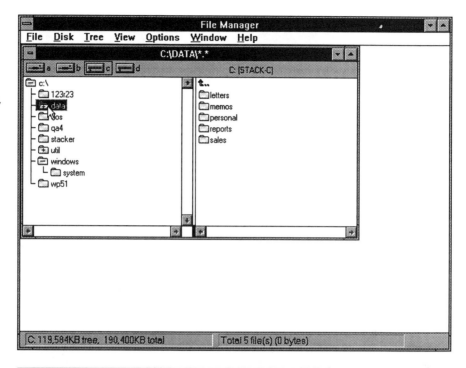

Part 4

Notice that the icon for the DATA directory now shows a minus sign instead of a plus sign. Notice also that one of DATA's subdirectories (REPORTS) itself has subordinates. To collapse an expanded branch of the tree, you double-click on its icon.

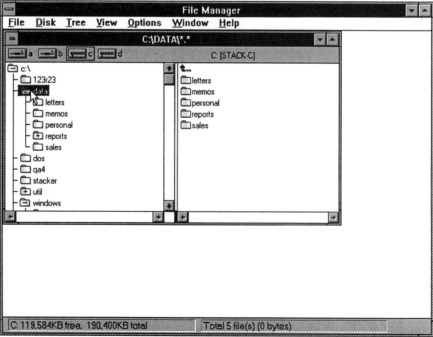

Figure 5-4   How to expand, collapse, and select directories in the tree pane (continued)

Part 5

The icon for the collapsed DATA directory shows a plus sign. You can issue the Expand Branch command from the Tree menu to expand the DATA branch to show all of its sub-directories, not just the first level of subdirectories.

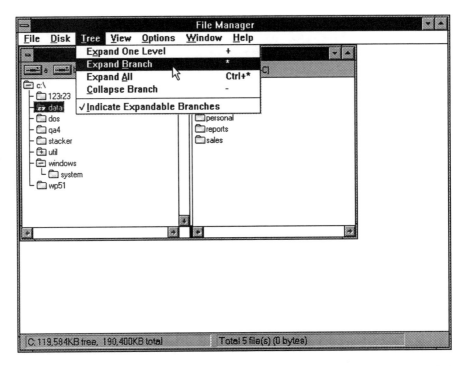

Part 6

With the DATA directory com-pletely expanded, notice that the subordinates of the REPORTS directory appear in the tree pane. Finally, to collapse the entire tree, you can double-click on the icon for the root directory.

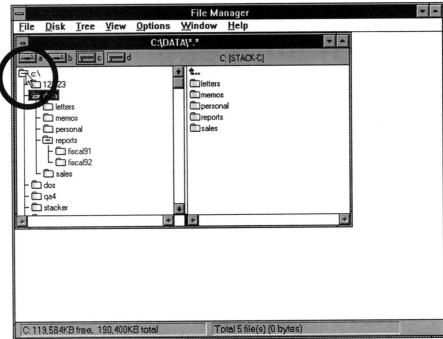

Figure 5-4   How to expand, collapse, and select directories in the tree pane (continued)

Part 7

Now, the entire tree is collapsed. Notice that the directory pane shows the directories and files that reside in the root directory, and the icon for the root directory in the tree pane shows a plus sign to indicate that it is expandable.

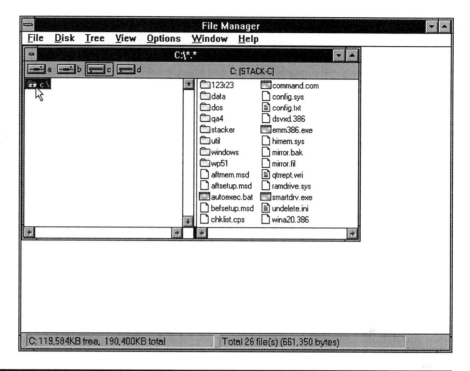

Figure 5-4   How to expand, collapse, and select directories in the tree pane (continued)

can see, the contents of the DATA directory are displayed in the directory pane, and the directory's name is displayed in the title bar.

You can exercise a lot of control over how much of a drive's directory structure you can see in the tree pane by expanding or collapsing its directories. If you can't see the subdirectories you're interested in, you can expand a directory one level at a time or all at once. If you think the tree pane is too cluttered, you can collapse a directory.

One way to expand a tree is to double-click on a directory icon. In part 3 of figure 5-4, you can see that the DATA directory has subdirectories because its icon appears with a plus sign. Then, when you expand the DATA directory one level by double-clicking on its icon, you get the results shown in part 4. As you can see, it has five subdirectories: LETTERS, MEMOS, PERSONAL, REPORTS, and SALES. To look at the contents of one of these subdirectories, you just click on its icon.

In part 4 of figure 5-4, you can see that the REPORTS subdirectory has its own subdirectories. They don't appear, however, because the DATA directory was expanded by only one level. If you want to see all of the subdirectories in a branch of the directory tree, you can use the Expand Branch command from the Tree menu as shown in part 5 of figure 5-4. When you issue this command, the File Manager expands the DATA directory as shown in part 6. Here, you can see all five of the directories that are immediately subordinate to the DATA directory, plus two more that are subordinate to the REPORTS subdirectory: FISCAL91 and FISCAL92.

To collapse an expanded directory, you can double-click on its icon in the tree pane. If you collapse the DATA directory shown in part 4 of figure 5-4, for example, the tree returns to the structure shown in part 3. If you want to collapse the entire tree, you can double-click on the icon for the root directory, as shown in part 6. The resulting tree structure is shown in part 7. Here, the tree pane shows only the highest-level directory on the drive, the root directory. In the directory pane, though, you can see the icons for the directories that the root directory contains along with the files that it contains.

If you want to display the directory structure for a different drive, click on its drive icon. When a directory window contains information for a hard disk drive, its contents are updated automatically. However, when a directory window contains information for a diskette drive, that may not be the case. For instance, if you remove a diskette that's represented in a directory window and replace it with another diskette, the contents of the directory window aren't updated. Instead, the directory window continues to show information for the first diskette, even though it's no longer in the drive. To update the diskette information displayed in the directory window, you can issue the Refresh command from the Window menu.

How to work with more than one directory window   To open an additional directory window, all you have to do is double-click on the icon for the drive you want. If you double-click on the icon for a drive that already has an open directory window, another window will open for that drive. This is useful when you want to look at or work with the contents of two or more directories on the same drive.

Figure 5-5 shows how you can open a second directory window for a different drive. In part 1 of the figure, only one directory window is open, and it contains information for the C drive. To open a second window for drive B, you double-click on its icon. You can see the results in part 2 of figure 5-5.

The File Manager lets you open many directory windows at the same time. The exact number depends on how other *Windows* programs are using *Windows* resources. However, the maximum number really doesn't matter because you probably will never approach it. Realistically, the largest number of directory windows you'll want to open at the same time is three or four because you can't fit more than that on the screen and still work with them effectively.

Part 1

To open a new directory window for a directory on a different drive, double-click on the drive icon.

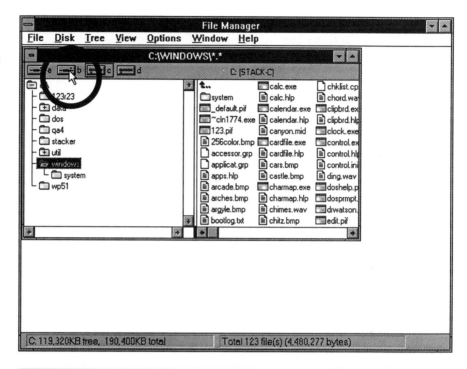

Part 2

The File Manager opens a second directory window on top of the first. Notice the drive and directory identifier in the title bar of each of the two directory windows.

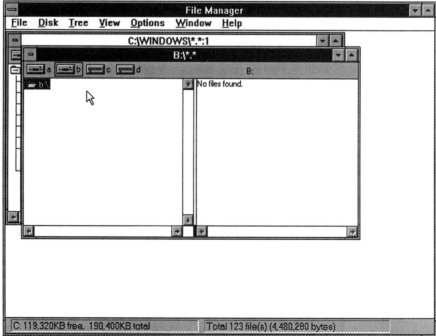

Figure 5-5   How to open a second directory window

No matter how many directory windows you have open, only one is the active window. This window has a highlighted title bar. And if the directory windows overlap, the active window is always the one on the top of the stack.

To make an inactive directory window the active window, you can click on it or select it from the File Manager's Window menu. When you pull down the Window menu, it displays a list of the titles of the open directory windows. To switch to another window, you just select the title of the window that you want.

If you work with more than one window, you often need to arrange them so you can use them efficiently. If so, you can use most of the same techniques that you learned for working with Program Manager windows. You can maximize directory windows within the File Manager's application window. You can minimize directory windows to special File Manager icons that appear at the bottom of the File Manager's application window. You can size and position directory windows by dragging their borders, corners, and title bars. And you can use the Tile and Cascade commands in the Window menu to organize the directory windows automatically.

Exercise 5-1

How to work with directories and directory windows

1. If it isn't already running, start *Windows* on your PC. Then, start the File Manager program from the Main group of the Program Manager. How many directory windows are open inside the File Manager's application window? There will be at least one, and there may be more.

2. Look at the drive icons that appear at the top of the active directory window. How many drives are there? How many are diskette drives? How many are hard disk drives? Are there any network drives?

3. Study the layout of the current directory window. What directory does it display? The name of that directory will appear in the window's title bar, and it will be highlighted in the tree pane.

4. Minimize all of the directory windows. Notice that each appears as an icon at the bottom of the File Manager's application window.

5. Restore the directory window that was active in step 3 by double-clicking on its icon.

6. Examine the contents of some of the directories that appear in the tree pane of the directory window. To do so, click once on each icon in the tree pane. As you do, the contents of the associated directory will appear in the directory pane. For each directory, note whether it contains subdirectories.

7. Collapse the entire tree by double-clicking on the icon for the root directory of the current drive. You may need to scroll the contents of the tree pane to see the icon for the root directory.

8. Expand the tree one level by double-clicking on the icon for the root directory. Did the tree return to the state it was in step 6? If the tree displayed any subdirectories in step 6, they should no longer be visible.

Continued on the next page...

Exercise 5-1 (continued)
How to work with directories and directory windows

9. If necessary, switch to the drive that the *Windows* files are stored on. Then, click on the icon for the WINDOWS directory and examine its contents in the directory pane. Does the WINDOWS directory contain any subdirectories? If the directory has any subdirectories (it will almost certainly contain one called SYSTEM), they will appear in the directory pane, but not in the tree pane.

10. Double-click on the icon for the WINDOWS directory in the tree pane to expand it one level. Now, the directories that are subordinate to the WIN-DOWS directory appear in both the tree and directory panes.

11. Click on the icon for the root directory to make it the current directory. Notice that its name now appears in the title bar of the directory window, and its contents appear in the directory pane.

12. Issue the Expand All command from the Tree menu. Then, use the scroll bar on the side of the tree pane to scroll through the expanded tree. Now, the entire directory structure for the current drive appears in the tree pane. The chances are that many directories and subdirectories appear in the tree pane. In most cases, you'll find it easier to work with a tree pane that shows only the directory branches you're interested in, not all of them that are present on your hard drive.

13. Make the root directory the current directory and issue the Collapse Branch command from the Tree menu to collapse the entire tree structure. (This command has the same result as double-clicking on the icon for the root directory.)

14. Double-click on the icon for the root directory in the tree pane to expand the tree one level. This has the same result as issuing the Expand One Level command from the Tree menu.

15. If the directory icons in the tree pane don't already indicate whether a directory has subordinates, issue the Indicate Expandable Branches command from the Tree menu. Now, those directories that contain subdirectories show a plus sign on their icons.

16. Double-click on the control-menu box in the File Manager's application window to exit from the File Manager program.

How to manage files and directories

Figure 5-6 summarizes the most useful procedures for managing files and directories with the File Manager. In the first three procedures, you start by selecting the directory, file, or files that you want to delete, copy, move, or rename. In the fourth procedure, you start by selecting the directory that you want to create a subdirectory for. Once you've made the selections, you can complete the operations by using the Delete key, a mouse operation, or one of the commands in the File menu.

How to select files and directories   To select a single file or directory, you just click on its icon. To select two or more files or directories, you hold down either the Shift or Ctrl key as you click on the icons you want. This is summarized in figure 5-7. As you can see, the Shift key lets you select a continuous range of files; the Ctrl key lets you select files that don't make up a continuous range. Although this figure just shows the selection of two files, you can continue to hold the Ctrl key down and click on additional files to select as many as you want for a single operation. The only limitation for selecting files is that all the files must be in the same directory window.

You can also select files with the keyboard. First, press the Tab key until the highlight is in the directory pane. Then, to select one file, use the arrow keys to move the highlight to its icon. To select a continuous range of files, hold down the Shift key, then use the arrow keys to "paint" the highlight over the files you want. Or, to select all of the items in the directory pane, type /.

If you want to use the keyboard to select two or more files that don't make up a continuous range of items in the directory pane, the procedure is a little more complicated. After you've moved the highlight into the directory pane, you press Shift+F8 to enter a special selection mode. When you're in this mode, the File Manager's highlight flashes. Then, for each item you want to include in the selection, you move the flashing highlight to its icon, and you press the Spacebar. After you've marked all of the items you want to include in the selection, press Shift+F8 again to leave this special selection mode.

Another way to select files is to use the Select Files command in the File menu. When you issue this command, the File Manager prompts you for a file specification. Normally, you respond by giving a file specification that includes a wildcard. Then, the command automatically selects all the files in the current directory that match your wildcard specification. If you know how to use wildcards, this method can save you time, and it reduces the chance that you'll miss a file. In just a moment, I'll illustrate the use of this command.

Function	How to do it
Delete	1. Select the files or directory. 2. Press the Delete key. 3. Click on the OK button in the Delete dialog box. 4. Respond to the confirmation dialog boxes.
Copy or Move	1. Select the files or directory. 2. Is the destination directory the same as the source directory? If not, use the mouse, or the mouse and a modifier key as shown in figure 5-9. If so, use the Copy command under the File menu as shown in figure 5-10. 3. Respond to the confirmation dialog box if one appears.
Rename	1. Select the files or directory. 2. Issue the Rename command from the File menu. 3. Supply a new name in the Rename dialog box. 4. Click on the OK button in the Rename dialog box.
Create Directory	1. Select the directory that you want the new directory to be subordinate to. 2. Issue the Create Directory command from the File menu. 3. Supply a name for the new directory in the Create Directory dialog box. 4. Click on the OK button in the Create Directory dialog box.

Figure 5-6   How to manage files and directories

How to delete a directory, a file, or more than one file   To delete the directory or files that you've selected, all you have to do is press the Delete key. Then, the File Manager displays one or more dialog boxes that ask you to confirm the deletion. If these boxes indicate that the right directory or files are going to be deleted, you can confirm the operation. Otherwise, you can cancel the operation.

When you delete a directory, all of the directory's contents are deleted including any subdirectories it contains and their contents. This has the potential to cause major problems if you make a mistake. Similarly, pressing the Delete key after you've selected a screenful of files has the potential for trouble. That's why it's worth taking the time to read the dialog boxes that ask you for confirmation.

How to copy or move a directory, a file, or more than one file   The easiest way to move or copy a directory or one or more files is to drag the selected icon or icons from one directory to another. To make this possible, you need to be able to see both the directory or files that you want to move or copy

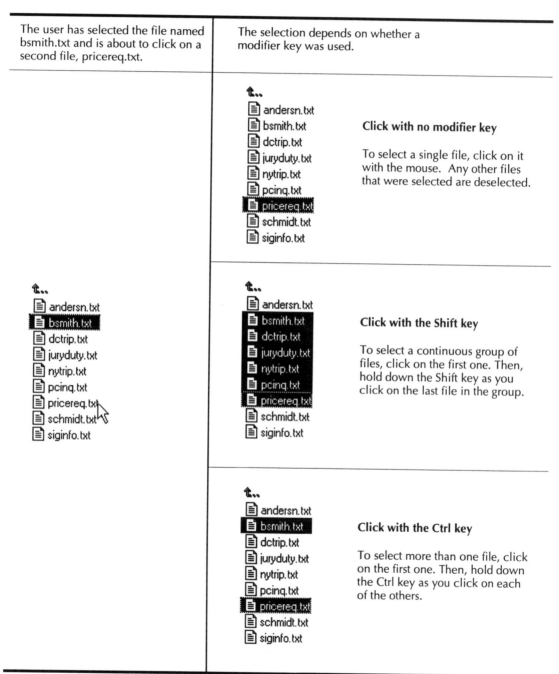

The user has selected the file named bsmith.txt and is about to click on a second file, pricereq.txt.

The selection depends on whether a modifier key was used.

Click with no modifier key

To select a single file, click on it with the mouse. Any other files that were selected are deselected.

Click with the Shift key

To select a continuous group of files, click on the first one. Then, hold down the Shift key as you click on the last file in the group.

Click with the Ctrl key

To select more than one file, click on the first one. Then, hold down the Ctrl key as you click on each of the others.

Figure 5-7   How to select files from the directory pane

and the directory that you want to move or copy them to. When you move or copy a directory, the directory including all its files and subdirectories is moved or copied.

Before you drag a file or directory, though, you need to be aware of the File Manager conventions for these operations as summarized in figure 5-8. If you drag an icon to a location that's on the same drive, the File Manager performs a move operation. If you drag an icon to a location that's on a different drive, the File Manager performs a copy operation. However, you can override these default operations by using the Ctrl or Shift key. If you want to copy a file or directory to a location that's on the same drive, just hold down the Ctrl key as you drag the icon. And if you want to move a file or directory to a different drive, hold down the Shift key as you drag the icon. Although this can be confusing at first, you'll quickly get used to it.

To help you with these operations, the File Manager tells you whether a drag operation will result in a copy or a move operation. After you drag an icon to its destination but before you release the mouse button, look closely at the icon. If there's a plus sign on it, the File Manager will copy your selection. Otherwise, the File Manager will move it. Also, before you release the mouse button, look back to the origin of the drag operation. If the source icon is still present, the File Manager is about to copy your selection. If the source icon is gone, the File Manager is about to move your selection. If you take another look at figure 5-8, you can see examples of how the icon changes its appearance during these operations.

If you have selected more than one file for a move or copy operation, you point the mouse to any one of the selected files to start the dragging action. Then, the icon that you drag indicates a stack of three files instead of a single file.

You can use this dragging technique for copy and move operations as long as they go from one directory to another. But if you want to make a copy of a file and store that copy in the same directory as the original file, you can't use this method. Instead, you have to use the Copy command in the File menu.

Figure 5-9 illustrates the use of the Copy command as well as the use of the Select Files command. In part 1, LETTERS is the current directory, and all of the files in that directory have the extension TXT. One way to select all of these files is to use the Select Files command in the Files menu. When you issue this command, you get the dialog box shown in part 2. Here, you can type a file specification that includes wildcards and click on the Select button. When the command is executed, the files that match the wildcard specification are marked with an outline as shown in part 3. Then, if your selection worked the way you wanted it to, you can click on the Close button in the dialog box. Otherwise, you can click on the Deselect button and type a new specification.

To **copy** a directory or files to a destination on the **same drive**:

1. Select the source icons.
2. Hold down the **Ctrl** key.
3. Drag the source icons to the destination icon.

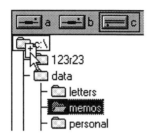

To **copy** a directory or files to a destination on a **different drive**:

1. Select the source icons.
2. Drag the source icons to the destination icon. (No modifier key is necessary.)

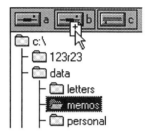

To **move** a directory or files to a destination on the **same drive**:

1. Select the source icons.
2. Drag the source icons to the destination icon. (No modifier key is necessary.)

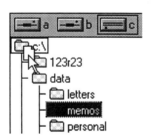

To **move** a directory or files to a destination on a **different drive**:

1. Select the source icons.
2. Hold down the **Shift** key.
3. Drag the source icons to the destination icon.

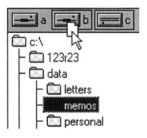

Figure 5-8   How to copy and move files and directories by dragging icons

Part 1

Here, the current
directory is
C:\DATA\LETTERS.

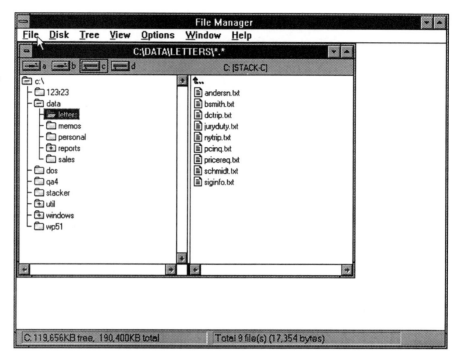

Part 2

When you issue
the Select Files
command in the
File menu, a
dialog box
appears. Then,
you can type in a
wildcard specifi-
cation, such as
*.txt, and click on
the Select
command button.

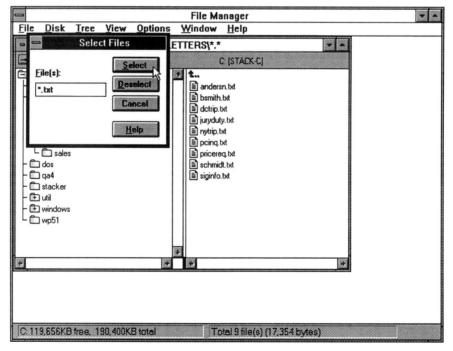

Figure 5-9   How to use the Select Files and Copy commands to copy files

Part 3

The File Manager marks the files it selects with outlines. If you're satisfied with the selection, you click on the Close button to close the Select Files dialog box.

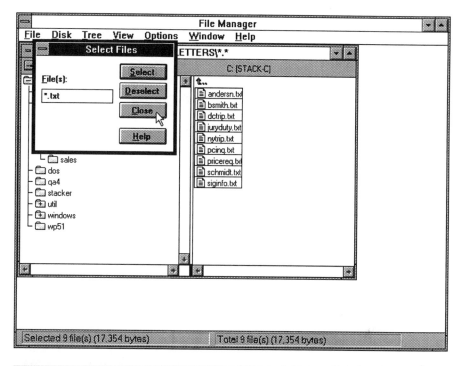

Part 4

Notice that all of the files with the extension .txt were selected in the directory pane. To make duplicates of these files in the same directory, you can issue the Copy command under the File menu.

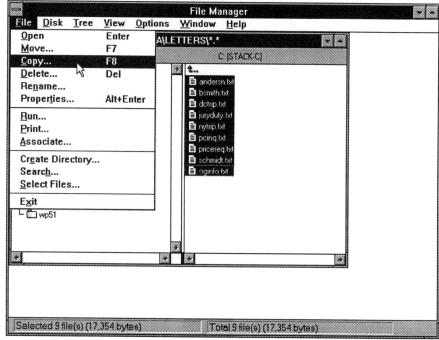

Figure 5-9   How to use the Select Files and Copy commands to copy files (continued)

Part 5

The new value of *.cpy specifies that the duplicate files will have the same name as the original files, but their extensions will be .cpy instead of .txt. To start the copy operation, click on the OK button.

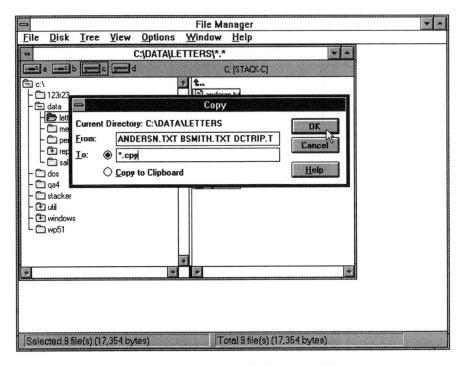

Part 6

When the copy operation is complete, the directory pane shows both the original files and the duplicates.

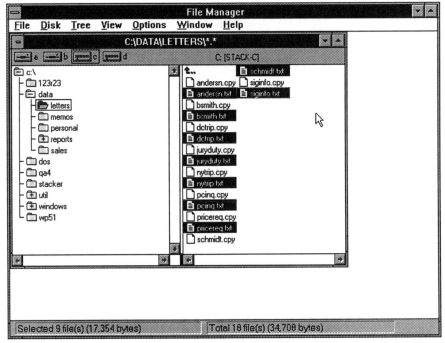

Figure 5-9   How to use the Select Files and Copy commands to copy files (continued)

After the files are selected, you can issue the Copy command in the File menu as shown in part 4 of figure 5-9. In the dialog box that appears in part 5, you have to type a file specification that includes a wildcard in order to name the copied files without duplicating the old names. In this example, the specification is entered as *.cpy, which means that all of the new files will have the same names as the old files, but with the extension CPY instead of TXT. To complete the Copy command, you click on the OK button and the files are copied as shown in part 6. Here, you can see that File Manager has made copies of all the selected files.

How to rename a directory, a file, or more than one file To rename the directory or files that you've selected, you use the Rename command in the File menu. Then, the File Manager displays the Rename dialog box to ask you what the new name or new names should be. If you're changing the name of only one directory or file, you just type the new name.

If you're renaming two or more files at the same time, though, you have to use wildcards in the file specification as illustrated by figure 5-10. In part 1 of this figure, all the files in the LETTERS directory are selected and all have an extension of TXT. In part 2, the Rename command in the File menu is selected. In part 3, a file specification of *.ltr is used to indicate that all of the files should be renamed with the extension LTR. In part 4, you can see the results of this operation.

How to create a directory To create a new directory, you use the Create Directory command in the File menu. Before you start this command, though, you must select the directory that you want the new directory to be subordinate to. If, for example, you want to create a directory that's subordinate to the root directory, you select the root directory. If you want to create a directory that's subordinate to the DATA directory, you select the DATA directory. When you issue the command, a dialog box asks you for the name of the new directory. After you type the name, you click on the OK button to complete the command.

Part 1

Select the files
you want to
rename. Here, all
of the files in the
C:\DATA\LETTERS
directory are
selected.

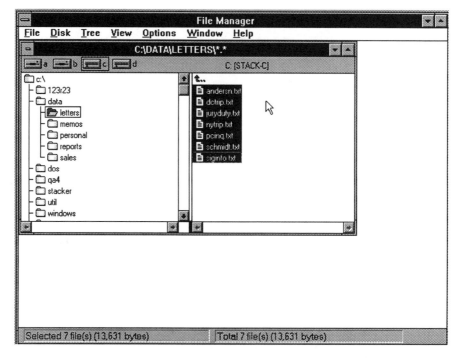

Part 2

Issue the Rename
command from
the File menu.

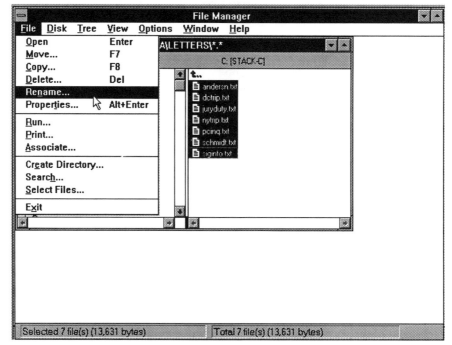

Figure 5-10   How to rename several files at the same time

Part 3

In the Rename dialog box, type the specification for the new name. Here, *.ltr will add an extension of LTR to the name of each file.

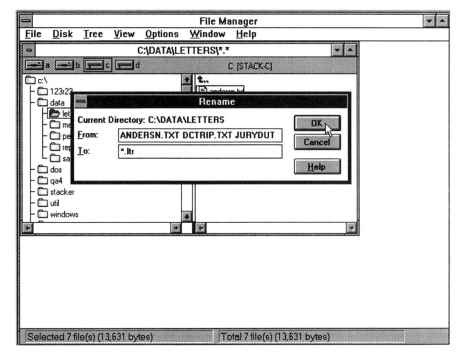

Part 4

When the operation is complete, all of the files have been renamed.

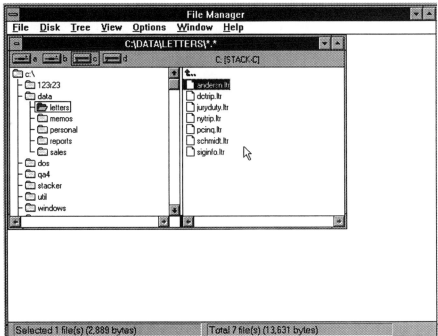

Figure 5-10   How to rename several files at the same time (continued)

Exercise 5-2

How to manage files and directories

1. If it isn't already running, start *Windows* on your PC. Then, start the File Manager program.

2. Click on the icon for the root directory of the C drive to make it the current directory.

3. Issue the Create Directory command under the File menu, and create a new directory called TEMPDIR (for temporary directory). This directory is a top-level directory that's subordinate to the root directory because of the selection you made in step 2. An icon for the new directory will appear in both the tree and directory panes of the directory window.

4. In the tree pane, click on the icon for the WINDOWS directory. The contents of the WINDOWS directory appear in the directory pane.

5. Scroll through the contents of the directory pane to find the icons for these two files: WINLOGO.BMP and ZIGZAG.BMP. These files contain graphics that you can edit with the Paintbrush accessory program that comes with *Windows.*

6. Select WINLOGO.BMP and ZIGZAG.BMP. To select these two files, and only these two files, click on one to select it. Then, press and hold down the Ctrl key as you click on the second one.

7. Copy WINLOGO.BMP and ZIGZAG.BMP from the WINDOWS directory to the TEMPDIR directory you created in step 3. To perform this copy operation with the mouse, you need to use a modifier key. So hold down the Ctrl key as you drag the icons from the directory pane into the tree pane and release them on top of the icon for the TEMPDIR directory. Respond to the Confirm Mouse Operation dialog box to show that you do want to *copy* these files.

8. Rename the copies of WINLOGO.BMP and ZIGZAG.BMP that are in the TEMPDIR directory to WINLOGO.CPY and ZIGZAG.CPY. To rename them:

    (a) Click on the icon for the TEMPDIR directory in the tree pane to make it the current directory.

    (b) Select WINLOGO.BMP and ZIGZAG.BMP in the directory pane. They should be the only files in the directory.

    (c) Issue the RENAME command from the File menu.

Continued on the next page...

Exercise 5-2 (continued)
How to manage files and directories

8. (Continued)

   (d) Type *.cpy for the To: file specification in the dialog box.

   (e) Click on the OK button to confirm the operation.

   (f) Check the directory window to verify the operation.

9. Move the entire TEMPDIR directory into the WINDOWS directory. To do this, simply drag the icon for TEMPDIR in the tree pane onto the icon for the WINDOWS directory that's also in the tree pane. Then, respond to the Confirm Mouse Operation dialog box.

10. Click on the icon for the WINDOWS directory in the tree pane to make it the current directory. The icon for the TEMPDIR directory should appear as a subdirectory in the directory pane.

11. Double-click on the icon for the WINDOWS directory in the tree pane to expand it one level, if it isn't already expanded. Now, the icons for all of the directories that are subordinate to WINDOWS, including TEMPDIR, should appear in both the tree pane and the directory pane.

12. Delete the TEMPDIR directory and its contents. To delete this directory:

    (a) Select the icon for the TEMPDIR directory in either the tree or directory pane.

    (b) Press the Delete key.

    (c) Confirm the Delete operation by responding properly to the dialog boxes that appear.

    (d) Check the directory window to make sure the deletion was done.

13. Double-click on the control-menu box in the File Manager's application window to exit from the File Manager program.

How to work with diskettes

If you use diskettes in your work, the Disk menu provides two commands that you may find useful. One lets you format a diskette of any size or capacity. The other lets you make a copy of a diskette and all of its files.

How to format a diskette   To *format* a diskette is to prepare it so it can store information. This involves: (1) creating and verifying a pattern of tracks for organizing the stored data, and (2) creating the root directory on the diskette. The File Manager lets you format all four kinds of diskettes that I described in chapter 1: 360KB and 1.2MB 5.25-inch diskettes, and 720KB and 1.44MB 3.5-inch diskettes.

Figure 5-11 shows you how to format a diskette. After you put the diskette in the drive, you issue the Format Disk command from the Disk menu, as shown in part 1. The resulting dialog box is shown in part 2. Here, you use drop-down boxes to tell the File Manager what diskette drive you're going to use to format the diskette and what the capacity of the diskette is.

You probably won't need any of the options in the Format Disk dialog box. But if you want to supply a volume label for the diskette, you can click in the Label box and type a label of up to 11 characters that will be stored on the diskette to help identify it. And if you want to make the disk you're about to format a system disk, you can click once in that check box. When a *system disk* is formatted, three DOS files are stored on it so you can start your PC from the diskette instead of from your hard disk.

The last option in the dialog box is Quick Format. You can use this if a diskette has already been formatted and all you want to do is reset the diskette's directory information. That has the effect of removing all of the files from the diskette. However, because this option doesn't actually format the diskette, you can't use it with an unformatted diskette.

Because formatting destroys any files that are stored on a diskette, the File Manager displays a dialog box to warn you about that. Then, if you confirm the operation, the formatting operation starts, and the File Manager displays another dialog box to report the progress of the operation. When the operation is completed, the File Manager displays a third dialog box to ask if you want to format another diskette.

How to copy a diskette   Occasionally, you may want to make a copy of an entire diskette. The easiest way to do that is to use the Copy Disk command in the Disk menu. When you use this command, the size and capacity of the source and destination diskettes must be the same. Then, the contents of the

Part 1

To format a diskette, insert the diskette into one of your PC's diskette drives, then issue the Format Disk command from the Disk menu.

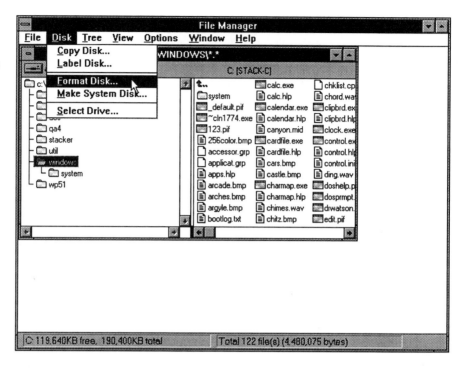

Part 2

In the dialog box that appears, use the drop-down boxes to specify the drive that contains the diskette you want to format (A or B) and the capacity of the diskette. Then, click on the OK button.

Figure 5-11 How to format a diskette

source diskette replace the contents of the destination diskette. When the operation is finished, the destination diskette is an exact copy of the source diskette.

When you issue the Copy Disk command as shown in part 1 of figure 5-12, the dialog box in part 2 appears. This dialog box asks you to identify the drive that's going to be used for the original diskette (Source In) and the drive that's going to be used for the diskette copy (Destination In). If your PC has two diskette drives and they're both the same capacity, you should select different drives for the source and destination. Then, you insert the source diskette in the source drive and the destination diskette in the destination drive, and you click on the OK button. Next, a dialog box warns you that any data on the destination diskette will be erased, and it gives you a chance to cancel the operation. If you confirm the operation, the File Manager starts the copying operation. As it copies, it displays another dialog box that reports the progress of the operation.

If your PC has only one drive for the capacity of diskette you want to copy, you have to specify it for both the Source In and Destination In drives as shown in part 2 of figure 5-12. Then, after you use the dialog box shown in part 3 to confirm that the source diskette is in the Source In drive, the File Manager reads its contents. Next, the File Manager prompts you to remove the source diskette and insert the destination diskette. After you confirm that this has been done, the File Manager proceeds by writing what it read from the source diskette onto the destination diskette.

Part 1

To copy a diskette, issue the Copy Disk command from the Disk menu.

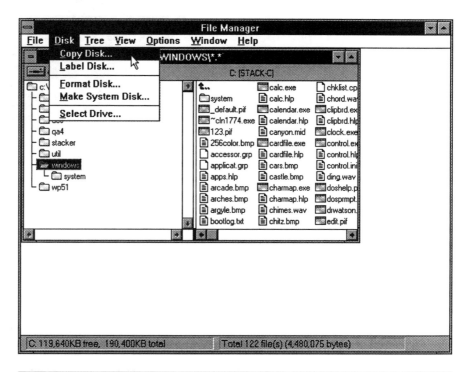

Part 2

In the dialog box that appears, use the drop-down boxes to specify the diskette drives for the source and destination diskettes. Then, click on the OK button to start the copy operation.

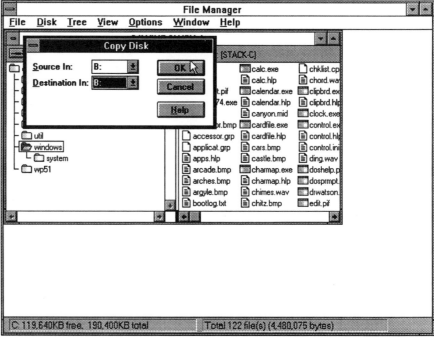

Figure 5-12   How to copy a diskette

Part 3

The File Manager displays dialog boxes to guide you through the copy operation.

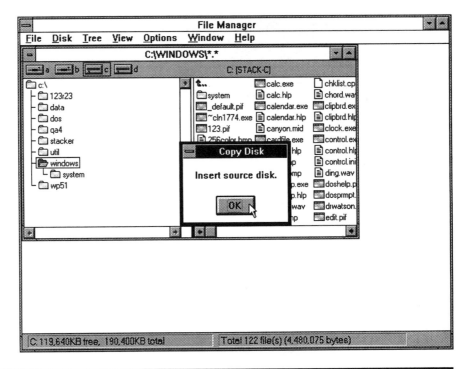

Figure 5-12 How to copy a diskette (continued)

Exercise 5-3

How to format and copy diskettes

For this exercise, you'll need two diskettes. Just be aware that if you use diskettes that have data on them, you'll lose that data.

1. If it isn't already running, start *Windows* on your PC. Then, start the File Manager program.

2. Format the first diskette. To format the diskette:

    (a) Insert one of the diskettes into the appropriate diskette drive.

    (b) Issue the Format Disk command from the Disk menu.

    (c) Select the correct values from the Disk In and Capacity drop-down boxes in the Format Disk dialog box.

    (d) Click on the OK button.

    (e) Respond to the dialog boxes that appear. In the last box, respond that you do want to format another diskette.

3. Format the second diskette. Dialog boxes will appear to lead you through the process.

4. Open a new directory window for the diskette you just formatted. To do this, double-click on the drive icon for the diskette you just formatted. Its directory pane should be empty.

5. Click on the directory window that was active before you opened the new directory window for the diskette.

6. Find and select the icons for the files WINLOGO.BMP and ZIGZAG.BMP in the WINDOWS directory. To select these two files, and only these two files, click on one to select it. Then, press and hold down the Ctrl key as you click on the second.

7. Copy the files WINLOGO.BMP and ZIGZAG.BMP from the WINDOWS directory to the diskette you just formatted. To do so, simply drag the selected file icons to the icon for the diskette drive at the top of the directory window. To copy these files, you don't need to hold down a modifier key because the destination drive is different from the source drive.

8. Switch back to the directory window for the diskette and verify that the two files were successfully copied. They should appear in the directory pane of the directory window for the diskette.

Continued on the next page...

Exercise 5-3 (continued)
How to format and copy diskettes

9.   Copy the second diskette, which now contains two files, to the first diskette that you formatted in step 2. To copy the diskette:

   (a)   Issue the Copy Disk command from the Disk menu.

   (b)   Select the correct source and destination disks from the drop-down boxes in the Copy Disk dialog box.

   (c)   Click on the OK button.

   (d)   Respond to the dialog boxes that prompt you through the process.

10.   Double-click on the control-menu box in the File Manager's application window to exit from the File Manager program.

Perspective

If you've used DOS commands or the DOS shell for managing files and directories, you probably realize already that the File Manager is a significant improvement over DOS. In general, the File Manager provides all of the functions that are available through DOS, but it does so with a graphic interface that lets you work without remembering so many details. In addition, the File Manager lets you perform most functions more efficiently than you can do them with DOS. If you don't already appreciate these benefits of the File Manager, I think you will once you start using it.

In chapter 7, you can learn how to get the most from the File Manager. There, you'll learn how to use the menu commands that I haven't introduced in this chapter. You'll learn how to customize a directory window. And you'll learn how to start programs from the File Manager by double-clicking on an icon for a program or the icon for a file that's associated with a program.

Summary

- To start the File Manager from the Program Manager, you double-click on its icon, which is in the Main program group.

- The File Manager always displays one document window, called a *directory window*. If the directory window hasn't been customized, the directory window contains a *tree pane* and a *directory pane*. The tree pane shows the directory structure for the selected drive; the directory pane lists the subdirectories and files that are stored in the selected directory.

- You can determine what portions of the *directory tree* are shown by *expanding* or *collapsing* portions of the tree. When you expand a directory, you display one or more levels of its subdirectories. When you collapse a directory, none of its subdirectories are shown.

- You can open more than one directory window at the same time. Then, you can arrange them using the same techniques that you learned to use for the document windows of the Program Manager.

- To select a directory or file, you click the mouse on it. To select more than one file, you can use the mouse while you hold down the Shift or Ctrl key. You can also use the Select Files command of the File menu to select files.

- To delete what you've selected, you use the Delete key. To copy or move what you've selected, you can use mouse techniques in combination with the Shift or Ctrl key. Or, you can use the Copy or Move commands of the File menu. To Rename what you've selected, you use the Rename command of the File menu. And to create a new directory, you use the Create Directory command of the File menu.

- To format or copy diskettes, you use the Format Disk or Copy Disk command of the Disk menu.

Other essential
Windows skills

The five chapters in this section present *Windows* skills that expand upon the skills you learned in section 2. In chapter 6, you can learn how to get the most from the Program Manager, and in chapter 7, you can learn how to get the most from the File Manager. Although you may never need all of the commands and functions presented in these chapters, you should at least know that they're available if you do need them.

Then, in chapter 8, you can learn how to manage your printers in case they're not working the way you want them to. In chapter 9, you can learn how to use the Control Panel to customize *Windows* so it works the way you want it to. And in chapter 10, you can learn more about using DOS programs under *Windows* so they work the way you want them to.

To make this section as useful as possible, all of its chapters are written as independent modules. That means you can read them in whatever sequence you prefer. If, for example, you're having trouble using your DOS programs under *Windows*, you can skip to chapter 10. Or if you want to learn more about the printer fonts that *Windows* uses, you can skip directly to chapter 8. In short, you can learn new *Windows* skills whenever you have ten or fifteen minutes to spare.

Chapter 6

How to get the most from the Program Manager

The default program groups and program items
A summary of the commands in the Program Manager's menus
> File menu
> Options menu
> Window menu

How to customize your program groups
> How to create, rename, or delete a program group
> How to move, copy, or delete a program item
> How to create a new program item
> How to change the properties of a program item

Four ways to start programs from the Program Manager
> Double-click on the icon for a program
> Double-click on the icon for a file that's associated with a program
> Use the Run command under the File menu
> Move the icon for a program into the StartUp group

Perspective
Summary

In chapter 3, you learned the basic skills for working with the Program Manager. Specifically, you learned how to use the mouse to start a program from its program icon. You learned how to use the Run and Exit commands of the Program Manager's File menu. And you learned how to use the commands of the Options and Window menus.

In this chapter, you can learn how to get the most from the Program Manager. To start, you'll be introduced to the program groups and program items that you'll find in a new *Windows* system. Next, you'll be introduced to all of the commands in the Program Manager's menus. Then, you'll learn how to use these commands to customize the program groups that you use with the Program Manager. Last, you'll learn two more ways to start programs from the Program Manager.

The default program groups and program items

Right after *Windows* is installed, the Program Manager has five standard *program groups*: Accessories, Games, StartUp, Applications, and Main. In figure 6-1, you can see each of these groups represented as a *program group icon* in the Program Manager's application window. You can also see each of these groups after its *group window* has been opened. Within each group window, you can see the *program items* that the group contains. These items are represented by *program item icons* (or just *program icons*).

The first group, Accessories, contains program icons for the 13 accessory programs (*applets*) that come with *Windows* 3.1. These programs include Write, Paintbrush, Cardfile, and Terminal. If your requirements are limited, you may find one or more of these programs useful. In chapter 11, you can learn more about these other accessories.

In the Games group in figure 6-1, you can see that *Windows* 3.1 comes with two games: Solitaire and Minesweeper. If you want to learn how to play them, you can do so easily by referring to the Help information that's available with them.

After you install *Windows*, the StartUp group is empty. But when you put an icon in this group, *Windows* loads the program and opens an application window for it at the start of each *Windows* session. So if you use the same program or programs for most of your work, you may want to put icons for those programs in the StartUp group. You'll learn how to do that later in this chapter.

When you install *Windows*, it searches for DOS programs on your hard drive, and it creates program icons for the ones it recognizes. It puts these icons in the Applications group. In figure 6-1, you can see that *WordPerfect* and *Lotus 1-2-3* are in this group along with three other DOS programs, but the

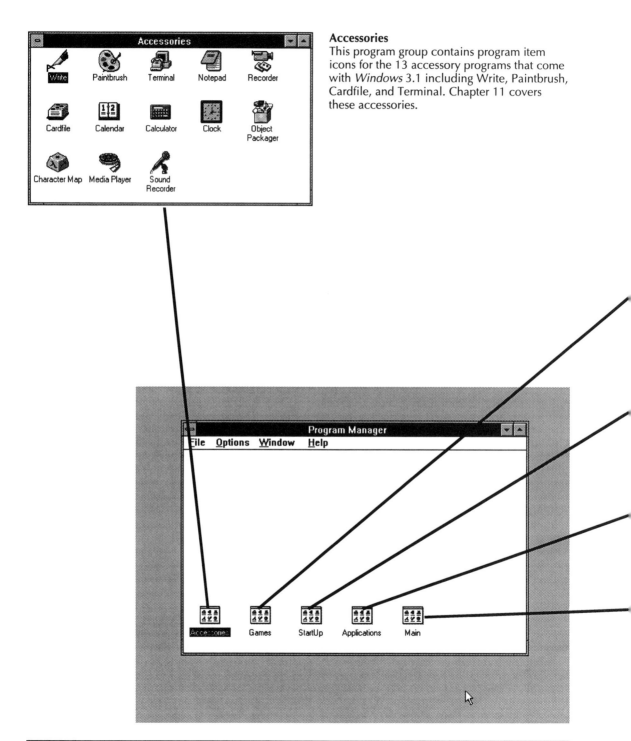

Accessories
This program group contains program item icons for the 13 accessory programs that come with *Windows* 3.1 including Write, Paintbrush, Cardfile, and Terminal. Chapter 11 covers these accessories.

Figure 6-1   Default program groups and program items

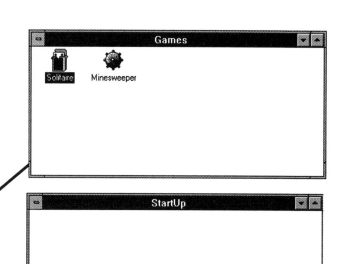

Games

This program group contains program item icons for the two game programs that come with *Windows* 3.1, Solitaire and Minesweeper. This book doesn't cover the game programs.

StartUp

This program group is empty after you install *Windows*. However, you can add program item icons to it for programs you want *Windows* to run automatically when you start a *Windows* session. This chapter shows how.

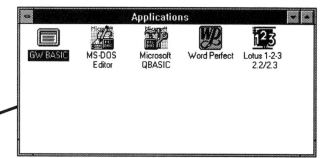

Applications

This program group contains program item icons for DOS programs that were on your PC when *Windows* was installed and that it recognized. The contents of this group vary from one PC to another. Chapter 10 describes how to prepare other DOS programs for use under *Windows*.

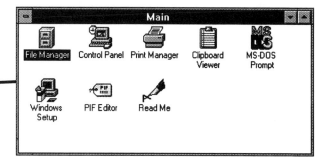

Main

This program group contains program item icons for the *Windows* system applications. You're likely to use some of these, like File Manager, often. Chapters 5 and 7 describe File Manager; chapter 9 describes Control Panel; chapter 10 describes MS-DOS Prompt, PIF Editor, and Windows Setup (for preparing a DOS program for use under Windows); and chapter 11 describes Clipboard Viewer and other functions of Windows Setup. Read Me represents a document file that's associated with an application program, and this chapter describes it.

contents of this group will vary from one PC to another. If *Windows* doesn't recognize one of your DOS programs or if you install a DOS program after you install *Windows*, you can learn how to create a program icon for it in chapter 10.

The last program group in figure 6-1 is the Main group. It contains program icons for the *Windows* system programs. The one you'll use the most is the File Manager, which you learned about in chapter 5 and can learn more about in chapter 7. As for the other programs in the Main group, chapter 8 describes Print Manager; chapter 9 describes Control Panel; chapter 10 describes MS-DOS Prompt, PIF Editor, and Windows Setup; and chapter 11 describes Clipboard Viewer and other functions of Windows Setup.

In addition to finding the default groups and their programs on a *Windows* 3.1 system, you'll find group and program items for the *Windows* applications that have been installed on the system. If, for example, *Word for Windows* and *Excel* are installed on your system, you'll find program group icons for each of them. And when you open these groups, you'll find two or more program item icons in each.

A summary of the commands in the Program Manager's menus

The Program Manager has four menus: File, Options, Window, and Help. Figure 6-2 shows the commands that are available under the first three menus, and figure 6-3 describes the function of each command. The fourth menu, the Help menu, offers the same commands that you'll find in any typical *Windows* program plus a Tutorial command that you won't have any need for, so I won't describe the Help commands in this chapter.

File menu   In chapter 3, you were introduced to the Run command for starting a program and the Exit (or Exit Windows) command for ending the Program Manager, so you shouldn't have any trouble using those commands. Later on, though, when I present the four ways for starting a program from the Program Manager, I'll briefly review the use of the Run command.

The New command lets you create new program groups and program items, and the Properties command lets you modify the properties of program groups and program items. You'll learn how to use these commands later in this chapter when I show you how to customize your program groups so you can work with them more efficiently.

The other commands under the File menu (Open, Move, Copy, and Delete) provide functions that you can accomplish more easily with simple mouse and keyboard actions. Instead of using the Open command, for example, you can double-click on an icon. And instead of using the Move command, you can use

File menu

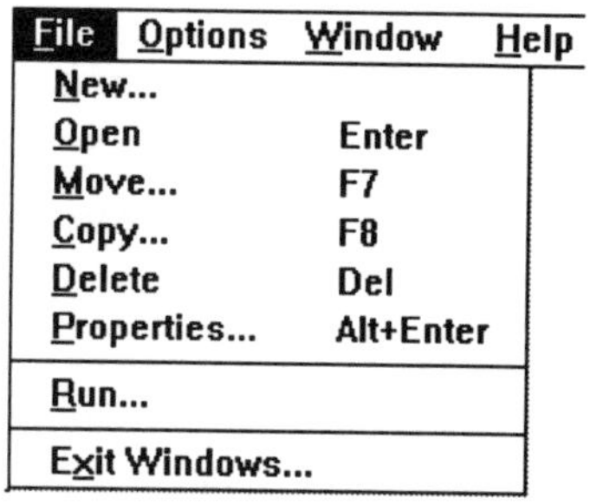

```
┌─────────────────────────────────────────────┐
│ File  Options  Window   Help                 │
│ ┌──────────────────────────────┐             │
│ │ New...                       │             │
│ │ Open            Enter        │             │
│ │ Move...         F7           │             │
│ │ Copy...         F8           │             │
│ │ Delete          Del          │             │
│ │ Properties...   Alt+Enter    │             │
│ ├──────────────────────────────┤             │
│ │ Run...                       │             │
│ ├──────────────────────────────┤             │
│ │ Exit Windows...              │             │
│ └──────────────────────────────┘             │
```

Options menu

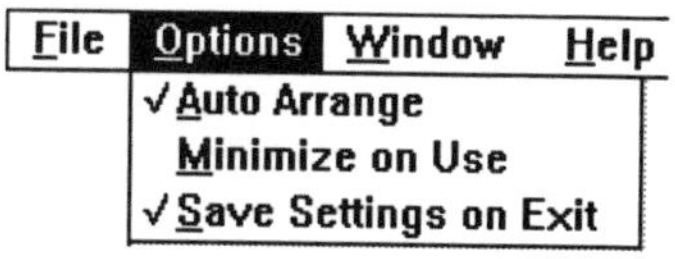

```
┌─────────────────────────────────────────────┐
│ File  Options  Window   Help                 │
│      ┌──────────────────────────┐            │
│      │ √ Auto Arrange           │            │
│      │   Minimize on Use        │            │
│      │ √ Save Settings on Exit  │            │
│      └──────────────────────────┘            │
```

Window menu

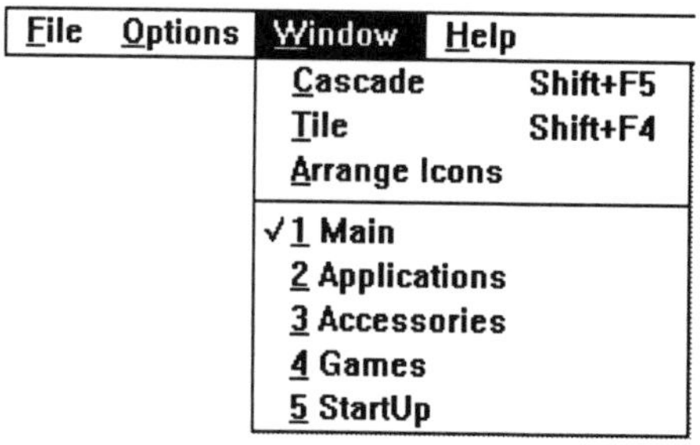

```
┌─────────────────────────────────────────────┐
│ File  Options  Window   Help                 │
│               ┌──────────────────────────┐   │
│               │ Cascade       Shift+F5   │   │
│               │ Tile          Shift+F4   │   │
│               │ Arrange Icons            │   │
│               ├──────────────────────────┤   │
│               │ √ 1 Main                 │   │
│               │   2 Applications         │   │
│               │   3 Accessories          │   │
│               │   4 Games                │   │
│               │   5 StartUp              │   │
│               └──────────────────────────┘   │
```

Figure 6-2   Program Manager menus

the mouse to drag a program icon from one program group to another. That's why you shouldn't ever need to use these commands, and that's why I'm not going to present them in this chapter.

Options menu   In chapter 3, I presented all three of the commands in the Options menu in figure 6-2, so I'll just review them briefly. A check to the left of an option indicates that it's on. To turn one of these options on or off, you just select the option. And once you turn one of the options on or off, it stays that way until you change it again.

Menu	Command	Function
File	New	Creates a new program group or a new program item within a group.
	Open	If a group icon is selected, the Open command opens a group window for it. If a program icon is selected, the Open command retrieves, loads, and starts the program associated with the icon.
	Move	Moves the selected program icon to another program group.
	Copy	Copies the selected program icon to another program group.
	Delete	Deletes the selected program item or program group.
	Properties	Lets you change the label for a program group. Lets you change the label, program, working directory, keyboard shortcut, and icon for a program item.
	Run	Starts an application program. If you specify a document that has an extension associated with an application program, the program is started, and the document is retrieved and loaded.
	Exit Windows	Ends the Program Manager. When the Program Manager is the shell program, this command also ends *Windows*.
Options	Auto Arrange	When active (checked), this option causes the Program Manager to reorganize the program icons in a group window when you move, add, or delete a program item, or you change the size of the group window.
	Minimize on Use	When active (checked), this option causes the Program Manager's application window to be minimized automatically to a desktop icon whenever you start an application program that runs in a window.
	Save Settings on Exit	When active (checked), this option causes the Program Manager to save the layout of all of its group windows and icons when it ends.
Window	Cascade	Resizes and moves open group windows so they overlap with their title bars visible.
	Tile	Resizes and moves open group windows so they're roughly the same size and do not overlap.
	Arrange Icons	Moves all program icons in the current group window so they align with a grid. If a group icon is selected, this command moves all group icons into one or more aligned rows at the bottom of the Program Manager's application window.
	group-window name	Opens a group window for the selected group. If a group window is already open for the group, this makes it the active group window.

Figure 6-3 How to use the Program Manager's menu commands

In general, I recommend that you keep the Auto Arrange and Save Settings on Exit options on. The Auto Arrange option automatically maintains the arrangement of the program icons in a group window. This is useful when you size a window or move an icon. The Save Settings on Exit option causes the Program Manager to record the arrangement of its icons and windows when you quit *Windows*. Then, when you start a new *Windows* session, the Program Manager windows are arranged just the way you left them at the end of your last session.

The Minimize on Use option determines whether the application window for the Program Manager should automatically be minimized when another application program starts. When this option is on, you have to open the Program Manager's application window whenever you want to start another program. For this reason, you'll probably want to keep this option off.

Window menu   In chapter 3, you learned how to use the commands under the Window menu in figure 6-2, so I'll just review them briefly. The Cascade and Tile commands organize all open group windows by sizing and moving them as shown in figure 6-4. Generally, the Cascade command is more useful because its windows are larger.

The Arrange Icons command aligns the group icons in the Program Manager's window if a group icon is selected. Otherwise, it aligns the program icons in a group window. But you don't need this command to align program icons if you activate the Auto Arrange command in the Options menu as I suggested a moment ago.

After the first three commands in the Window menu, you'll find a list of names for all the program groups that the Program Manager has. If you select one of these names, its group window is opened if it isn't already open, and it becomes the active window.

How to customize your program groups

After you've worked with *Windows* for a while, it often makes sense to take the time to customize the program groups so you can work with them more efficiently. As part of this process, you can create new program groups, consolidate two or more program groups, delete program groups, delete program items that you never use, and so on.

How to create, rename, or delete a program group   Figure 6-5 summarizes the procedures for creating, renaming, or deleting a program group. As you can see in the second and third procedures, you have to select the group

Before, the group windows are arranged and
sized randomly.

After the Cascade command, the group windows
are the same size and overlap so their title bars
are visible.

After the Tile command, the group windows are
the same size and arranged so they don't
overlap.

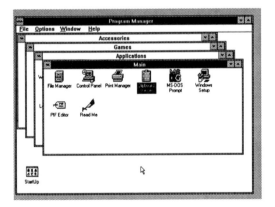

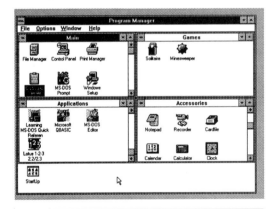

Figure 6-4   Results of the Cascade and Tile commands

icon before you can rename or delete the group. If the group window is open,
you need to close it. Otherwise, your actions will affect a program item in the
group, not the group itself. To select a group icon with the mouse, click on it;
then, click on it again. If you prefer to use the keyboard to select the group icon,
hold down the Ctrl key while you press the Tab key repeatedly. When the
highlight is on the group icon you want, release the Ctrl key to select the group.

How to create a new program group

1. Issue the New command from the File menu.
2. Select the Program Group option from the New Program Object dialog box.
3. Supply the name that will appear as the new program group's label in the Description text box in the Program Group Properties dialog box. It's not necessary to supply a value for the Group File text box.
4. Click on the OK command button.

How to rename a program group

1. Select the program group icon you want to rename.
2. Issue the Properties command from the File menu.
3. Change the value in the Description text box in the Program Group Properties dialog box to the new name. Don't change the value in the Group File text box.
4. Click on the OK command button.

How to delete a program group

1. Select the program group icon you want to delete.
2. Press the Delete key.
3. Reply Yes to the confirmation request in the Delete dialog box.

Figure 6-5   How to create, rename, or delete a program group

Figure 6-6 shows you how to create a new program group. After you issue the New command from the File menu, the Program Manager displays the New Program Object dialog box as shown in part 1. Then, you click on the Program Group option button to show that you want to create a program group, and you click on the OK command button. When the Program Group Properties dialog box appears as shown in part 2, you type the label you want to use for the new group in the Description text box. This label will appear under the icon for the group when it's closed and in the title bar of the group's window when it's open. You don't have to enter anything into the Group File text box because the Program Manager creates a value for it automatically. Instead, you just click on the OK command button to create the new group.

If you want to rename a program group, just select the group icon. Then, issue the Properties command from the File menu. In the dialog box that appears, type in the new name you want in the Description text box. When you click on the OK command button, the group is renamed.

Part 1

To create a new program group, issue the New command under the File menu. Then, choose the Program Group option from the New Program Object dialog box and click on the OK command button.

Part 2

In the Program Group Properties dialog box, supply the label for the new program group in the Description text box, then click on the OK command button

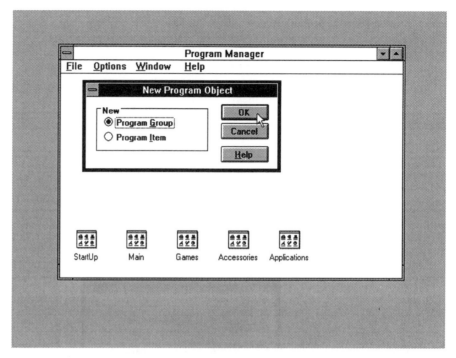

Figure 6-6   How to create a program group

How to move a program item

Drag the program item icon into the group window (or on top of the program group icon) where you want to move it.

How to copy a program item

1. Press and hold down the Ctrl key.
2. Drag the program item icon into the group window (or on top of the program group icon) where you want to copy it.
3. Release the Ctrl key.

How to delete a program item

1. Select the program item icon you want to delete.
2. Press the Delete key.
3. Reply Yes to the confirmation request in the Delete dialog box.

Figure 6-7   How to move, copy, or delete a program item

To delete a program group, you select its icon, and press the Delete key. Then, you confirm the operation in the dialog box that appears. When you confirm the operation, the group icon and any program icons it contains are deleted. So before you delete a group, make sure you don't need any of the program icons in it. Or move the program icons to another group or groups before you delete the group icon.

How to move, copy, or delete a program item   Figure 6-7 summarizes the procedures for moving, copying, or deleting a program item. Although you can use the Move, Copy, and Delete commands of the File menu to perform these functions, figure 6-7 shows you how to do them more efficiently by using mouse actions.

Figure 6-8 illustrates the use of the mouse for copying a program item. In this example, the File Manager icon is copied from the Main program group to the StartUp program group. As a result, the File Manager will be started whenever *Windows* is started.

Before you start a copying function like the one in figure 6-8, you should make sure that the destination group is visible on the desktop. This group doesn't have to be open, but you should at least be able to see its icon. Then, you hold down the Ctrl key while you drag the icon from one group to another as shown in part 1 of this figure. In part 2, you can see that the mouse pointer

Part 1

To make a copy of a program item, hold down the Ctrl key, and drag the icon to the destination. You can use this technique to make a copy of the File Manager program item icon.

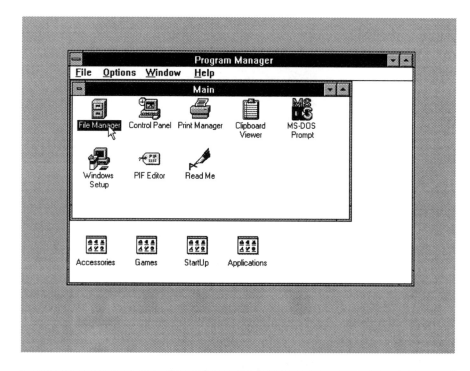

Part 2

If you drag the icon out of a program group window but not onto a program group icon, the mouse pointer appears as a circle with a diagonal bar. This indicates that you can't "drop" the icon in this position.

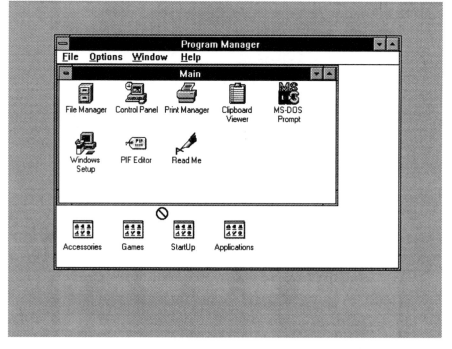

Figure 6-8   How to copy a program item with the mouse

Part 3

When you've moved the pointer on top of a valid destination (a program group window or icon), it appears as an outline of the original icon. That indicates that the destination is valid. Then, you can release the mouse button, and the Program Manager will make a copy of the icon in the destination group.

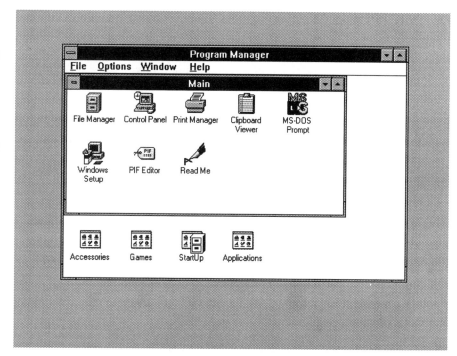

Part 4

Now, icons for the File Manager appear in both the Main and StartUp program groups.

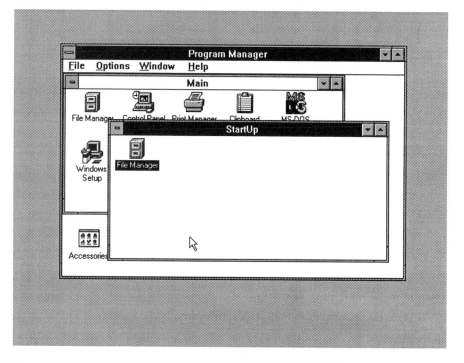

Figure 6-8   How to copy a program item with the mouse (continued)

appears as a circle with a line through it while you're dragging the icon over an area where it can't be released. In part 3, you can see how the mouse pointer looks when it's over an area where it can be released. And in part 4, you can see the result of the operation after you release the mouse button and end the dragging action.

To move an icon instead of copying it, you use the same dragging action. But you don't hold down the Ctrl key. You'll often use the move function when you want to combine the program items from more than one group into a single group.

To delete a program item, you just select it by clicking on it with the mouse or by using the arrow keys to move the highlight to it. Then, you press the Delete key, and you confirm the operation by responding to the dialog box that appears. This function is useful when you want to get rid of the icons that you don't use. When you install a new *Windows* program, for example, a new program group is created that may contain some program icons that you don't need like the icons for Read Me files. Once you've read a Read Me file, you probably won't ever need to read it again, so you can delete it.

When you delete a program icon from the Program Manager, you should realize that you've deleted only the icon, not the program itself. Instead, the program file remains on the hard disk, and you'll be able to find an icon for that program when you use the File Manager.

How to create a new program item   Most of the program icons that you need are created when you install *Windows* or a *Windows* application. Occasionally, though, you may want to create a new program icon for an application that doesn't have one, such as a DOS application, or for a frequently used document that's associated with an application program.

Although you can use the New command to create a new program item, it's easier to use the mouse technique that's summarized in the first procedure in figure 6-9. With this procedure, you just drag a program icon from a File Manager window to the appropriate group window of the Program Manager. When you do this, the Program Manager creates a new program icon with properties based on the File Manager icon. In this case, you don't have to use the Ctrl key as part of the copy operation; you just use the mouse.

If you work frequently on a document that's associated with a program, you may want to drag its file icon to the Program Manager instead of dragging the icon for the program file. Then, when you double-click on the resulting icon in the Program Manager, *Windows* loads the program and opens your document in one operation. If, for example, you use a *Lotus 1-2-3* spreadsheet frequently, you can drag the spreadsheet's icon from the File Manager to the

---

How to create a program item

1. Start the File Manager.
2. Arrange the File Manager and Program Manager windows so you can see the File Manager icon for the program (or a file associated with the program) as well as the program group that you want to add the program icon to.
3. Drag the File Manager icon to the program group that you want to put the icon in.

How to modify a program item

1. Select the program item you want to modify.
2. Issue the Properties command from the File menu.
3. Change the information about the program in the Program Item Properties text box.
4. Click on the OK command button.

Figure 6-9   How to create or modify a program item

Program Manager. Then, when you double-click on the resulting icon in the Program Manager, *Windows* loads *Lotus 1-2-3* and your spreadsheet at the same time. You'll learn more about this when I present the four ways for starting a program from the Program Manager later in this chapter.

How to change the properties of a program item   The second procedure in figure 6-9 shows you how to use the Properties command of the File menu to change the properties of a program item. Although you won't need to do this often, it occasionally makes sense.

In figure 6-10, you can see how the Properties command is used to change three of the properties of the program item for the Notepad accessory program. In part 1, you can see the default properties that *Windows* assigns the Notepad accessory. In this case, no default working directory is given for the files that you use when you're using Notepad, and no shortcut key is specified for starting Notepad.

In part 2 of figure 6-10, you can see the modifications that were made. First, the description was modified to include Notepad's function so the icon's label will contain the words *Text editor* in parentheses.

Second, a working directory is specified so C:\DATA\MEMOS is the default directory for the files that are used when working with Notepad. If you don't specify a working directory here, *Windows* assumes that the program's working directory is the same as the one that the program file resides in. For an accessory program, that directory is the *Windows* directory (usually, C:\WINDOWS).

Part 1

When you issue the Properties command from the File menu, the properties of the selected program item appear in a dialog box. This example shows the starting properties for the Notepad program item in the Accessories program group.

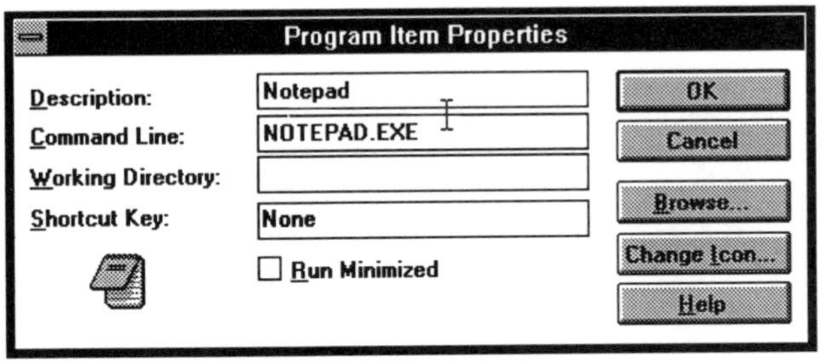

Part 2

Here, most of the properties for the Notepad program's icon have been changed (the description, the working directory, and the shortcut key).

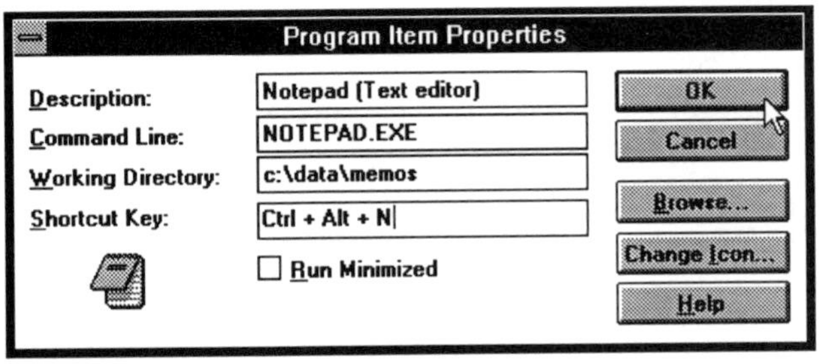

Figure 6-10   How to modify a program item's properties

Third, the shortcut key combination of Ctrl+Alt+N is assigned to the program. This means that you can start the program from the Program Manager by using that combination. When you assign a shortcut key combination, it must start with Ctrl+Alt, Crtl+Shift, or Ctrl+Alt+Shift. To make the assignment, you hold down one of these key combinations and press the key that you want to use with it.

As you can see in figure 6-10, another property you can set is whether the program runs minimized. If you activate this option, the program runs as an icon at the bottom of your desktop when it starts. One use of this option is for the programs you put in the StartUp group. If you have more than one program there, you may not want them all to start in application windows. Also, some programs run perfectly well as icons. When the Clock accessory runs minimized, for example, you can easily tell its time.

Normally, you don't have to change the command line when you modify a program item's properties. So the command line in both parts of figure 6-10 is the same. In this case, no path is required because Notepad resides in the *Windows* directory. If you do have to provide a path, you can just type it into the command line, or you can use the Browse command button to access a dialog box that lets you build the path for the working directory.

Although there's rarely a reason for doing so, the fourth command button in the Program Item Properties dialog box lets you change the icon for a program item. This is illustrated in figure 6-11, which shows you how to change the icon for the File Manager. In part 1, you select the Change Icon button from the dialog box for the Properties command. In part 2, you can see the current icon and some others that are immediately available. If you don't like one of these, you can use the Browse command button as shown in part 3 to access a whole library of icons that comes with *Windows*. This library is stored in a file named MORICONS.DLL in the *Windows* directory. In the dialog box in part 4, you can view the icons, click on the one you want to represent the File Manager, and click on the OK button to confirm your selection.

Four ways to start programs from the Program Manager

Figure 6-12 lists the four ways you can use for starting a program from the Program Manager. In chapter 3, you learned how to use the first and third way, so I'll just review them briefly. But I'll describe the other two ways in more detail.

Double-click on the icon for a program   The simplest way to start a program is to double-click on its program icon. When you do, the Program Manager uses the icon's command line property to locate the program file for the application. Then, *Windows* retrieves the program file from disk, loads it into internal memory, creates a new application window, and starts the program in the window.

Double-click on the icon for a file that's associated with a program   The command line property for a program icon can point to a document file as well as to a program file. When you double-click on this kind of program icon, the Program Manager retrieves the data file and opens it along with the application program that's *associated* with it.

To illustrate, please refer back to figure 6-1. Here, you can see that the Read Me program icon in the Main group is the same as the Write icon in the Accessories group. In figure 6-13, though, you can see that the command line properties for these program items are not the same. The command line for Write is WRITE.EXE so the Write program is launched when you double-click on that item. In contrast, the command line for Read Me is README.WRI, which is a data file, not the Write program file. However, the Program Manager can tell by the WRI extension that the data file is associated with the Write program. So when you double-click on the Read Me icon, the Program Manager loads Write, then opens the README.WRI file.

Part 1

To access the Change Icon dialog box, issue the Properties command for the selected program item; then, click on the Change Icon command button. This is the first dialog box you see if you want to change the File Manager's icon.

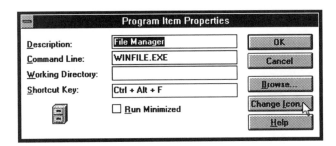

Part 2

The Change Icon dialog box shows all of the icons that are associated with the selected program item. To see other icons, click on the Browse command button.

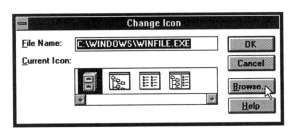

Part 3

Navigate in the Browse dialog box to the file MORICONS.DLL in the WINDOWS directory. Then, click on the OK command button to access that file.

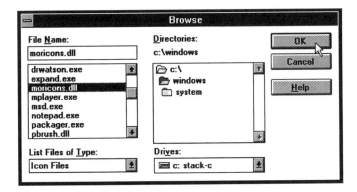

Part 4

You can look through many alternative icons. Here, one that looks like a filing cabinet with an open drawer is selected. Click on the OK command button after you've selected the icon you want to use.

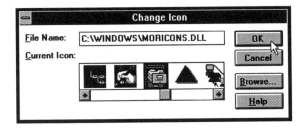

Figure 6-11   How to change the icon for a program item

1. Double-click on the icon for a program.
2. Double-click on the icon for a file associated with a program.
3. Use the Run command under the File menu.
4. Move the icon for a program item into the StartUp group so it starts automatically when *Windows* starts.

Figure 6-12   Four ways to start a program from the Program Manager

Windows lets you start applications through their data files because it maintains a list of the associations between data file extensions and the related application programs in a file named WIN.INI. At the bottom of figure 6-13, you can see the list of WIN.INI associations that are in place on a newly installed *Windows* system. However, the installation procedures for *Windows* applications often add their own associations to WIN.INI. On my PC, for example, the WIN.INI file contains more than 40 associations. If you want to add associations to this list or modify any of the existing associations, you can do so by using the File Manager as explained in the next chapter. If, for example, you don't like the association of the extension TXT with the Notepad program, you can change the association to Write or to another text-processing application like *Word for Windows*.

If you work with the same data files frequently (like a template document or a large spreadsheet), you may want to create program icons that let you access the files along with their programs. The easiest way to do this is to drag the icon for the document file from the File Manager to the Program Manager. Then, if necessary, you can use the Properties command to modify the properties of the program item.

Use the Run command under the File menu   In chapter 3, you learned how to use the Run command for starting programs that don't have icons. After you issue the Run command, *Windows* displays the Run dialog box shown in figure 6-14. Here, you type the command line necessary to start the program in the Command Line text box. In this example, the command line will start the program named INSTALL.EXE from the diskette in the B drive.

If you have to specify a path with the command in the command line, you can select the Browse button in the dialog box. Then, a dialog box is displayed that lets you build the path by navigating through the directories on a drive to locate the program file you want to run. When you reach the file, you click on the OK button and the complete path for the file appears in the Command Line text box of the Run dialog box.

Properties of the Write and Read Me program item icons

The Command Line property for the
Write program item names the
WRITE.EXE program file.

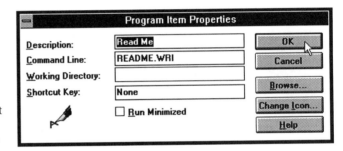

The Command Line property for the
Read Me program item names the
README.WRI file. *Windows* looks in
its WIN.INI file for an association of
the file's extension, WRI, with an
application program. The association
of the WRI extension with the Write
program is one of ten associations that
are in place on a new *Windows*
system. As you install other programs,
their installation procedures create
more associations.

Associations that are already in place in the WIN.INI file on a newly installed *Windows* system

Extension	Associated application program
cal	calendar.exe
crd	cardfile.exe
trm	terminal.exe
txt	notepad.exe
ini	notepad.exe
pcx	pbrush.exe
bmp	pbrush.exe
wri	write.exe
rec	recorder.exe
hlp	winhelp.exe

Figure 6-13   How the Command Line property of a program item identifies the program to be
started

When you issue the Run command from the Program Manager's File menu, the Run dialog box appears. Then, in the Command Line text box, you can type the command line you'd enter at the DOS prompt to run the program you're interested in.

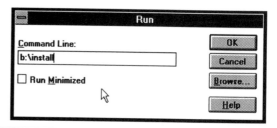

Figure 6-14   How to start a program with the Program Manager's Run command

Move the icon for a program into the StartUp group   If you want to run a specific program in each *Windows* session, you can put the program icon for it in the StartUp program group. Then, when *Windows* starts, it will automatically start the application program too. If, for example, you want to run the File Manager in each *Windows* session, you can copy its icon from the Main group to the StartUp group as illustrated in figure 6-8.

Perspective

One way to make *Windows* your own is to customize the Program Manager so you can quickly access the programs and documents you work with most often. At the least, you're likely to want to delete program groups and program items that you no longer use. You may also want to change the properties of a program item so it works the way you want it to. Or, you may want to move a program item into the StartUp group so it starts automatically. No matter what you want to do, though, you shouldn't have any trouble doing it using the techniques presented in this chapter.

Summary

- The Program Manager organizes your programs into *program groups*, which can be displayed in windows called *group windows*. When a group window isn't open, a program group is displayed as a *program group icon*, or just *group icon*. When a group window is open, the *program items* within it are displayed as *program item icons*, or just *program icons*.

- You can use the New and Rename commands of the File menu to create or rename a program group. You can delete a program group by selecting it and pressing the Delete key.

- You can move or copy a program item by using mouse techniques. You can delete a program item by selecting it and pressing the Delete key. You can also use the Move, Copy, and Delete commands for these functions, but the mouse techniques are more efficient.

- You can create a new program item by dragging an icon from a File Manager directory window to a Program Manager group. The File Manager icon you drag can be the icon for the program file or the icon for a file that's *associated* with the program. Another way to create a new program item is to issue the New command from the File menu, but the dragging technique is more efficient and less error-prone.

- You can use the Properties command of the File menu to change the *properties* of a program item. The most important property is the *command line* because *Windows* uses it to start the program. Other properties include the program icon's description, its working (default) directory, the shortcut key combination you can use to start the program, and the picture used for the icon.

- One way to start a program is to double-click on the icon for a file that's *associated* with a program. Then, the program is started and the file is opened in one operation. To make this possible, the WIN.INI file in the *Windows* directory contains a list of the associations between file extensions and programs.

- If you want to have *Windows* start a program automatically in each session, you can put a program icon for it in the StartUp group.

Chapter 7

How to get the most from the File Manager

An introduction to the menus of the File Manager
How to use the commands of the File menu
> The Open command
> The Move, Copy, and Delete commands
> The Rename command
> The Properties command
> The Run command
> The Print command
> The Associate command
> The Create Directory command
> The Search command
> The Select Files command
> The Exit command

How to use the commands of the Disk menu
> The Disk commands
> The Select Drive command
> Networking commands that may appear under the Disk menu

How to use the commands of the Tree menu
How to use the commands of the View menu
> How to display only one of the panes in a directory window
> How to change the width of the tree and directory panes
> How to change the file information that's displayed in a directory pane
> How to change the sequence of files in a directory pane
> How to limit the types of files that appear in a directory pane

How to use the commands of the Options menu
    The Confirmation command
    The Font command
    The other commands

How to use the commands of the Window menu
    The New Window command
    The Cascade and Tile commands
    The Arrange Icons command
    The Refresh command
    The directory names at the bottom of the menu

Three ways to start a program from the File Manager
    Double-click on the icon for a program
    Double-click on the icon for a file associated with a program
    Use the Run command under the File menu

How to change your shell program from the Program Manager to the File Manager
Perspective
Summary

In chapter 5, you learned the basic skills for working with the File Manager. If you've been using the File Manager for a while, you probably realize that it is a significant improvement over DOS. Specifically, the File Manager makes it easier for you to perform routine jobs like copying files, formatting diskettes, and managing your system's directories.

This chapter expands on what you learned in chapter 5 by showing you how to get the most from the File Manager. First, this chapter presents all of the File Manager's commands, menu by menu, and it gives you detailed examples of how to use the most useful commands. Then, this chapter shows you the three ways to start application programs from the File Manager. Last, this chapter shows you how to make a simple change to one of your *Windows* initialization files so *Windows* will use the File Manager instead of the Program Manager as its shell program.

An introduction to the menus of the File Manager

Figure 7-1 shows you the seven menu names in the menu bar for the File Manager. In chapter 5, you learned how to use the most important commands in the File, Disk, and Tree menus, and in chapter 4, you learned how to use the standard commands of the Help menu. In this chapter, you'll learn how to use all of the other commands in the first six menus of the File Manager.

If you're using DOS 6.0, your File Manager's menu bar may include another menu called Tools. This menu lets you access three DOS 6.0 utility programs (Backup, Antivirus, and DoubleSpace Information). However, because the Tools menu doesn't appear if you haven't upgraded to DOS 6.0, this chapter doesn't cover it. For more information about the DOS 6.0 utilities, an excellent source is Doug Lowe's *The Only DOS Book You'll Ever Need*, 2nd edition. You can find ordering information for it at the end of this book.

How to use the commands of the File menu

Figure 7-2 shows the File menu and summarizes each of its commands. Some of these commands like Copy and Create Directory replace DOS commands; others like Open and Run let you start application programs; and still others like Search and Select Files help you find and select files. Now, I'll present these commands in the order that they appear in the menu, and I'll briefly review the commands you learned how to use in chapter 5.

The Open command   You probably won't use the Open command much because you can do all of its functions more easily by using the mouse to double-click on an icon. Even so, you may be curious to know what the functions of this command are.

Figure 7-1 The File Manager's menus

The function of the Open command depends on where the File Manager's highlight is when you issue it. If the highlight is on a directory icon in the tree pane, the Open command either expands the tree so you can see the first level of its subdirectories (if it's closed), or it collapses the tree to hide its subdirectories (if it's open). But you can accomplish the same function more easily by double-clicking on the icon. Similarly, if the highlight is on a drive icon at the top of a directory window, the Open command opens a new directory window for that drive, but double-clicking on the drive icon does the same thing. And if the highlight is on a program icon in the directory pane (or an icon for a document associated with a program), the Open command starts the program (or the program along with the document), but double-clicking on the icon is easier.

The Move, Copy, and Delete commands   In chapter 5, you learned how to move and copy directories and files by dragging their icons with the mouse. You also learned how to delete directories and files by pressing the Delete key after you have selected them. Although you can use the Move, Copy, and Delete commands to perform these functions too, you usually won't want to use these commands because the mouse techniques are more efficient.

In two cases, though, you have to use the Copy command. First, you need to use this command when the copies of the files are going to be stored in the same directory as the originals. Then, the new files must be given different names than the originals. Second, you need to use this command when you want the copies to have different names than the originals, whether or not they're in the same directory. When you use mouse techniques to copy files, the originals and copies always have the same names.

The Rename command   In chapter 5, you learned how to use the Rename command. When its dialog box is displayed, you can give the new name that you want to use for a file, or you can give a wildcard specification to rename more than one file with a single command.

| File | Disk | Tree | View | Options | Window | Help |

Open	Enter
Move...	F7
Copy...	F8
Delete...	Del
Rename...	
Properties...	Alt+Enter
Run...	
Print...	
Associate...	
Create Directory...	
Search...	
Select Files...	
Exit	

Command	Function
Open	If a program icon is selected in the directory pane, Open starts the program. If a data file icon is selected in the directory pane and a program is associated with its extension, Open starts the program and opens the data file. If a disk icon is selected, Open creates a new directory window for the current directory on that disk. If a directory icon is selected in the tree pane, Open expands that directory one level or, if it's already expanded, collapses it.
Move	Moves the selected items to a destination you specify in a dialog box.
Copy	Copies the selected items to a destination you specify in a dialog box.
Delete	Deletes the selected items.
Rename	Displays a dialog box that lets you specify names for the selected items.
Properties	Lets you change the DOS attributes (read only, hidden, archive, and system) for the selected files.
Run	Starts the specified application program. If you specify a document whose extension is associated with an application program, the program is started and the document is opened.
Print	Prints the selected document on the default printer, if the document is associated with a program.
Associate	Lets you associate the extension of the selected file with a specific application program so you can start the program through the data file.
Create Directory	Creates a new directory subordinate to the current directory.
Search	Searches the specified directory (and optionally, its subdirectories) for files that you specify in a dialog box.
Select Files	Selects a group of files based on a file specification you provide in a dialog box.
Exit	Ends the File Manager. When the File Manager is the shell program, this command also ends *Windows*.

Figure 7-2   The commands of the File menu

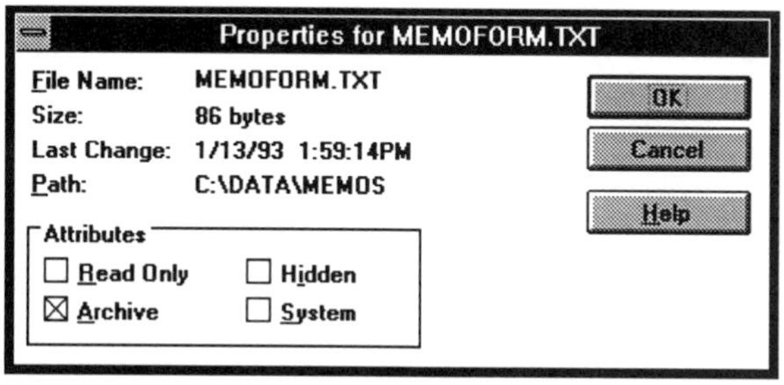

Properties for MEMOFORM.TXT

File Name: MEMOFORM.TXT
Size: 86 bytes
Last Change: 1/13/93 1:59:14PM
Path: C:\DATA\MEMOS

OK
Cancel
Help

Attributes
☐ Read Only   ☐ Hidden
☒ Archive   ☐ System

Figure 7-3   The Properties dialog box

The Properties command   The Properties command lets you change one or more of the four DOS attributes of files: the read only, hidden, archive, and system attributes. If you're like most PC users, you won't need to worry about these attributes, so you won't ever need to use this command.

If you do want to change the DOS attributes, though, you can issue the Properties command after you select the files that you want to change the attributes for. Then, the File Manager displays a dialog box like the one in figure 7-3. If you select more than one file before you issue the Properties command, the dialog box looks slightly different than the one in this figure, but it still lets you set the four attributes for the selected files. To turn an attribute on or off, just click on its check box.

By the way, you shouldn't confuse the File Manager's Properties command with the Program Manager's Properties command. In the Program Manager, the Properties command has nothing to do with DOS attributes. Instead, it lets you manage the characteristics of your group and program icons.

The Run command   One of the three ways to start an application program from the File Manager is to use the Run command. When you issue it, *Windows* displays a Run dialog box that lets you specify the DOS command for starting a program. This is similar to using the Run command for the Program Manager, and you'll learn how to use this command later in this chapter.

The Print command   The Print command lets you print a single copy of a document from the File Manager without explicitly starting the program that created the document. Before you issue the Print command, you select the icon for the file that you want to print. This icon must have horizontal lines on it to show that it is associated with the program that created it. Then, when you issue the Print command, *Windows* starts the program that's associated with the file, opens the document file, and invokes the program's print function. At that

---

1. Select the icon for a file that has the extension you want to associate with an application.

2. Issue the Associate command from the File menu.

3. Find the application with which you want to associate the extension. If necessary, use the Browse command to look for the program on your hard disk drive.

4. Click on the OK command button to complete the operation.

Figure 7-4   How to associate a file extension with an application program

point, you'll see the standard Print dialog box from the application program. When you confirm the print operation, the document is printed and the program ends.

The Associate command   *Windows* uses *associations* to relate data files (through their extensions) with application programs. When you install *Windows* or a *Windows* application, standard associations are established. For instance, the extension TXT is associated with the Notepad accessory program, and the extension DOC is associated with *Word for Windows*. Once an association is established, you can start an application program by double-clicking on the icon for an associated data file, and you can use the Print command to print the data file.

To create or change an association, you use the Associate command. If, for example, you want to abandon Notepad and use *Word for Windows* when you access files with the extension TXT, you just change the TXT association from Notepad to *Word for Windows*. Figure 7-4 gives the procedure for doing that.

Figure 7-5 illustrates the use of the Associate command for changing the TXT association from Notepad to Write. In part 1, a file with the TXT extension is selected, and the Associate command is issued. In part 2, the dialog box shows that the TXT extension is already associated with the Notepad program (notepad.exe). Then, to change this association to another program, you can click on the Browse button to navigate through the files on your system. In part 3, you can see the Browse dialog box after the program file for the Write accessory (write.exe) has been reached. To complete the command, you click on the OK command button once for the Browse dialog box and once for the Associate dialog box.

Part 1

To associate a program with a file extension, select a file with that extension (like setup.txt), then issue the Associate command from the File menu.

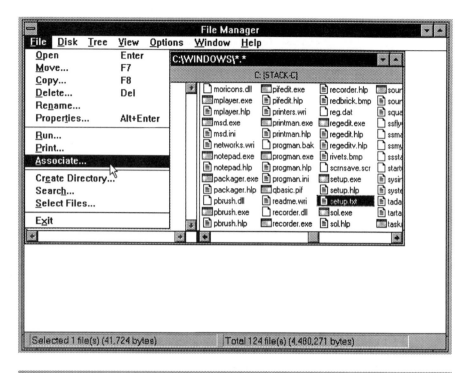

Part 2

The Associate dialog box lists associations that are already in place. As you can see, the extension TXT is already associated with the Notepad program. To create a different association, you can click on the Browse command button to select a different program from those on your hard disk.

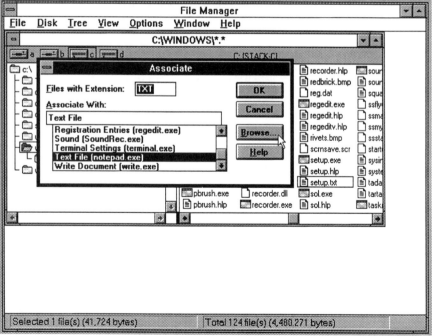

Figure 7-5   How to associate a file extension with an application program

Part 3

You navigate through your disk's directory structure to find the executable file you want to associate with the extension. Here, the program file for the Write accessory is selected. Then, you click on the OK command button to confirm the association.

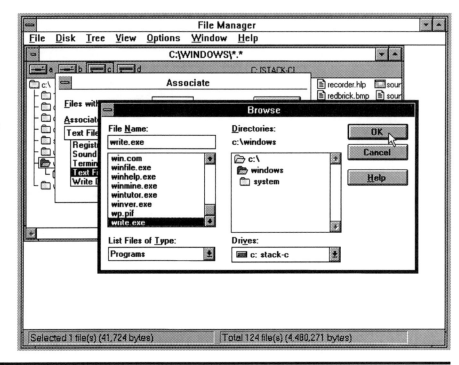

Figure 7-5   How to associate a file extension with an application program (continued)

The Create Directory command   You learned how to use the Create Directory command in chapter 5. Before you issue this command, you select the directory that you want the new directory to be subordinate to. Then, you issue this command and supply the name for the new directory in its dialog box.

The Search command   The Search command is useful when you've forgotten where you saved one or more files, as illustrated by figure 7-6. Before you issue this command, you select the directory that you want the search to start from. Then, when you issue the command, the File Manager displays the dialog box shown in part 1 of this figure. In this example, the Search For text box says that the File Manager should search for all files named P&LNOTES, no matter what the extension is (p&lnotes.*); the Start From text box says that the search should start with the root directory on the C drive (C:\); and the Search All Subdirectories check box indicates that the search should continue through all subdirectories. When you select the OK command button, the search starts.

Part 1

After you issue the Search command from the File menu, the File Manager prompts you for the search string you want to use and the directory where you want the search to begin. Here, the File Manager will search for files named p&lnotes with any extension on the entire C drive (the root directory and all of its subdirectories).

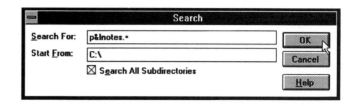

Part 2

When the search is complete, the File Manager displays the files it found in the Search Results window. Here, you can select any or all of the files for subsequent action.

Figure 7-6   How to use the Search command

In part 2 of figure 7-6, you can see what the Search Results window looks like when this command is finished. Here, you can see the four files that have been found along with the directory for each file. When the Search Results window is displayed, you can select one or more of the files for a subsequent action like renaming or deleting the files.

The Select Files command   The Select Files command lets you select files in the current directory by entering a selection string rather than by tagging all of the files individually. When you issue this command, the File Manager displays a Select Files dialog box like the one in part 1 of figure 7-7. Then, you can enter a file specification to identify the files that you want to select. In this example, the specification includes a wildcard (*.bmp) to show that all files with BMP as the extension should be selected. To complete the command, you can click on the Select command button.

Part 1

Before you issue the
Select Files command
from the File menu, you
need to choose the
directory that contains
the files you want to
select. Then, when you
issue the command, the
File Manager prompts
you for the selection
string you want to use.
Here, all files with the
extension BMP will be
selected.

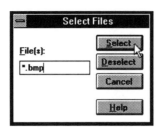

Part 2

When the selection is
complete, all of the files
that met the specification
are selected in the
directory pane.

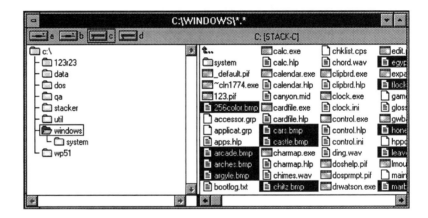

Figure 7-7   How to use the Select Files command

In part 2 of figure 7-7, you can see that the selected files are highlighted
in the directory pane. At that point, you can use other File Manager techniques
to move, copy, delete, or rename the files. Or, you can use the Select Files
command again to change the selection.

If you want to select all of the files in a directory, you can use the Select
Files command with *.* as the file specification. But it's easier to do this by
pressing the slash (/) key when the highlight is in the directory pane.

The Exit command   The Exit command under the file menu ends the File
Manager. If the File Manager is also the *Windows* shell, this command ends
Windows too.

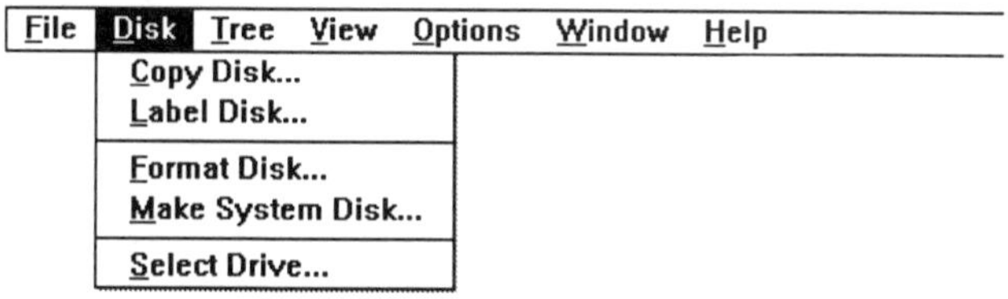

| File | **Disk** | Tree | View | Options | Window | Help |

Copy Disk...
Label Disk...

Format Disk...
Make System Disk...

Select Drive...

Command	Function
Copy Disk	Copies the files and directories from one diskette to another.
Label Disk	Changes the volume label on a hard disk or diskette.
Format Disk	Formats a diskette.
Make System Disk	Creates a diskette with MS-DOS system files that you can use to boot a PC.
Network Connections	On some networks, lets you manage connections between your PC and network drives. Not always available.
Connect Network Drive	On some networks, lets you establish connections between your PC and network drives. Not always available.
Disconnect Network Drive	On some networks, lets you end connections between your PC and network drives. Not always available.
Select Drive	Changes the current drive. This command produces the same result as clicking on a drive icon.

Figure 7-8   The commands of the Disk menu

How to use the commands of the Disk menu

Figure 7-8 shows the standard commands of the Disk menu. If your PC is part of a network, you may also see network management commands under this menu.

The Disk commands   The first four commands of the Disk menu provide basic functions that replace DOS commands for disk functions. In chapter 5, you learned how to use the Copy Disk and Format Disk commands to copy and format diskettes. These are replacements for the DOS Diskcopy and Format commands, so I won't say anything more about them in this chapter.

The Label Disk command lets you change the volume label on a diskette or a hard disk drive. The volume label is assigned to a disk when it's formatted, and it appears to the right of the disk icons in the directory window for the disk. If, for example, you look back to part 2 of figure 7-7, you can see that the C drive's volume label is STACK-C. Because you usually don't need to change the volume label for a hard disk or diskette, you may never need the Label Disk command. But if you do need to use it, you just select the appropriate disk icon and issue the command. Then, you supply a new label of up to 11 characters in the Label Disk dialog box.

The Make System Disk command copies three DOS files to a diskette. This makes the diskette a *system diskette* that you can use for starting your PC. Although you normally start your PC from the DOS files on a hard disk, you'll need to start it from a system diskette if your hard disk drive fails.

The Select Drive command   The easiest way to select a drive is to click on its icon in the directory window. As a result, you probably won't ever use the Select Drive command. When you issue this command, the File Manager displays a dialog box that contains a list box with one entry for each disk drive you have access to, including local hard disk drives, network drives, and diskette drives. Then, to switch to a different drive in the current directory window, you select the drive from the list and click on the OK command button.

Networking commands that may appear under the Disk menu   If your PC is part of a network, you may have other commands under the Disk menu like Connect Network Drive or Disconnect Network Drive. However, these commands vary from one network to another. If you need more information about the network commands on your system, you should get help from a colleague or your network administrator.

How to use the commands of the Tree menu

Figure 7-9 presents the commands available under the File Manager's Tree menu. In chapter 5, you were introduced to all of them. The first four commands let you expand or collapse the selected directory. But if you want to expand a directory just one level or if you want to collapse a directory, it's easier to double-click on the directory. The last command sets an option that puts a plus or minus sign on each directory that has subdirectories. If this option is on, a check appears to the left of Indicate Expandable Branches.

How to use the commands of the View menu

The commands in the View menu are summarized in figure 7-10. Although there are 12 commands in this menu, eleven of them just let you set options that determine how the directory windows should be displayed and what information they should include. In the menu in this figure, for example, the check marks show that both the tree pane and the directory pane should be displayed,

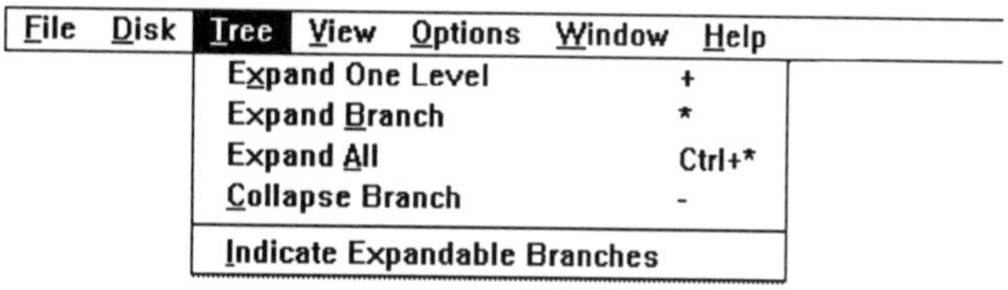

File	Disk	**Tree**	View	Options	Window	Help

Expand One Level   +
Expand Branch   *
Expand All   Ctrl+*
Collapse Branch   -

Indicate Expandable Branches

Command	Function
Expand One Level	Displays one level of subdirectories under the selected directory in the tree pane.
Expand Branch	Displays all subdirectories under the selected directory in the tree pane.
Expand All	Displays the entire directory structure of the current disk in the tree pane.
Collapse Branch	Hides all subdirectories under the selected directory in the tree pane.
Indicate Expandable Branches	Displays a plus sign on the icons of directories with subdirectories that don't appear in the tree. Displays a minus sign on the icons of directories with subdirectories that do appear in the tree.

Figure 7-9   The commands of the Tree menu

that all of the file details should be displayed in the directory window, and that the files in that window should be in sequence by name.

How to display only one of the panes in a directory window   If you want to see only the tree or directory pane of a directory window, you select the Tree Only or the Directory Only command. If, for example, you select Directory Only as shown in part 1 of figure 7-11, the resulting directory window looks like the one in part 2. To restore a directory window so it shows both panes, you just select the Tree and Directory command. When you use one of these commands, it applies only to the current directory window, not to all directory windows.

The Directory Only command is useful when you work with a directory that contains many files and you want to see more of them at once. Although the tree directory isn't available in the directory window, you can still navigate through the directory structure. To change the current directory, you can click on a directory icon to navigate "down" in the directory structure. Or, you can click on the up arrow that's the first item in the directory list to navigate "up" in the directory structure.

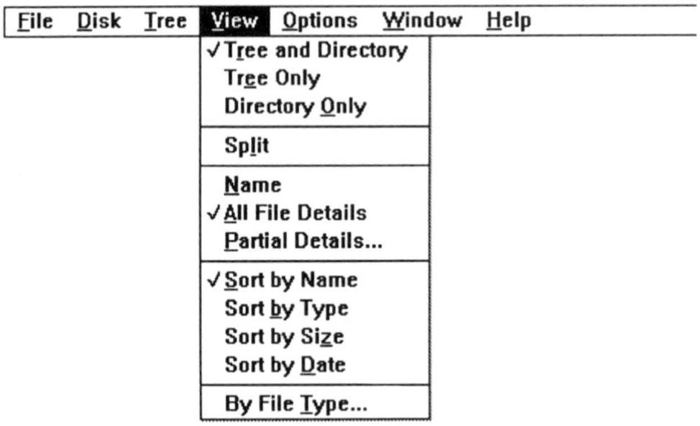

| File | Disk | Tree | View | Options | Window | Help |

√ Tree and Directory
Tree Only
Directory Only

Split

Name
√ All File Details
Partial Details...

√ Sort by Name
Sort by Type
Sort by Size
Sort by Date

By File Type...

Command	Function
Tree and Directory	Displays both the tree and directory panes of the current directory window.
Tree Only	Displays only the tree pane of the current directory window.
Directory Only	Displays only the directory pane of the current directory window.
Split	Lets you resize the directory and tree panes by moving the split bar that separates them.
Name	Displays only the names of files and directories in the directory pane.
All File Details	Displays the name, size, last modification date, last modification time, and attributes of files that appear in the directory pane.
Partial Details	Lets you select what information appears in the directory pane. You use a dialog box to specify whether size, last modification date, last modification time, and attributes appear.
Sort by Name	Specifies that the files in the directory pane should appear in file-name sequence.
Sort by Type	Specifies that the files in the directory pane should appear in exten-sion sequence, and where extensions are the same, filename se-quence.
Sort by Size	Specifies that the files in the directory pane should appear in size sequence, largest first.
Sort by Date	Specifies that the files in the directory pane should appear in modifi-cation date sequence, most recent first.
By File Type	Lets you specify what items should appear in the directory pane. You can specify directories, application program files, data files associated with programs, and all other files. Plus, you can specify a comparison string to further restrict the files that appear.

Figure 7-10   The commands of the View menu

Part 1

You can issue the Tree Only command or the Directory Only command from the View menu to show only one pane of a directory window.

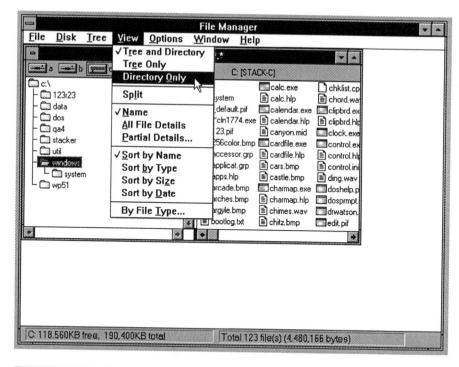

Part 2

Here, the directory window shows only the directory pane, but it's still possible to navigate through the directory structure. You can click on a directory icon that appears in the window (like *system* here) to go to a subdirectory or on the up arrow (the first item in the list) to go to the parent directory.

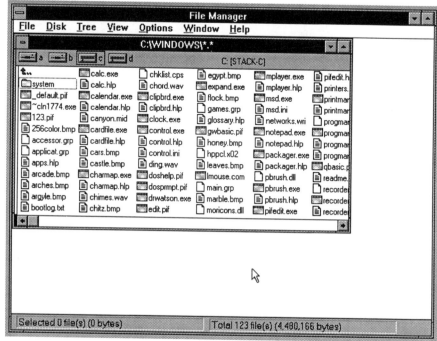

Figure 7-11   How to display only one pane of a directory window

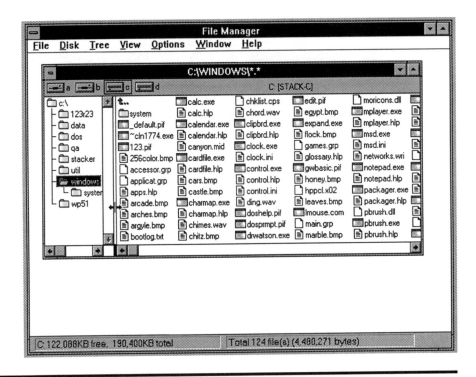

Figure 7-12   A directory window after the widths of the tree and directory panes have been changed

How to change the width of the tree and directory panes   The easiest way to change the width of the panes in a directory window is to use the mouse to drag the *split bar* that separates the two panes of a normal window. Another way is to use the Split command under the View menu. After you select this command, you can move the split bar with the mouse or with the left and right arrow keys. When you get the split bar where you want it, you can click the mouse or press the Enter key to complete the command. Figure 7-12 shows a directory window after the pane widths have been changed.

How to change the file information that's displayed in a directory pane   The Name, All File Details, and Partial Details commands let you change the information that's displayed for each file in a directory pane. Unless you specify otherwise, the Name option is on so the File Manager lists only file names in the directory pane. But if you select the All File Details command, the directory pane also shows each file's size, last modification date, last modification time, and file attributes.

If you want to display some of the file details, but not all of them, you can use the Partial Details command as illustrated in figure 7-13. In part 1, you can

Part 1

When you issue the Partial Details command under the View menu, this dialog box is displayed.

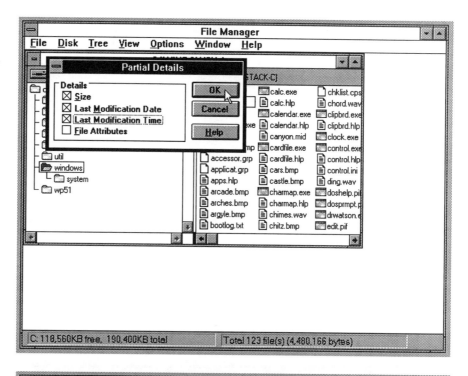

Part 2

When file information other than the file names appears in the directory pane, the File Manager uses one line per item. As a result, more information is available, but you have to scroll more to find and select files.

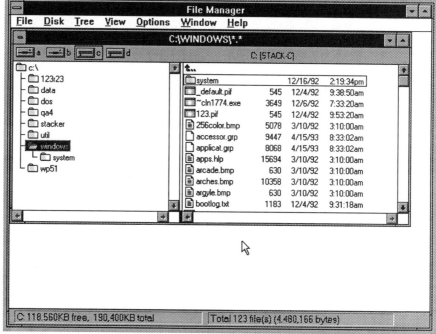

Figure 7-13   How to change the file information that's displayed in the directory pane of a directory window

Files appear in extension sequence when they're sorted by type.

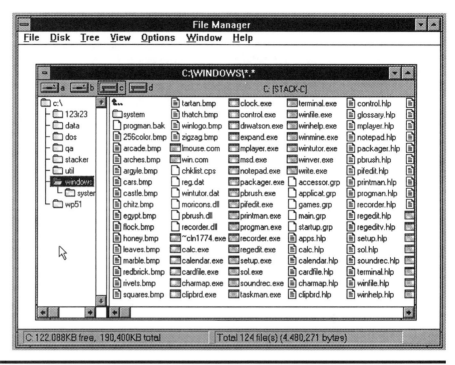

Figure 7-14   A directory pane after the Sort by Type command has been issued

see the dialog box for this command. Then, you can check the items of information that you want displayed. In part 2 of this figure, you can see how the directory pane looks when all details except the file attributes are displayed.

How to change the sequence of files in a directory pane   The Sort commands (Sort by Name, Type, Size, and Date) let you change the sequence of the items in the directory pane. These options can be useful when you want to see the files you've worked on most recently (use Sort by Date) or all files with a particular extension (use Sort by Type). For example, figure 7-14 shows a directory pane after the Sort by Type command has been issued.

How to limit the types of files that appear in a directory pane   The File Manager's default is to display all of the directories and files (except hidden and system files) in a directory pane. But if you want to limit this, you can use the By File Type command as illustrated in figure 7-15. In part 1, you can see the dialog box for this command. In this example, only the box for Programs has been checked. In the resulting directory pane in part 2, you can see that only programs are listed (those files with EXE, PIF, COM, and BAT extensions).

Part 1

When you issue the By File Type command under the View menu, a dialog box like this appears. The default is for the File Manager to display all subdirectories and files for the current directory, but you can use this dialog box to exclude some categories.

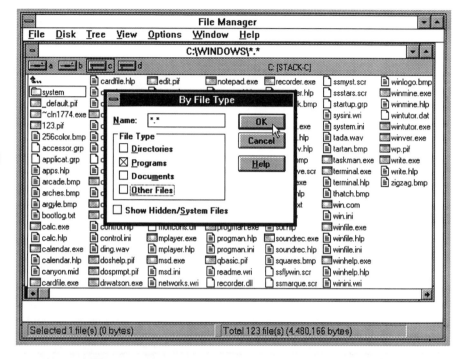

Part 2

Only program files appear in this directory pane. This can be misleading, though, because directories, documents, and other files are still present in the current directory, even though you can't see them.

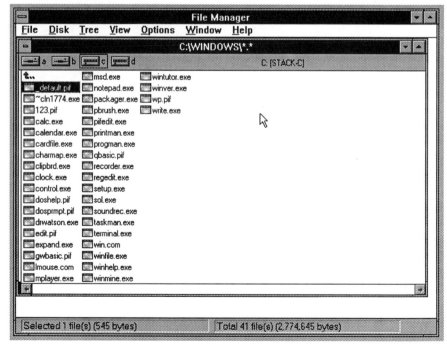

Figure 7-15   How to limit the files that appear in the directory pane of a directory window

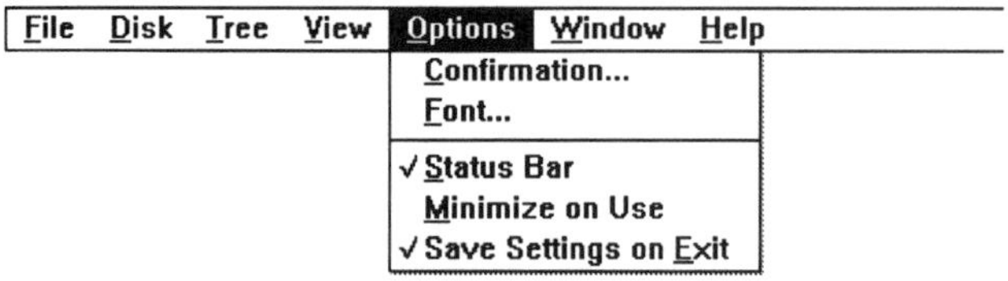

| File | Disk | Tree | View | **Options** | Window | Help |

Confirmation...
Font...

✓ Status Bar
Minimize on Use
✓ Save Settings on Exit

Command	Function
Confirmation	Lets you specify which categories of confirmation dialog boxes should appear when you perform file management operations.
Font	Lets you specify the typeface, style, and size for the text that appears in all directory windows.
Status Bar	When active (checked), this option causes the File Manager's status bar to appear at the bottom of its application window.
Minimize on Use	When active (checked), this option causes the File Manager's application window to be minimized automatically to a desktop icon whenever you use the File Manager to start an application program that runs in a window.
Save Settings on Exit	When active (checked), this option causes the File Manager to save the layout of all of its directory windows and icons when you quit the program.

Figure 7-16   The commands of the Options menu

If you work with directories that contain many files, using the By File Type command can make it easier to find specific files. However, it's easy to be confused by a directory pane that doesn't show all of the files in the directory. It can mislead you into thinking that some files are lost or misplaced when they're just excluded from the pane.

How to use the commands of the Options menu

Figure 7-16 summarizes the commands of the Options menu. For most users, the File Manager's default settings are best, so you probably won't ever have to use these commands. But you should at least know what they are in case someone else changes the settings on your system.

The Confirmation command   Figure 7-17 shows the dialog box that appears when you issue the Confirmation command from the Options menu. Here, you can turn off the warning messages for five categories of File Manager actions. Unless you want to live dangerously, though, you should leave these options on because it's all too easy to press the Delete key accidentally or drag

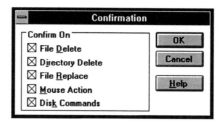

Figure 7-17   The Confirmation dialog box

the icon for a directory to a place you didn't intend. All five types of confirmation boxes give you a chance to double-check your requests and avoid aggravating mistakes.

The Font command   The default font that the File Manager uses in its directory windows is too small for some users to read easily. That's especially true on systems that use SuperVGA monitors where the high resolution can make text seem very small. So if you're not satisfied with the readability of the text in the File Manager, you can use the Font command to make it readable.

Figure 7-18 illustrates the use of the Font command. In part 1, you issue this command from the Options menu. Then, the File Manager displays a Font dialog box like the one in part 2. Here, you can see that the default font *Windows* 3.1 uses is MS Sans Serif in Regular style in 8-point size. You can use this dialog box to change the font as shown in part 3. Here, the font is changed to Arial in 11-point size, and the check in the Lowercase box is removed so all capital letters will be used. The result of this command is shown in part 4.

The other commands   The last three commands under the Options menu set options that are either on or off as indicated by a check to the left of the command. When the Status Bar command is on, the File Manager's application window shows a status bar along its bottom border. The status bar shows statistics for the current selection and the current directory. Unless you need the little bit of space the status bar takes, there's no good reason to turn this option off.

The Minimize on Use command automatically minimizes the File Manager's application window when you start an application program from it. That means that you have to re-open the File Manager's application window each time you want to use it. As a result, you probably won't want to use this option.

The Save Settings on Exit command causes the File Manager to record the arrangement of its icons and windows when it ends. Then, when you restart the

Part 1

To change the
font the File
Manager uses,
issue the Font
command under
the Options
menu.

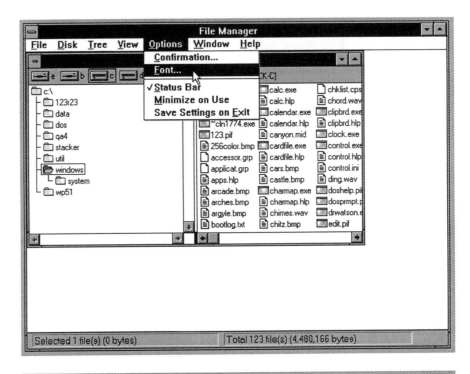

Part 2

The Font dialog
box lets you
change from the
default font (8-
point regular MS
Sans Serif). It also
lets you specify
whether the text
the File Manager
displays should be
upper- or lower-
case. The default
is lowercase.

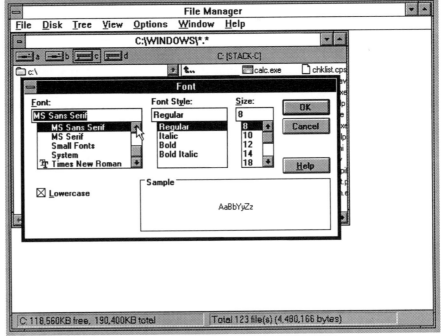

Figure 7-18   How to change the font that the File Manager uses

Part 3

Here, the font has been changed to 11-point Arial. Also, the Lower-case checkbox has been deacti-vated. You can preview the new font in the Sample box. When you're satisfied with it, click on the OK command button.

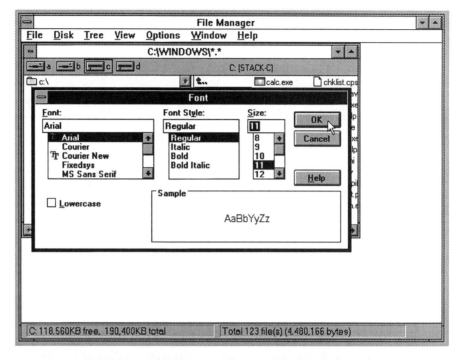

Part 4

The new font applies to the tree and directory panes of all directory win-dows and to the drive icon labels.

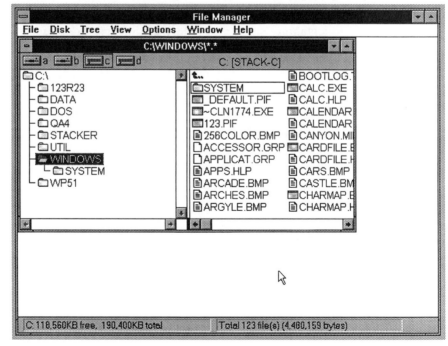

Figure 7-18   How to change the font that the File Manager uses (continued)

File Manager, it's just the way you left it the last time you used it. Because you'll probably appreciate this feature, you'll want to make sure that this option is on.

How to use the commands of the Window menu

Figure 7-19 summarizes the commands of the Window menu. These commands are similar to the Window menu commands that you learned for the Program Manager in chapter 3, so I'll go through them quickly.

The New Window command   When you issue the New Window command, the File Manager creates a new directory window that duplicates the current directory window. Because it's easier to create a new directory window by double-clicking on one of the drive icons, you probably won't want to use this command.

The Cascade and Tile commands   These commands provide the easiest ways to organize open directory windows. They work similarly to the Cascade and Tile functions of the Program Manager and the Task Manager, but the Tile command can be used in two forms with the File Manager.
    Figure 7-20 shows the three results that are possible with these commands. In part 1, you can see the results of the Cascade command. In part 2, you can see the results of the Tile command, which tiles the windows with a horizontal orientation. But if you hold the Shift key down when you issue the Tile command, the directory windows are arranged so they're oriented vertically, as shown in part 3.

The Arrange Icons command   When you minimize a directory window, an icon for it appears at the bottom of the File Manager's application window. If you want to align those icons, you can issue the Arrange Icons command. It moves all minimized directory window icons into a row at the bottom of the File Manager's application window and aligns them so they're evenly spaced. Because you probably won't find the need to minimize many directory windows, you may never need this command.

The Refresh command   The File Manager updates directory windows for hard disk drives immediately when their contents change. However, for network drives, there can be a substantial delay before these updates occur. And for diskette drives, the updates aren't automatic. Even if you remove a diskette from a drive and replace it with another, the directory window for that drive continues to show the contents of the first diskette. In these cases, you can

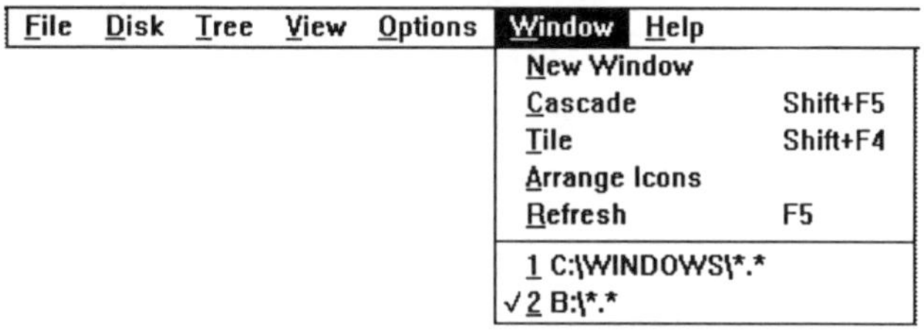

File	Disk	Tree	View	Options	**Window**	Help

```
New Window
Cascade                    Shift+F5
Tile                       Shift+F4
Arrange Icons
Refresh                    F5
────────────────────────────────────
1 C:\WINDOWS\*.*
√ 2 B:\*.*
```

Command	Function
New Window	Creates a new directory window with the same contents and settings as the active directory window.
Cascade	Resizes and moves open directory windows so they overlap with the title bar of each visible.
Tile	Resizes and moves open directory windows so they're roughly the same size and do not overlap. By default, the windows are arranged so they span the File Manager's application window horizontally. If you want to arrange the windows so they span the application window vertically, hold down the Shift key as you issue this command.
Arrange Icons	Aligns all minimized document window icons along the lower border of the application window.
Refresh	Updates the contents of the active directory window. This is useful for diskettes and drives on networks.
directory-window name	Makes the specified directory window the active window. If the window has been reduced to an icon, choosing its name restores the window.

Figure 7-19   The commands of the Window menu

issue the Refresh command to bring the current directory window up to date. Or, you can use the keyboard shortcut for the Refresh command (F5) to refresh the current window.

The directory names at the bottom of the menu   If you're working with just one or two directory windows, you'll probably use the standard *Windows* techniques to switch from one directory window to another. But if you're working with a number of directory windows, you may find it more efficient to select the directory name at the bottom of the Window menu for the window you want to switch to. This is an efficient switching technique because it doesn't require you to move, resize, or close other windows.

Part 1

You can issue the Cascade command to organize all open directory windows so they overlap and you can read the title bar of each.

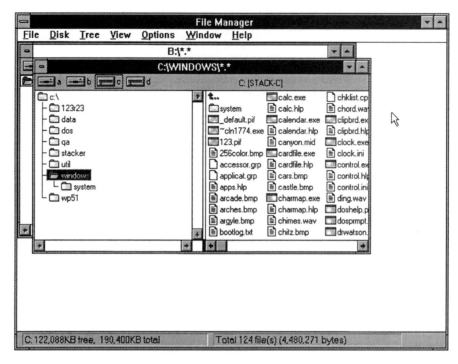

Part 2

If you issue the Tile command without holding the Shift key down, the File Manager orients the open directory windows horizontally.

Figure 7-20   The effects of the Cascade and Tile commands

Part 3

If you hold the
Shift key down
when you issue
the Tile com-
mand, the File
Manager orients
the directory
windows verti-
cally.

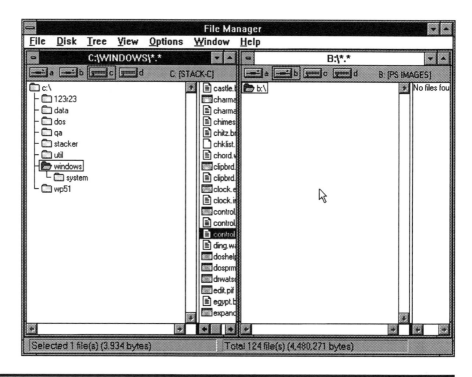

Figure 7-20   The effects of the Cascade and Tile commands (continued)

Three ways to start a program from the File Manager

Figure 7-21 lists the three methods for starting a program from the File
Manager. These are analogous to three ways for starting a program from the
Program Manager, so I will present them quickly.

Double-click on the icon for a program   The simplest way to start a
program with the File Manager is to double-click on the icon for its program
file in the directory pane. When you do, *Windows* retrieves the program file
from disk and starts it. This is illustrated in figure 7-22.

Double-click on the icon for a file associated with a program   When
you double-click on the icon for a document that's associated with a program,
the File Manager starts the associated program and opens the data file. This is
illustrated by figure 7-23. Here, the Write program is started by double-

---

1. Double-click on the icon for a program.
2. Double-click on the icon for a document file associated with a program.
3. Use the Run command under the File menu.

Figure 7-21   Three ways to start a program from the File Manager

clicking on the WININI.WRI file because the WRI extension is associated with the Write program. To associate an extension with a program, you use the Associate command as I explained earlier in this chapter.

Use the Run command under the File menu   A third way to start a program from the File Manager is to use the Run command. Before you issue this command, you should change the current directory to the one that contains the program that you want to start. Then, when you issue the command, a dialog box like the one in figure 7-24 is displayed, and you can type the DOS command for starting the program in the Command Line text box. Because you can start a program more easily just by double-clicking on its icon in the directory pane, you probably won't ever want to use this command.

How to change your shell program from the Program Manager to the File Manager

If you work with many programs and many files, you may want to use the File Manager instead of the Program Manager as your shell program. To make this change to your system, you have to edit the SYSTEM.INI file that resides in the *Windows* program directory. To edit this file, you can start Notepad, and open SYSTEM.INI. Near the top of the file, look for a line that reads

```
shell=progman.exe
```

and change it to

```
shell=winfile.exe
```

Then, save the file and restart *Windows*. When you do, the Program Manager won't start, but the File Manager will.

Part 1

To start the Write accessory program, you can double-click on the File Manager icon for its program file (WRITE.EXE).

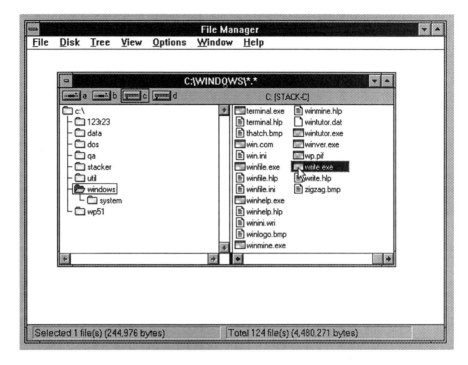

Part 2

When you do, *Windows* retrieves the WRITE.EXE file, loads it into internal memory, and opens a new application window for it.

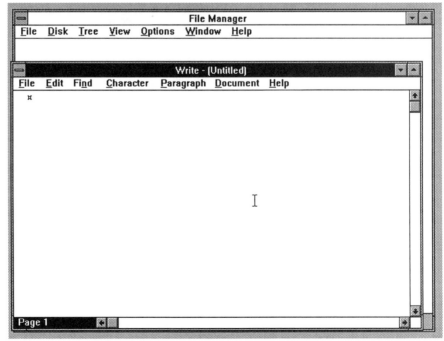

Figure 7-22   How to start a program by double-clicking on its program icon

Part 1

You can start an application program by double-clicking on the File Manager icon for a data file that's associated with the program. For example, you can double-click on the icon for WININI.WRI to start the Write accessory program.

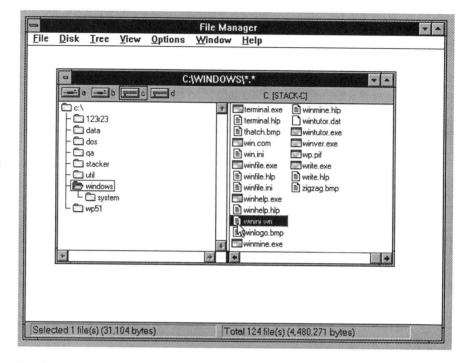

Part 2

Then, *Windows* retrieves and launches the Write application and opens the data file with it.

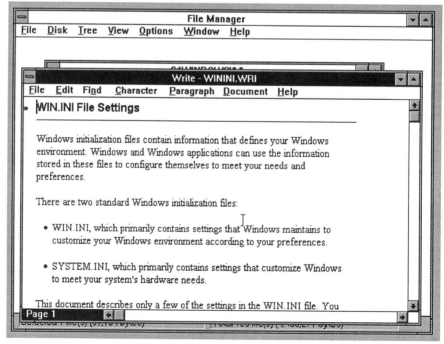

Figure 7-23   How to start a program by double-clicking on the icon for a data file that is associated with the program

When you issue the Run command, the File Manager displays a dialog box. There, you supply the file name for the program. Then, when you OK the dialog box, the File Manager looks for the program in the current directory. To set the current directory to the one that the program is in, you can select the directory before you issue the Run command.

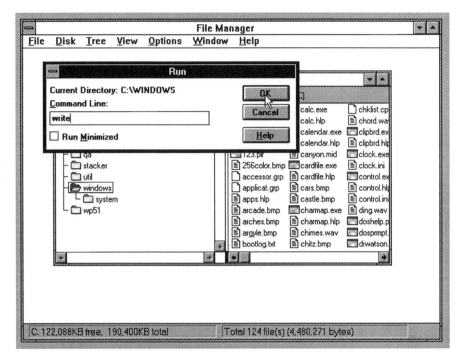

Figure 7-24　　How to start a program with the Run command

Perspective

Now that you know how to use all of the commands for the File Manager, you can set it up so it's most efficient for your purposes. For instance, you can set up two directory windows for the same hard disk so you can have two different views of its directories and files. One directory window can be set up as usual with two panes; the other window can be set up with only a directory pane that shows all of the file information for each file, but only for the files that have the extension DOC. Then, you can use the first window to manage all of the directories and files on the disk drive, and the second window to manage just your word processing files.

Summary

- The File Manager's menus always include the commands this chapter presents. But if you're running DOS 6.0, the File Manager may include a Tools menu that lets you start some DOS 6.0 utility programs. And if your system is part of a network, the File Manager may include some network management commands under the Disk menu.

- The most useful commands in the File menu are Copy (when the file names of the copies are different than the original names), Rename, Print, Associate, Create Directory, Search, and Select Files.

- The most useful commands in the Disk menu are Copy Disk and Format Disk, which you can use for copying and formatting diskettes.

- You can use the commands in the View menu to customize the layout of directory windows and specify what information appears in them.

- You can use the commands in the Options menu to set several File Manager options, like what confirmation messages are displayed and what font is used in the directory windows. Usually, though, the defaults are set the way you want them.

- You can use the commands in the Window menu to arrange directory windows (Cascade and Tile), to update the directory windows for network drives or diskettes (Refresh), and to switch to another directory window.

- You can start a program from the File Manager in three ways: (1) double-click on the icon for a program file, (2) double-click on the icon for a file associated with a program, (3) use the Run command under the File menu.

- To use the File Manager instead of the Program Manager as the *Windows* shell, you have to change the SYSTEM.INI file.

Chapter 8

How to work with printers and fonts

How to use the Print Manager to control your print jobs
How to access the Print Manager
How to manage the print queue
How to use menu commands

How to install and set up a printer
How to install a printer driver
How to set the default printer
How to set advanced printer options

How to select the fonts for printed documents
When to use TrueType fonts
When to use printer fonts
When and how to use PostScript fonts

Perspective
Summary

In chapter 4, you learned the standard techniques for printing from a *Windows* application. If your PC is set up so it prints the way you want it to, that may be all you need to know about printing from *Windows* applications. If your printer doesn't work the way you expect or if you need to install a new printer on your PC, this chapter tells you more about working with printers and the fonts that are used for printing.

To start, you'll learn how to use the Print Manager to control the printing of your print jobs. Then, you'll learn how to use the Print Manager to install a new printer on your PC. Last, you'll learn how to select the fonts that you use when printing from a *Windows* application.

How to use the Print Manager to control your print jobs

When you print a document, your application program doesn't send it directly to the printer. Instead, your program creates a temporary *print file* that *Windows* sends to the Print Manager. Then, the Print Manager, not your application program, controls the printing that's done.

The advantage of using the Print Manager is that it runs in the *background*, so you can go on with your work while a document prints. You can even send other documents to the Print Manager while the first document is printing. As it receives print files, the Print Manager adds them to its *print queue*. Then, it prints the files from the queue in the order it received them. After a job finishes printing, the Print Manager deletes its print file. And when there are no print files left in the queue, the Print Manager ends.

If you need to, you can intervene in the operations of the Print Manager. For instance, you can change the order of your print jobs in the queue and monitor their progress as they print. The Print Manager also alerts you if there's a problem so you can correct it and continue printing. In addition, you can control options that affect the speed of the Print Manager and the kind of information it displays for each print job.

When you print documents to a *local printer* (that is, one that's attached directly to your PC), it's appropriate for the Print Manager to handle all printing operations. However, when you print documents on a *network printer*, *Windows* usually bypasses the Print Manager and sends the print file directly to the network server. Then, the server manages its network print queue and controls the network printers directly. This eliminates the double-queuing of a print file (once on your PC by the Print Manager and again on the network server by the network printing software).

How to access the Print Manager   Most of the time, you won't need to start the Print Manager explicitly because *Windows* starts it automatically whenever you print a document. When the Print Manager is active, you can access it through its minimized application icon at the bottom of the desktop or with any of the other *Windows* techniques for switching from one program to another.

If you want to change the Print Manager options when the Print Manager isn't running, you can start it by double-clicking on its program icon in the Main program group. Part 1 of figure 8-1 shows the Print Manager's icon, and part 2 shows its application window. In this example, only one local printer is available to the system, and no documents are printing.

How to manage the print queue   Figure 8-2 shows how you can control the Print Manager's operations. After you access the Print Manager, its application window appears. In this example, the PC has access to several printers. For each print job, the Print Manager shows the application that created it, its size, and the date and time the file was sent to print.

In part 1 of figure 8-2, one document (a *PowerPoint* presentation) is printing on the HP LaserJet IIP Plus printer, and the print job is 5 percent complete. You can tell which file is currently printing because a printer icon is displayed next to the name of the print file.

To pause a print job, delete a job, or change its sequence in the print queue, you first select the job by clicking on it. Then, you either use the command buttons at the top of the window or mouse techniques to complete the task. In part 2 of figure 8-2, printing for the *PowerPoint* document was paused. Notice that an icon that looks like a hand appears next to the name of the printer to show that it's suspended. To resume the job, you click on the Resume command button. To delete the job, you click on the Delete command button. If you delete the job, the print file disappears from the queue, as shown in part 3. Then, the Print Manager proceeds with the next file in the queue. In this example, the next job is a *PageMaker* document.

If you want to change the order of the jobs in the print queue, all you have to do is drag an entry in the list to where you want it to go. When you "drop" the item in the new position, the Print Manager renumbers and rearranges the other jobs. You can use this technique if you need a printed copy of a document right away, but other long print jobs are ahead of it in the queue.

How to use menu commands   Most of the time, you don't have to use the menu commands of the Print Manager because the chances are that the default printing options will be satisfactory for you. But in case you do need to change them, figure 8-3 summarizes the Print Manager's menu commands. As you see, some of the commands are relevant only if your PC is attached to a network.

Part 1

To start the Print Manager, double-click on its icon in the Main group.

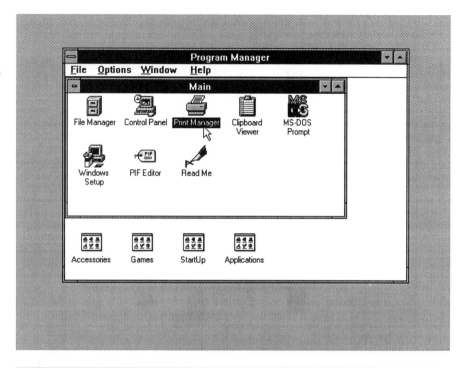

Part 2

The Print Manager's application window.

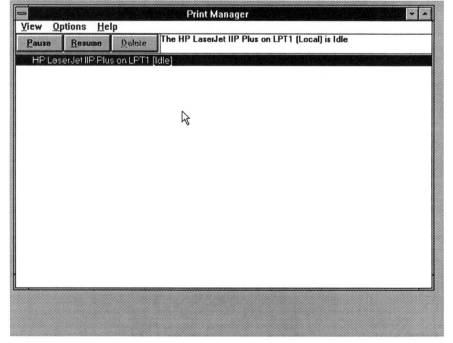

Figure 8-1   How to start the Print Manager

Part 1

The Print Manager displays information that identifies each printer, the current print job, the progress of the current print job, the size of each print job, and the date and time each was sent to print.

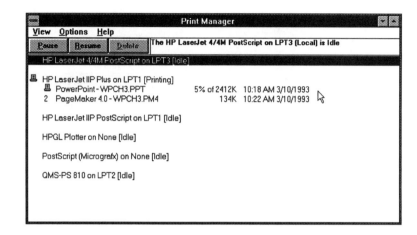

Part 2

To control a print job, select it. Then, use the Pause, Resume, or Delete command buttons.

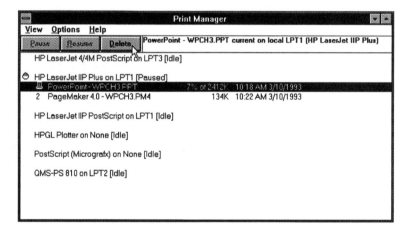

Part 3

When the current print job ends (or if it's deleted), the job entry disappears from the screen, and the next job in the queue prints.

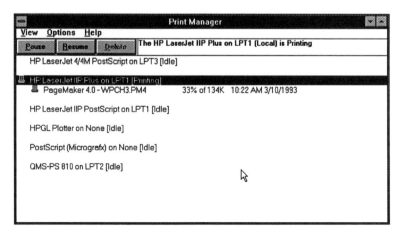

Figure 8-2   How to control printing with the Print Manager

The View menu commands let you control the information that appears in the Print Manager's application window. If the Time/Date Sent and Print File Size options are enabled (as they are by default), this information appears for each print queue entry. You should probably leave these options on because they provide information that's useful if you want to delete or change the sequence of the jobs in the queue.

The next three View menu commands (Refresh, Selected Net Queue, and Other Net Queue) are available only if your PC is attached to a network that supports these commands. You can use these commands to get information about the status of network print queues. The Refresh command updates the network queue displays. You may want to use this command if your network software doesn't automatically update the status of its queues as often as you want.

Unless you specify otherwise, the only print queue entries that the Print Manager displays for a network printer are the files you printed. But if you want to see all of the files that are queued to print on a network printer, you can move the highlight to the line for the printer and issue the Selected Net Queue command. Then, you can use this information to decide if you want to use that network printer or choose another one.

If you want to see the activity on a network printer that you're not connected to, you can use the Other Net Queue command. When you issue it, you have to type the network path to the printer you're interested in. Of course, this varies from one network to another.

The first three Options menu commands (Low Priority, Medium Priority, and High Priority) let you control how quickly jobs print. Because the Print Manager works alongside your application programs, it has to share your system's resources. If you leave the default option, Medium Priority, in effect, *Windows* tries to divide the processor's time equally among competing tasks. This option gives about half of your processor's time to the Print Manager and half to the current application program. Of course, it isn't that simple, but that's a logical way to think about it. The other options let you give less processor time (Low Priority) or more processor time (High Priority) to the Print Manager.

Generally, you should leave the default option, Medium Priority, on. However, this option may slow your application programs down so much that using them is difficult. If so, you can specify the Low Priority option to give a larger share of your system's resources to your program. Or, if you're printing a complicated document that requires the Print Manager to process and send a large amount of data to the printer, you can use the High Priority option to speed up the process.

View menu		
Time/Date Sent		Includes the time and date that a document was sent to the printer in the Print Manager display. (Default setting.)
Print File Size		Includes the sizes of print files in the Print Manager display. (Default setting.)
Refresh	**(Network)**	Updates the Print Manager display.
Selected Net Queue	**(Network)**	Shows every file queued for printing on the network printer that you're connected to, not just the print files you sent.
Other Net Queue	**(Network)**	Shows the files queued for printing on a network printer that you're not connected to.
Exit		Ends the Print Manager program.
Options menu		
Low Priority		Assigns less processor time to the Print Manager than to your applications.
Medium Priority		Assigns roughly equal amounts of processor time to the Print Manager and to your applications. (Default setting.)
High Priority		Assigns more processor time to the Print Manager than to your applications.
Alert Always		Displays a message whenever user intervention is necessary.
Flash if Inactive		Flashes the Print Manager icon or its window title bar if user intervention is necessary. (Default setting.)
Ignore if Inactive		Doesn't display a message or flash when user intervention is necessary if the Print Manager is not the active program.
Network Settings	**(Network)**	Adjusts how frequently the display for the network print queue is updated and specifies whether the Print Manager should be bypassed when printing to a network printer.
Network Connections	**(Network)**	Controls the connections to network printers.
Printer Setup		Lets you install printer drivers, specify your default printer, and set advanced printer options.

Figure 8-3   How to use Print Manager menu commands

If you have to intervene in the operation of your printer, the Print Manager will generate a message to advise you. The next three Option menu commands (Alert Always, Flash if Inactive, and Ignore if Inactive) let you control how those messages are presented if the Print Manager isn't the active program. Alert Always means the Print Manager will display a dialog box that contains the message regardless of what program is active. Flash if Inactive, the default setting, means the Print Manager icon (or, if it's running in an inactive window, the window title bar) will flash until you make it the current program. The third command, Ignore if Inactive, means nothing will happen until you return to the Print Manager. You should realize, though, that some messages will be displayed automatically regardless of which of these options is active. For example, if the Print Manager tries to print to an off-line printer, a dialog box will always appear immediately.

The next two commands under the Options menu, Network Settings and Network Connections, let you adjust how the Print Manager deals with network printing. The Network Settings command lets you specify whether the network queues should be updated automatically and whether the Print Manager should be used or bypassed for network printing. The Network Connections command lets you choose a different network printer. As with the other network commands, though, you need to know how your specific network operates to use these commands properly. So if you have any questions, you should talk with your network administrator.

How to install and set up a printer

Windows makes it easy for you to install a new printer, set a default printer, and set printer options. To do so, you can use the last command under the Print Manager's Options menu, the Printer Setup command. You can also use the Printers option of the Control Panel that's presented in the next chapter. They work the same way, though, so the techniques that follow are all that you need.

How to install a printer driver   When you get a new printer, the installation process has two parts. First, you need to attach the printer to your computer physically. This means you have to use the right printer port or network connection and the right cable. Second, you need to make sure that the right *printer driver* software is installed within *Windows*. A printer driver is a program that controls how your computer and printer interact. It provides information about the connection between the computer and the printer and about the printer's fonts and other features.

Figure 8-4 illustrates how to install a printer driver with the Print Manager. From the Options menu, you issue the Printer Setup command as shown in part 1, and you click on the Add command button on the Printers dialog box as shown in part 2. Then, the Print Manager expands the dialog box with an Install command button and a list of available drivers as shown in part 3. Since *Windows* comes with over 250 different drivers, it's likely that the driver you need is available in the list. If it is, you select your printer from the list and click on the Install button. At that point, *Windows* will probably prompt you to insert one of its installation disks so it can retrieve the appropriate printer driver as shown in part 4. To complete the operation, you insert the diskette in the drive and follow the directions in the dialog box.

If the printer you want to install doesn't appear in the list, you can still use it if you have a driver disk from your printer's manufacturer or if your printer *emulates* a standard printer that's in the list. To use a manufacturer-supplied disk, click on the Install Unlisted or Updated Printer item in the list box and proceed from there. To use printer emulation, install the driver for the printer you want to emulate. If, for example, you have a Texas Instruments microLaser Plus printer, which doesn't have a driver packaged with *Windows*, you can emulate the HP LaserJet IIP and install its *Windows* printer driver. If your printer emulates a standard printer, you can find out which standard driver to use by looking in the documentation that came with your printer.

How to set the default printer   If you have access to more than one printer, the *default printer* is the one *Windows* uses unless you specifically request a different one. To set the default printer, you issue the Printer Setup command from the Options menu. Then, you select the printer you want to use from the list that appears in the Printers dialog box as shown in figure 8-5. To complete the operation, you click on the Set As Default Printer button.

When you set the default printer through the Print Manager, you would expect it to apply to all *Windows* programs and to stay in force unless changed through the Print Manager. But that may or may not work the way you expect. Sometimes, a change to the default printer in an application program also changes the default printer for *Windows*. Other times, the default printer in the application program overrides the default printer for *Windows*.

How to set advanced printer options   The Printer Setup command lets you set advanced printer options such as resolution, dithering, intensity, and print quality. However, it's unlikely that you'll ever need to change these settings because the defaults that *Windows* sets generally work well. If you do need to change these options, though, the best source of information about them is the documentation that came with your printer. Then, you can change the options

Part 1

Issue the Printer Setup command from the Options menu.

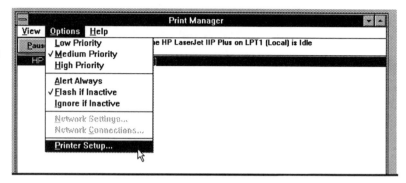

Part 2

Click on the Add command button in the resulting dialog box.

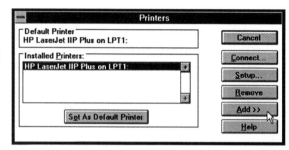

Part 3

Select the printer you want to install from the List of Printers; then, click on the Install command button.

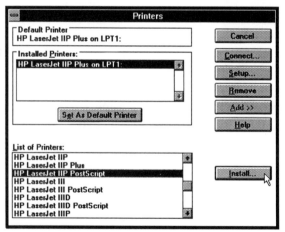

Part 4

You may need to use one of the *Windows* installation diskettes to complete installing the printer driver.

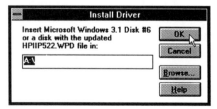

Figure 8-4   How to install a printer driver

To set the default printer, issue the Printer Setup command from the Options menu of the Print Manager. Then, select the printer from the Installed Printers list and click on the Set As Default Printer button.

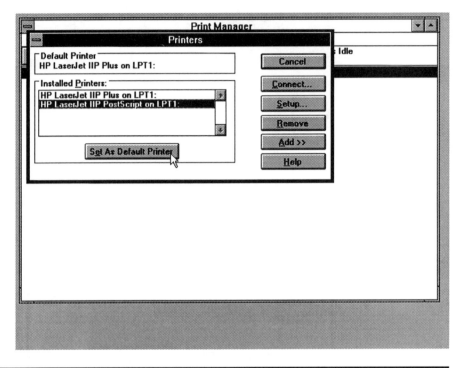

Figure 8-5   How to set the default printer

by issuing the Printer Setup command from the Options menu, clicking on the Setup command button, and clicking on the Options button. The resulting dialog box shows the options you can change.

How to select the fonts for printed documents

A *font* is a set of character shapes comprised of letters, numbers, signs, and symbols. Most *Windows* programs have formatting commands that let you let you assign a font to a block of text in a document. For example, figure 8-6 shows the Font dialog box that the Write accessory program displays to let you format a text block. As you can see, you can choose the font itself (like Times New Roman), the type style (regular, italic, bold, and bold italic are common options), and the type size in points (a *point* is 1/72 inch).

When you use a *Windows* application, you usually have the choice of at least two types of fonts: (1) the *TrueType fonts* that come with *Windows* and (2) the fonts that come with your printer (*printer fonts*). In addition, some application programs add fonts to your system when you install them. And you

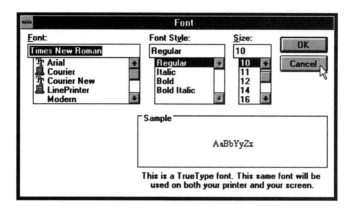

Figure 8-6   The Font dialog box from the Write accessory program

can buy and install fonts from software publishers like Bitstream, Agfa, or Adobe.

To help you identify the types of fonts that are available to you, many *Windows* applications display small icons in the dialog boxes. In figure 8-6, for example, the TT icon next to the first and third fonts means that those are TrueType fonts. The printer icon next to the second and fourth fonts means that those are printer fonts. And the omission of an icon before the fifth choice (Modern) usually means that the font is a screen font that's unlikely to print satisfactorily.

When you choose a font for a portion of text, you normally do so based on the appearance of the font. However, you should also be aware that the font type matters because it can affect the way the font looks on the screen, the way it looks when it's printed, and how efficiently your printer can print it. On that basis, you should usually work with either TrueType fonts or printer fonts. Or, in the special case of Postscript printers, you should use a combination of the two.

When to use TrueType fonts   One of the benefits that you get from using *Windows* is that all of the *Windows* applications have access to its TrueType fonts. When you use these fonts, you can be sure that what you see on the screen is what you're going to get on the printer. Also, these fonts are designed to provide high quality printing no matter what point size they're printed in. Last, the fonts are *scalable*, which means they can be printed in a wide continuous range of point sizes. If, for example, you want to print a 56-point headline, you can do so, and it will print in the highest quality that's possible on your printer.

Arial   (like PostScript Helvetica)

ABCDEFGHIJKLMNOPQRSTUVWXYZabcdefghijklmnopqrstuvwxyz1234567890

Courier New   (like PostScript Courier)

ABCDEFGHIJKLMNOPQRSTUVWXYZabcdefghijklmnopqrstuvwxyz1234567890

Times New Roman   (like PostScript Times)

ABCDEFGHIJKLMNOPQRSTUVWXYZabcdefghijklmnopqrstuvwxyz1234567890

Symbol   (like PostScript Symbol)

ΑΒΧΔΕΦΓΗΙϑΚΛΜΝΟΠΘΡΣΤΥςΩΞΨΖαβχδεφγηιφκλμνοπθρστυϖωξψζ1234567890

Wingdings

✂✁✆✇☎✉✂✃✄✌☺☹☻✪✧✈→☼❀✿✝✞✠✡☧☨☩☪♌♍♎♏✙✚✛✜❀✫&✱●○■□◻□□□◆◇✦✧•◙◘

Figure 8-7   The TrueType fonts that come with *Windows* 3.1

Figure 8-7 shows the five TrueType font families that come with *Windows* 3.1: Arial, Courier New, Times New Roman, Symbol, and Wingdings. The first three are text fonts and are available in four different styles: regular, bold, italic, and bold italic. In contrast, the Symbol and Wingdings fonts consist entirely of symbols. As you can see in figure 8-7, four of these fonts are like PostScript typefaces that have nearly become the industry standard for page design and typography. You'll learn more about PostScript fonts in a moment.

To illustrate the difference between a TrueType font and a printer font, figure 8-8 shows the Write program's Font dialog box for two similar fonts: Courier (a printer font) and Courier New (a TrueType font). As you can see, the dialog box for Courier shows that the font is available in just two sizes (10-point and 12-point). As a result, you can't use it for high quality output in other sizes. If, for example, you want to print 40-point text with the Courier font, the image will be poorly rendered as shown in the sample box in part 1. In contrast, if you use a TrueType font like Courier New, you can select any font size, even if it doesn't appear in the Size list box. As you can see in part 2, for example, the text for 40-point New Courier is rendered in high quality on the screen, and it will be on the printer too.

The disadvantage of using TrueType fonts is that they may slow you down because *Windows* has to send the font images to the printer; it doesn't just tell the printer what printer fonts to use. As a result, your PC may work more slowly because of the additional processing it has to do to prepare the TrueType font

Part 1

Courier is a printer font that's available in only two sizes: 10-point and 12-point. A request for a different size results in distorted characters.

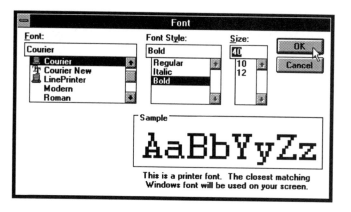

Part 2

In contrast, Courier New is a TrueType font that's available in a continuous range of sizes. You can specify a size that doesn't appear in the Size drop-down list box and still get perfectly rendered characters.

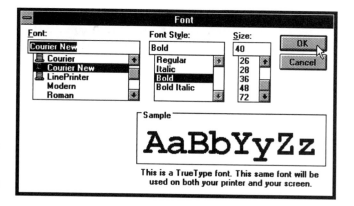

Figure 8-8   A TrueType font is freely scalable, but most printer fonts aren't

images for the printer. In addition, your printer may work more slowly because it has to print graphics output rather than use its own printer fonts, which are optimized for speed. The actual effect of using TrueType fonts in your documents, though, depends on your system. If you're using a fast PC, you may not even notice the overhead that TrueType imposes.

Because of the benefits that you get from using TrueType fonts, I recommend that you start by using those fonts for all your documents. Then, if you feel that the use of these fonts is slowing down your system, you can experiment with printer fonts to see if they can improve your system's performance.

When to use printer fonts   Printer fonts usually produce excellent output at the fastest possible speed because they and the printer are designed to work together. The main disadvantage of using these fonts is that they often aren't as scalable as TrueType fonts so you can't print them in as many point sizes. Also, if you try to print them in some sizes, the print quality is reduced. This is illustrated by the 40-point Courier font in part 1 of figure 8-8.

When and how to use PostScript fonts   A special case that may affect you involves laser printers that use Adobe's *PostScript* fonts. Like TrueType fonts, PostScript fonts can be scaled to a wide continuous range of point sizes and still produce excellent printed output. When you use PostScript fonts, though, the printer prepares the font images for printing; *Windows* doesn't. As a result, the fonts that *Windows* uses to represent PostScript fonts on the screen may not look exactly like those that are printed.

You can get around this screen display problem and still use PostScript fonts by selecting TrueType fonts that closely simulate the standard PostScript fonts. Then, when you print a document, *Windows* replaces the TrueType fonts with requests for the related PostScript fonts in the job that it sends to the printer. These relationships between TrueType fonts and the standard PostScript fonts are shown in figure 8-9. If, for example, you want to prepare a document to be printed with the PostScript fonts named Times and Helvetica, you should use the TrueType fonts named Times New Roman and Arial.

As you can see in figure 8-9, *Windows* 3.1 doesn't come with TrueType fonts that parallel all of the fonts that are standard on PostScript printers. If you want to print a document with the Palatino PostScript font, you won't find a TrueType font that parallels it in the fonts that come with *Windows* 3.1. However, Microsoft's *TrueType Font Pack*, which you can purchase separately, does include the TrueType fonts that you need. In figure 8-10, you can see all of the fonts that come in this package. Besides those that match the PostScript fonts, you get the Lucida family of fonts that produce excellent output, especially on dot-matrix printers.

Perspective

Although the Print Manager and the TrueType fonts that come with *Windows* 3.1 plus the *TrueType Font Pack* make it easy for you to get the most out of your printer, there are many other products on the market that can enhance your printing capabilities. For example, hundreds of other TrueType fonts are available, and many are inexpensive. As a result, you can build a large library of TrueType fonts for use in your documents.

To print with this font on your PostScript printer	Use the TrueType font	Available with
Helvetica	Arial	*Windows* 3.1
Courier	Courier New	*Windows* 3.1
Times	Times New Roman	*Windows* 3.1
Symbol	Symbol	*Windows* 3.1
Narrow Helvetica	Arial Narrow	*TrueType Font Pack*
Palatino	Book Antiqua	*TrueType Font Pack*
Bookman	Bookman Old Style	*TrueType Font Pack*
Avant Garde	Century Gothic	*TrueType Font Pack*
New Century Schoolbook	Century Schoolbook	*TrueType Font Pack*
Zapf Chancery	Monotype Corsiva	*TrueType Font Pack*
Zapf Dingbats	Monotype Sorts	*TrueType Font Pack*

Figure 8-9   TrueType fonts and their PostScript equivalents

Also, because Hewlett-Packard laser printers are so common, Microsoft has developed an add-on product for *Windows* to provide even better support for them. It is called the *Windows Printing System*. This product increases printing speeds and makes it easier for you to control your HP laser printer.

In the next chapter, you can learn how two of the Control Panel options apply to printing. As you will see, the Fonts option lets you manage the fonts on your system, and the Printers option duplicates some of the functions of the Print Manager. In addition, the Printers option lets you disable the Print Manager. Although you usually don't want that, it makes sense in some circumstances.

Summary

- When you print a document, your program creates a temporary *print file* that *Windows* sends to the Print Manager. Then, the Print Manager sends the print file to the printer. Because the Print Manager runs in the *background*, you can go on with your work while your documents print.

- When you print documents on a *network printer*, *Windows* may bypass the Print Manager and send the print file directly to the *network server*.

- You can use the Print Manager to delete jobs from a *print queue* and to change the sequence of the jobs in the queue.

Arial Narrow (like PostScript Narrow Helvetica)

ABCDEFGHIJKLMNOPQRSTUVWXYZabcdefghijklmnopqrstuvwxyz1234567890

Book Antiqua (like PostScript Palatino)

ABCDEFGHIJKLMNOPQRSTUVWXYZabcdefghijklmnopqrstuvwxyz1234567890

Bookman Old Style (like PostScript Bookman)

ABCDEFGHIJKLMNOPQRSTUVWXYZabcdefghijklmnopqrstuvwxyz1234567890

Century Gothic (like PostScript Avant Garde)

ABCDEFGHIJKLMNOPQRSTUVWXYZabcdefghijklmnopqrstuvwxyz1234567890

Century Schoolbook (like PostScript New Century Schoolbook)

ABCDEFGHIJKLMNOPQRSTUVWXYZabcdefghijklmnopqrstuvwxyz1234567890

Lucida Blackletter

ABCDEFGHIJKLMNOPQRSTUVWXYZabcdefghijklmnopqrstuvwxyz1234567890

Lucida Bright

ABCDEFGHIJKLMNOPQRSTUVWXYZabcdefghijklmnopqrstuvwxyz1234567890

Lucida Calligraphy

ABCDEFGHIJKLMNOPQRSTUVWXYZabcdefghijklmnopqrstuvwxyz1234567890

Lucida Fax

ABCDEFGHIJKLMNOPQRSTUVWXYZabcdefghijklmnopqrstuvwxyz1234567890

Lucida Handwriting

ABCDEFGHIJKLMNOPQRSTUVWXYZabcdefghijklmnopqrstuvwxyz1234567890

Lucida Sans

ABCDEFGHIJKLMNOPQRSTUVWXYZabcdefghijklmnopqrstuvwxyz1234567890

Lucida Sans Typewriter

ABCDEFGHIJKLMNOPQRSTUVWXYZabcdefghijklmnopqrstuvwxyz1234567890

Monotype Corsiva (like PostScript Zapf Chancery)

ABCDEFGHIJKLMNOPQRSTUVWXYZabcdefghijklmnopqrstuvwxyz1234567890

Monotype Sorts (like PostScript Zapf Dingbats)

✿✛✢✣✤✦✧☆✪☆★★★★☆✳✱✲✳✴✵✶✷✸✹✿✪✺✻✽✽✻✽✼✽✾✿●○■□▢▣□▲▼◆✤▶▮▮∞➡✔✔

Figure 8-10 The fonts in Microsoft's *TrueType Font Pack* and how they relate to PostScript fonts

- To set up a printer, you need to install the right *printer driver* for it. *Windows* comes with printer drivers for hundreds of printers, and new printers usually come with the printer drivers that *Windows* needs.

- *Windows* can print documents using *TrueType fonts* or *printer fonts*. TrueType fonts are freely scalable fonts that *Windows* uses to generate high-quality output on both your screen display and your printer. Printer fonts are usually less scalable, but they may improve the performance of your printing operations.

- With *PostScript* printers, you can use TrueType fonts for screen display and PostScript fonts for printing because *Windows* maps TrueType fonts to their PostScript equivalents.

Chapter 9

How to use the Control Panel to customize *Windows*

How to access the Control Panel options
A summary of the Control Panel options
How to set the most useful Control Panel options
>Date/Time
>Mouse
>Keyboard
>Printers
>Fonts
>Desktop

Perspective
Summary

The Control Panel program provides options that let you customize the way *Windows* works and looks. For instance, you can use these options to set the date and time for your PC, to set the sensitivity of the keyboard or mouse, and to set the colors and patterns that are used on your desktop display. You can also use these options to activate or deactivate *Windows* features like the Print Manager and Fast Alt+Tab Switching.

When you set an option, the setting is stored in the *Windows* directory in an initialization file named WIN.INI. As a result, the new setting remains in effect from one *Windows* session to another. In other words, it becomes the default setting for your PC.

In this chapter, you'll learn how to access and set Control Panel options. Then, you'll get specific information about setting the options that you're most likely to need. As you will see, though, you probably won't ever need most of the Control Panel options.

How to access the Control Panel options

Unless your system has been customized, you'll find the program icon for the Control Panel in the Main program group of the Program Manager as shown in part 1 of figure 9-1. Then, when you start the Control Panel, an application window like the one in part 2 is displayed. In this window, you can see an icon for each Control Panel option that's appropriate for your PC. In this figure, the icons for 12 options are displayed.

To find out what an options does, you can select it by clicking on its icon. Then, you can read its description in the bottom line of the Control Panel's window. To access an option, you can double-click on its icon. Or, you can use the Settings menu. This menu lists all of the available options.

When you access an option, it may lead to a single dialog box where you can adjust a setting. Or it may lead to dialog boxes and settings that are several layers deep. Although the dialog boxes are usually easy to understand, you can get more information by clicking on the Help command button in a dialog box whenever one is available.

A summary of the Control Panel options

Figure 9-2 summarizes the Control Panel options that are likely to be available on your PC. However, you probably won't ever need to change most of these options because the *Windows* installation program does a good job of setting the defaults so they work the way you want them to. Similarly, if you add new hardware to your system, the installation program will probably set appropriate defaults so you won't have to change them either.

Part 1

To access the
Control Panel,
double-click on
its icon in the
Main group of the
Program Man-
ager.

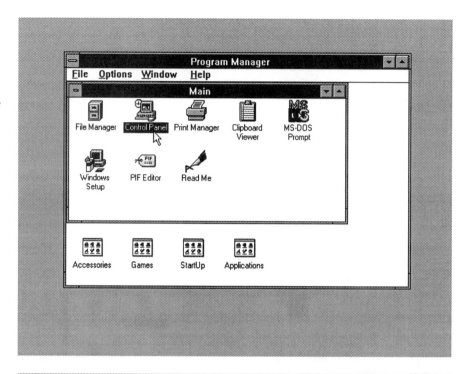

Part 2

To access an
option, double-
click on its icon,
or pull down the
Settings menu and
select its name.

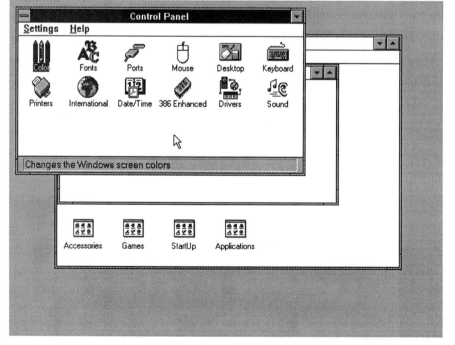

Figure 9-1   How to access the Control Panel and its options

The six most useful options

Date/Time	Sets your PC's internal clock.
Mouse	Adjusts the sensitivity of the mouse.
Keyboard	Adjusts the sensitivity of the keyboard.
Printers	Manages the printer installation of printers and their use, including whether or not documents are sent to the Print Manager before printing.
Fonts	Manages the installation of fonts and their use.
Desktop	Sets the options for the desktop display, including the selection of a screen saver.

Five options you probably won't need to change

International	Sets the options that vary from country to country, like date, time, number, and currency formats.
Color	Sets the colors for desktop elements.
Ports	Sets the options for serial (COM) ports.
Drivers	Manages the device drivers for special input and output devices, not including your monitor, keyboard, mouse, and printers.
Sound	Associates sounds with system events.

Other options you may have in the Control Panel, but probably won't need to change

Network	Sets options for network connections.
386 Enhanced	Sets options that are available in 386 enhanced mode, such as virtual memory. (These options are not available on 286 PCs.)
MIDI Mapper	Sets MIDI (Musical Instrument Digital Interface) options.

Figure 9-2   A summary of the Control Panel options

On the other hand, there are times when you need to change the Control Panel options to correct system information, to make your hardware run more smoothly, or to get *Windows* to work the way you want it to. For these purposes, you're most likely to use the six options in the first group in figure 9-2. I'll present them in more detail in a moment.

In the second group in figure 9-2, the International and Color options are easy to change. On most PCs, though, the International options are set the way you want them during installation so there's no need to change them, and the Color options are satisfactory so there's no benefit to changing them. In contrast, changing the Ports, Drivers, and Sound options requires more technical knowledge, but you probably won't ever need to change them either.

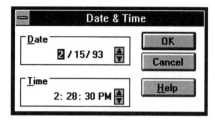

Figure 9-3   The dialog box for the Date/Time option

The third group in figure 9-2 presents three options that you don't find on all PCs. The Network option is only available if your PC is part of a network. The 386 Enhanced option is available if you're using a PC with a 386 or better processor chip, but not if you're using a 286. And the MIDI Mapper option is only available if your PC has sound capabilities. Here again, changing these options requires some technical knowledge, but you probably won't need to change them.

How to set the most useful Control Panel options

The options that you're most likely to want to set are the six in the first group in figure 9-2. So these are the only ones that I'll describe in detail in this chapter.

Date/Time   If you notice that the date or time on your PC is incorrect, you can use this option to correct it. When you double-click on the Date/Time icon in the Control Panel window, the dialog box in figure 9-3 appears. Then, you can change the date or time, and select the OK command button to complete the operation.

Mouse   When you select the Mouse option, the dialog box in figure 9-4 appears. Here, the Mouse Tracking Speed option lets you adjust how fast the mouse pointer moves across the screen, and the Double-Click Speed option lets you adjust the double-click rate. To test to see whether you've got the double-click option set the way you want it, you can double-click in the Test box. Each time that your double-click is successful, the background in this box changes. This lets you experiment with this option until you get it right.

If you're left-handed, you may want to switch the mouse buttons so they're easier to use. To do this, you can click in the check box for this option. Then, the right mouse button, not the left button, is the one you use for most mouse actions.

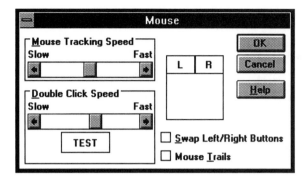

Figure 9-4   The dialog box for the Mouse option

On some PCs, you can use the Mouse Trails check box to activate an option that causes a temporary trail behind the mouse pointer as it moves across the screen. This option can make it easier to use *Windows* on a laptop PC when the refresh rate of the screen isn't fast enough to continuously display the mouse pointer as it moves across the screen. However, this option is only available if your mouse driver software supports it.

Keyboard   When you access the Keyboard option, a dialog box like the one in figure 9-5 is displayed. These options let you adjust the sensitivity of the keyboard. Here, you can use the Delay Before First Repeat option to set how long you have to hold down a key before it starts to repeat. And you can use the Repeat Rate option to set how quickly it repeats. Then, you can experiment with these settings by typing in the Test box.

Printers   When you access the Printers option, a dialog box like the one in figure 9-6 is displayed. With one exception, the options in this dialog box duplicate the functions of the Print Manager that are presented in chapter 8. As a result, you can use these options to install a printer, select a default printer, and set printer options. If you want to perform any of these functions, though, please refer to chapter 8 because these functions work the same whether you do them through the Print Manager or the Printers option of the Control Panel.

The one exception is the Use Print Manager check box at the bottom of the Printers dialog box in figure 9-6. This check box determines whether or not the Print Manager is used by your *Windows* system. When the box is checked, the Print Manager controls all the printing that is done by your system. This usually improves your productivity because you don't have to wait for the printer to finish printing a file before you can continue working on your PC.

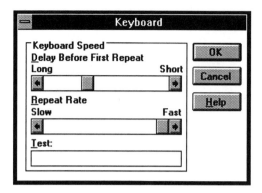

Figure 9-5   The dialog box for the Keyboard option

In some cases, though, using the Print Manager doesn't improve your efficiency. If, for example, you print a large file (like a complex graphics file), your PC first has to send the job to the Print Manager and then send it from the Print Manager to the printer. This duplication can slow down the entire process, even after the Print Manager takes control of the job. In fact, your PC may run so slowly while the job is printing that you won't want to continue working until the job is finished. In a case like this, turning off the Print Manager can sometimes speed up printing and increase your overall productivity.

Fonts   When you access the Fonts option, a dialog box like the one in figure 9-7 is displayed. The options in this box let you inspect the fonts that are available on your system, install new fonts, and remove fonts you don't want to keep.

Usually, you don't have to use the Fonts option to install new fonts because they are added automatically during other installation procedures. Eventually, though, you may find that you have so many fonts on your PC that they clutter the font menus of your applications or take up too much space on your hard disk. In figure 9-7, for example, you can see that the Arial font uses 67KB of disk space, and that's only one of four font files that make up the complete Arial font family.

If you decide that you want to remove some of the fonts from your system, you can inspect them as shown in figure 9-7 by selecting one at a time in the Installed Fonts box. Then, if you decide that you won't ever need a font, you can remove it from the system by clicking on the Remove button.

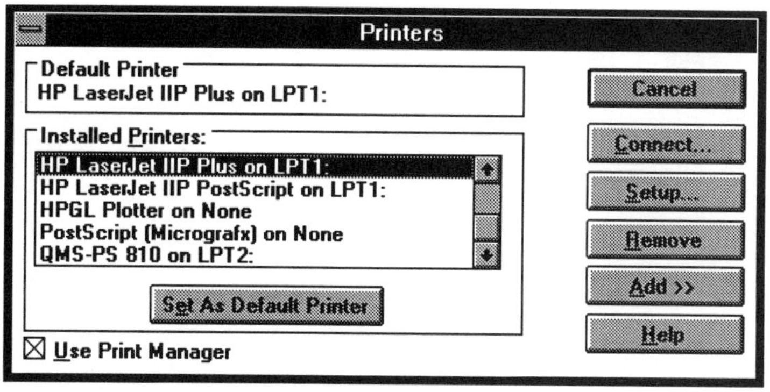

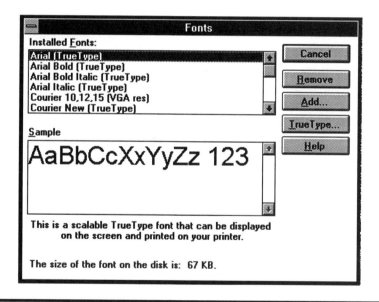

Figure 9-6   The dialog box for the Printers option

Figure 9-7   The dialog box for the Fonts option

If you don't want to delete fonts to reclaim disk space but you do want to simplify your font menus, you can consider using a Microsoft program called the *TrueType Font Assistant*. It's available as part of a separate product called the *Microsoft TrueType Font Pack 2*. This product lets you create customized groups of fonts. Then, you can select the font groups that are appropriate for the work you're doing. This can make it easier for you to use your application programs because they only show you the fonts from the groups that you've selected.

Desktop   When you access the Desktop option, a dialog box like the one in part 1 of figure 9-8 is displayed. The most important control in this box is a check box that lets you turn Fast Alt+Tab Switching on or off. When it is on, as indicated by the check in figure 9-8, you can use the Alt+Tab key combination to switch from one program to another as described in chapter 3.

The Screen Saver box in the middle of the Desktop dialog box lets you select a *screen saver* program. This type of program displays images on your monitor after your PC has been idle for a specified period of time. In part 1 of figure 9-8, you can see that the Marquee screen saver has been selected for display whenever the PC has been idle for two minutes. This protects your monitor from being "etched" by displaying the same static image for a long time. Then, to remove the screen saver from the screen and return to the program that you're working with, you move the mouse or press any key.

Windows comes with five screen savers. To see what each one looks like after you select it in the Name box, you can click on the Test button. To set other screen saver options, you can click on the Setup command button. This leads to a dialog box like the one for the Marquee screen saver that's shown in part 2 of figure 9-8. In the box for this saver, you can type a message that will move across the screen while the screen saver is active.

If you want to set up the screen saver so it doesn't leave the screen until you type a password, you can use the Password Options of the Setup dialog box. This option hides what you're working on and prevents others from using your PC without your consent. If you do use a password, though, be sure to remember it. If you forget it, you have to reboot your PC to get out of the screen saver, which means that you'll lose any work that you haven't saved.

The other options in the Desktop dialog box are easy to use, but they have little or no effect on your work. For instance, the Pattern option lets you select a pattern for the desktop background; the Wallpaper options let you select a background that looks like wallpaper; and the Icons options let you change the spacing of the icons and the form of their titles. Although experimenting with options like these can be interesting, it is also non-productive. So if you have no trouble seeing the components on your desktop, I recommend that you leave these options the way they are.

Part 1

To configure a screen saver, select it in the Name drop-down list box. Then, click on the Setup command button.

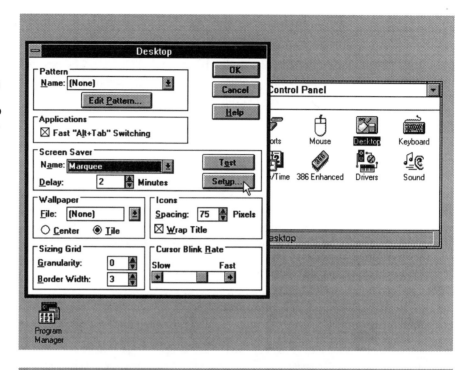

Part 2

To set a password, enable the Password Protected check box; then, click on the Set Password command button.

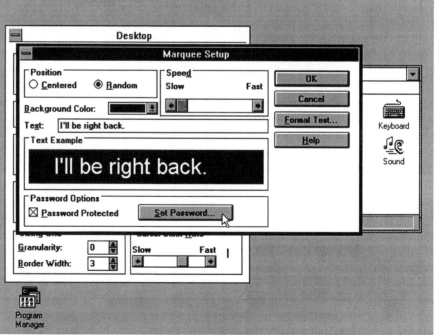

Figure 9-8   How to use the Desktop option to set up a screen saver

Perspective

Most of the Control Panel options are easy to understand and change as illustrated by the dialog boxes in this chapter. The others are easy to change if you have the required technical background. On most PCs, though, you shouldn't ever need to change any of the more technical options.

Summary

- The Control Panel lets you customize the way *Windows* operates. You can access it through its program icon in the Main program group.

- *Windows* stores the options you set through the Control Panel in a file named WIN.INI that's stored in the *Windows* directory. As a result, the Control Panel options become the default options for the system.

- The most useful Control Panel options are:

  Date/Time, for resetting your PC's internal clock;

  Mouse, for changing the sensitivity and operation of your mouse;

  Keyboard, for changing the sensitivity of your keyboard;

  Printers, for turning the Print Manager on or off;

  Fonts, for removing fonts from your system; and

  Desktop, for turning Fast Alt+Tab Switching on or off and for setting up one of the *Windows* screen savers.

Chapter 10

How to run your DOS programs under *Windows*

How to start a DOS program
From the Program Manager
From the File Manager
From MS-DOS Prompt

Other skills for using DOS programs under *Windows*
How to change from full-screen display to a window when running
   in 386 enhanced mode
How to switch from a DOS program to another program
How to close the window for a DOS program

How to copy and paste data through the clipboard when using DOS programs
In standard mode
In 386 enhanced mode

How to create a PIF and icon for a DOS program
When *Windows* recognizes the DOS program
When *Windows* doesn't recognize the DOS program

How to modify a PIF
Perspective
Summary

When you convert from DOS to *Windows*, you may be reluctant to abandon your DOS programs completely. For instance, you may want to continue to use a few of your DOS programs while you learn how to use the *Windows* versions of your other DOS programs. Or, you may want to continue to use a DOS program because there is no *Windows* replacement for it.

The good news is that you can use DOS programs under *Windows* and still get some of the benefits of using *Windows*. In particular, *Windows* lets you run two or more programs at the same time, whether they're DOS programs or not. *Windows* also makes it easier for you to transfer data to or from a DOS program by using the clipboard.

In this chapter, you'll learn how to start your DOS programs from the Program Manager, the File Manager, or the MS-DOS Prompt program. Next, you'll learn the other skills that you need when running DOS programs under *Windows*. Then, you'll learn how to use the *Windows* clipboard with your DOS programs so you can transfer data to or from a DOS program. Last, in case some of your DOS programs don't work quite the way you want them to under *Windows*, you'll learn how to create and modify the information files that *Windows* needs for running DOS programs.

How to start a DOS program

Figure 10-1 summarizes the many ways that you can start a DOS program under *Windows*. In general, you can use the same methods for starting DOS programs that you use for starting *Windows* programs. In addition, you can start DOS programs from the MS-DOS Prompt program that *Windows* provides.

From the Program Manager   When you install *Windows*, it creates program item icons for the DOS programs on your PC that it recognizes. It puts these icons in the Applications program group for the Program Manager. Then, you can start one of these DOS programs by double-clicking on its icon as illustrated in figure 10-2. When the program starts, it may take up the entire screen as it does when it runs under DOS. Or, it may be displayed in a window as shown in part 2 of this figure.

The other three methods in figure 10-1 for starting a DOS program from the Program Manager are described in more detail in chapter 6. If there isn't an icon for the DOS program that you want to start, you can use the Run command in the Program Manager's File menu for starting the program. Sometimes, though, the DOS program won't run the way you want it to when you start it from the Run command. In that case, you may have to create a Program Information File (PIF) for the program. You'll learn how to do that later in this chapter.

From the Program Manager

1. Double-click on a program item icon.
2. Double-click on an icon for a file that's associated with the program.
3. Use the Run command in the File menu.
4. Move the icon for the program into the StartUp group so the program is started whenever *Windows* is started.

From the File Manager

1. Double-click on an icon for the program file. (The file extension can be COM, EXE, PIF, or BAT.)
2. Double-click on an icon for a file that's associated with the program.
3. Use the Run command in the File menu.

From MS-DOS Prompt

Double-click on the icon for MS-DOS Prompt in the Main group of the Program Manager. Then, enter the DOS commands for starting the program.

Figure 10-1   How to start a DOS program under *Windows*

From the File Manager   The three methods in figure 10-1 for starting a DOS program from the File Manager are explained in more detail in chapter 7. Of these, the first method is the easiest one to use. You just double-click on the icon for the program that you want to start. This can be a program file with a COM, EXE, or BAT extension, or it can be a program information file that has a PIF extension. In figure 10-3, for example, you can see a file named 123.PIF in the *Windows* directory and a file named 123.EXE in the 123R23 directory. In this case, double-clicking on the icon for either file will start *Lotus 1-2-3* release 2.3 for DOS.

If you've read chapter 7, you know that you can start a *Windows* application from an icon that represents a data file that's associated with the program. This is also true for DOS programs. If, for example, files with the WK1 extension are associated with the *Lotus 1-2-3* program, you can start the program by double-clicking on the icon for any file with the WK1 extension. Then, when *Lotus 1-2-3* starts, it also opens the data file. In chapter 7, you can learn how to make an association like this.

Part 1

To start a DOS
program from the
Program Manager,
you can double-
click on its
program icon.

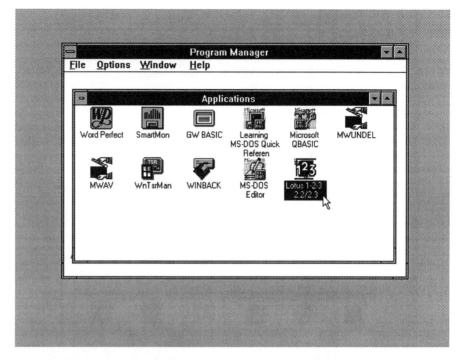

Part 2

When the DOS
program starts, it
can fill the entire
screen or it may
open in a
window, as
shown here.

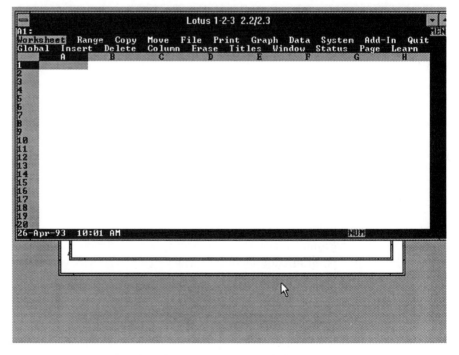

Figure 10-2   How to start a DOS program from the Program Manager

By default, the program information file for a DOS program is stored in the *Windows* directory. To start the related program, you can double-click on the icon for the PIF.

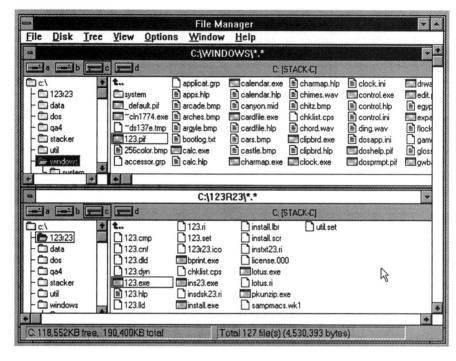

Figure 10-3   How to start a DOS program from its program information file in the File Manager

From MS-DOS Prompt   Another way to start a DOS program is to use the MS-DOS Prompt program that's in the Main program group of the Program Manager. This is illustrated in figure 10-4. When you start MS-DOS Prompt, *Windows* simulates a DOS environment by providing the DOS command prompt on a full screen or in a window like the one in part 2 of this figure. Then, you can issue the DOS commands that are necessary to start your program.

In general, though, DOS programs don't work as well when you start them from MS-DOS Prompt as they do when you customize them. I'll explain this more fully later in this chapter. As a result, you should only use MS-DOS Prompt for starting DOS programs that you use infrequently. Then, if the programs don't work the way you want them to, you need to create customized program information files for them.

Part 1

To start MS-DOS Prompt, double-click on its icon in the Main group of the Program Manager.

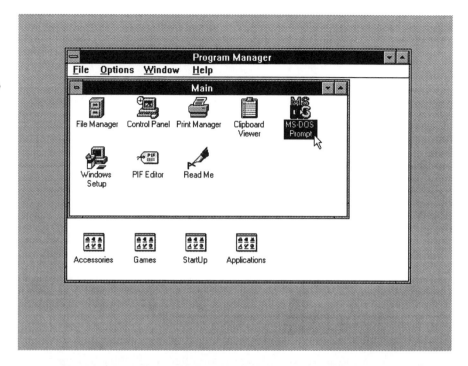

Part 2

When the DOS prompt is displayed, enter the commands for starting the DOS program.

Figure 10-4   How to start the MS-DOS Prompt program

Other skills for using DOS programs under *Windows*

For the most part, your DOS programs will work under *Windows* just as they do when you run them directly under DOS. That means the skills that you've already mastered with these programs carry over into the *Windows* environment. Beyond that, you just need to know: (1) how to switch from full-screen display to a window if that's possible on your PC, (2) how to switch from a DOS program to another program, and (3) how to close the window for a DOS program after you exit from it.

How to change from full-screen display to a window when running in 386 enhanced mode   Some of the features that *Windows* provides for DOS programs depend on the operating mode that *Windows* runs in. If your PC has a 286 processor, *Windows* runs in *standard mode*. If your PC has a 386 or higher processor, *Windows* can run in *386 enhanced mode*. As you will see, *Windows* provides more features for programs running in 386 enhanced mode. To find out which operating mode your PC uses, you can access the Help menu from either the Program Manager or the File Manager and issue the About command.

To switch from full-screen display to window display and back again, you use the Alt+Enter key combination. If you study part 2 of figure 10-4, you can see this key combination listed in the box at the top of the window that's opened by MS-DOS Prompt. You can use this key combination whenever you're using a DOS program in 386 enhanced mode.

How to switch from a DOS program to another program   Figure 10-5 summarizes the methods that you can use for switching from a DOS program to another program. These are the standard *Windows* methods that you learned in chapter 3. Obviously, though, you can't use the methods that require windows when you're running a DOS program in full-screen display. Fast Alt+Tab Switching is preferred by many people who use DOS programs because it works whether or not the programs are in windows.

How to close the window for a DOS program   When you finish working with a DOS program under *Windows*, you exit from it just as you do when you're running it under DOS. For most programs, this returns you to the Program Manager or File Manager. It also closes the window that your program was running in. In that case, you don't have to worry about closing the DOS window.

If you're running the program in full-screen display

1.   Use Fast Alt+Tab Switching to cycle through the programs that are running.
2.   Type Alt+Esc to switch to the next program.
3.   Type Ctrl+Esc to display the Task List. Then, select the program you want to switch to.

If you're running the program in a window in 386 enhanced mode

1.   Click on a visible portion of an inactive application window.
2.   Double-click on an unoccupied portion of the desktop to display the Task List. Then, select the program you want to switch to.
3.   Issue the Switch To command from the DOS window's control menu to display the Task List. Then, choose the program you want to switch to.

Figure 10-5   How to switch to or from a DOS program

Some programs, however, are set up so their windows don't close when they end. Then, to close one, you have to issue the Close command from the window's control menu or double-click on the window's control-menu box. Most programs aren't set up this way, but if you run into one that is, you can easily change the setup so the window closes when the program ends. I'll show you how to do this later in this chapter.

When you end a program that you started from MS-DOS Prompt, you are always returned to a DOS window or full screen that shows the command prompt. Then, to return to the Program Manager or File Manager, you must type *exit* at the prompt and press the Enter key. This closing technique is summarized when you start MS-DOS Prompt as shown in part 2 of figure 10-4, but this information isn't available when you are returned to the DOS prompt. It's something that you have to remember.

How to copy and paste data through the clipboard when using DOS programs

You can use the clipboard to copy and paste data between DOS applications and between DOS and *Windows* applications. The techniques you use depend on whether you're operating in standard or 386 enhanced mode. As you will see, using the clipboard with DOS programs is harder than using it with *Windows* programs. Also, the features for working in standard mode are more limited than those for 386 enhanced mode.

In standard mode   Figure 10-6 summarizes the techniques for copying and pasting when a DOS program is running in standard mode. In this mode, you can copy and paste text only. You can't work with graphic images.

To copy text to the clipboard from a DOS program, you just press the Print Screen key. When you do, *Windows* copies all of the text on the full screen to the clipboard. You can't select the portions of text that you want to copy.

To paste text from the clipboard into the document for a DOS program, you use the five step procedure in figure 10-6. In step 1, you move the insertion point to where you want the clipboard text pasted. In step 2, you switch to the Program Manager. When you do, an icon for your DOS application appears on the desktop. (If you're using MS-DOS Prompt, you'll see an icon for it instead of an icon for your program.) In step 3, you click on the icon for the DOS program to pop up its control menu. In step 4, you issue the Paste command from this control menu. In step 5, you double-click on the icon for the DOS program to restore it to working size.

In 386 enhanced mode   If you're running in 386 enhanced mode, you can use the clipboard to copy graphics as well as text. Also, if you run your DOS program in a window, you can select what you want to copy from the screen; you don't have to copy the whole screen. However, you still can't paste graphics into a DOS program.

Figure 10-7 lists the techniques you can use to copy data to and paste data from the clipboard in 386 enhanced mode. As you can see, the options that are available depend on whether you're running your program in full-screen display or in a window. In full-screen display, you press the Print Screen key to copy the entire screen of text *or* graphics to the clipboard, but you still can't select what you want to copy. Also, pasting data from the clipboard still requires a cumbersome technique. For those reasons, you'll probably want to run your DOS program in a window when you copy data from it or paste data into it.

When you run a DOS program in a window, you use the Edit command in the window's control menu to help you copy and paste. When you issue this command, a subordinate menu with the Mark, Copy, and Paste commands appears. Then, you can use the Mark command to select the data you want to copy; the Copy command to copy what you've selected to the clipboard; and the Paste command to paste the clipboard into a DOS application's window at the insertion point.

In figure 10-8, you can see how the procedures in figure 10-7 are used to copy data from a DOS application, *Lotus 1-2-3*, to a *Windows* application, the Write accessory program. In parts 2 and 4, you can see the Edit menu that is subordinate to the control menu for the DOS window. In parts 2 and 3, the Mark command in the Edit menu is used to select the data to be copied to the

Function	How to do it
Copy text to the clipboard	Press the Print Screen key to capture the text of the entire screen.
Paste text from the clipboard	1. In the DOS document, position the insertion point where you want the text on the clipboard to be pasted. 2. Switch back to the Program Manager. An icon for the DOS application will appear on the desktop. 3. Click on the icon for the DOS application to display the control menu. 4. Issue the Paste command. 5. Double-click on the icon for the DOS application to switch back to it. The text from the clipboard has been pasted into the document.

Figure 10-6   How to copy and paste text in a DOS program when *Windows* is running in standard mode

clipboard. In part 4, the Copy command is used to copy the data. In parts 5 and 6, the Paste command is used in the *Windows* Write program to paste the data from the clipboard into the Write document.

This example illustrates that you can copy data between a DOS application and a *Windows* application. It also shows that you can copy data between two different types of programs like a spreadsheet program and a word processing program. Unfortunately, though, the destination application doesn't always interpret the pasted data the same way that the source application does, so the copy operation doesn't always work the way you want it to. Often, you have to experiment with your programs to find out what works and what doesn't.

How to create a PIF and icon for a DOS program

In order to run a DOS program efficiently, *Windows* requires information about how the program uses your PC's resources including how the program uses internal memory, ports, and the monitor. *Windows* gets this information through a *Program Information File*, or *PIF*. As part of its installation procedure, *Windows* creates a PIF and an icon for each DOS program it recognizes. It puts the icon for the program in the Applications group of the Program Manager, and it stores the PIF for the program in the *Windows* directory. Then, when you start a DOS program from its icon, *Windows* accesses the related PIF file to get the information it needs for running the program.

When the DOS program is running with full-screen display

Function	How to do it
Copy text or graphics to the clipboard	Press the Print Screen key. If the screen is a text screen, its characters are placed on the clipboard. If the screen is a graphics screen, the image is placed on the clipboard as a bit map.
Paste text from the clipboard	1. Position the insertion point where you want the data on the clipboard to be pasted. 2. Switch back to the Program Manager. An icon for the DOS application will appear on the desktop. 3. Click on the icon for the DOS application to display its control menu. 4. Issue the Edit command from the control menu to access the Edit menu. 5. Issue the Paste command from the Edit menu. 6. Double-click on the icon for the DOS application to switch back to it. The data from the clipboard has been been pasted into the document.

When the DOS program is running in a window

Function	How to do it
Copy the graphic image of the entire desktop to the clipboard	Press the Print Screen key.
Copy the graphic image of the current window to the clipboard	Press the Alt+Print Screen key combination.
Copy selected text or graphics to the clipboard	1. Issue the Edit command from the DOS application window's control menu. 2. Issue the Mark command from the Edit menu. 3. Drag the selection highlight over the data you want to copy. 4. Press the Enter key. Or, issue the Edit command from the Control menu; then, issue the Copy command.
Paste text from the clipboard	1. Position the insertion point where you want the data on the clipboard to be pasted. 2. Issue the Edit command from the window's control menu. 3. Issue the Paste command from the Edit menu.

Figure 10-7   How to copy and paste data in a DOS program when *Windows* is running in 386 enhanced mode

Part 1

Here, you can see that a DOS version of *Lotus 1-2-3* and the Write accessory are both running under *Windows*, and *Lotus 1-2-3* is the active program.

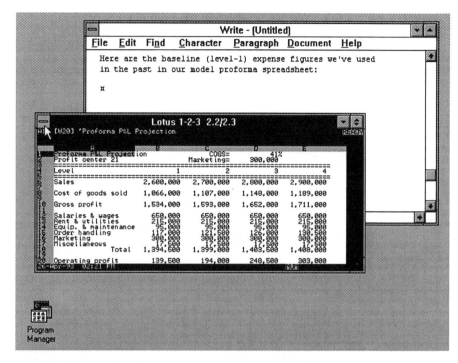

Part 2

To copy data from a DOS window, access the window's control menu. Then, issue the Edit command. Next, issue the Mark command.

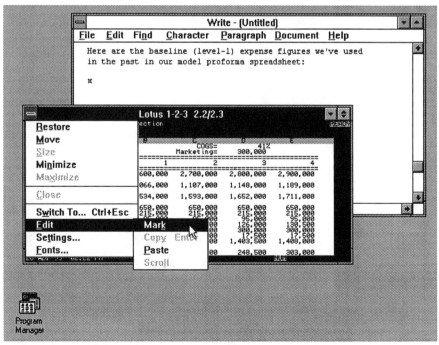

Figure 10-8 How to copy data from a DOS program and paste it into a *Windows* program in 386 enhanced mode

Part 3

Use the mouse to select data by dragging the highlight over it. After you mark the data, pull down the control menu.

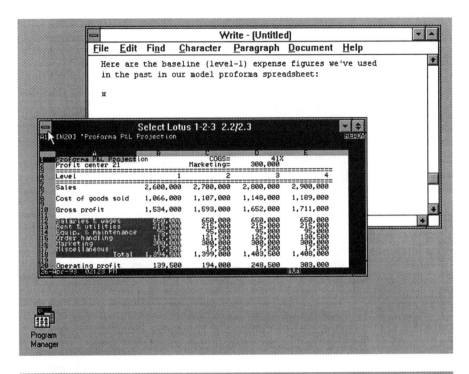

Part 4

From the control menu, issue the Edit command followed by the Copy command.

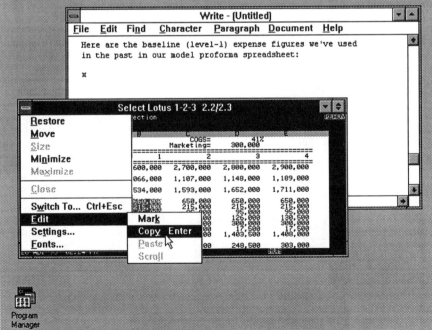

Figure 10-8   How to copy data from a DOS program and paste it into a *Windows* program in 386 enhanced mode (continued)

Part 5

Switch to the destination program and mark the insertion point. In a *Windows* application like Write, you can paste from the clipboard by issuing the Paste command from the Edit menu or using the Ctrl+V key combination.

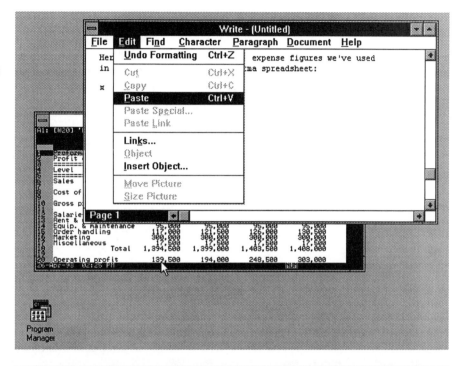

Part 6

This shows the selected *Lotus* data after it has been inserted into the Write document.

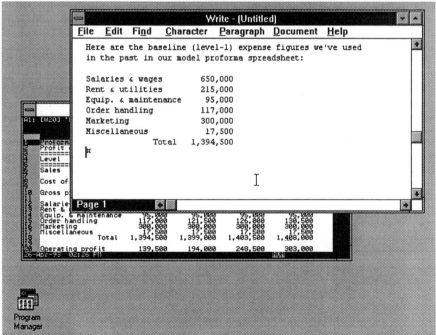

Figure 10-8   How to copy data from a DOS program and paste it into a *Windows* program in 386 enhanced mode (continued)

Because *Windows* recognizes most of the popular DOS programs, it's likely that it created PIFs and icons for all your DOS programs. However, if *Windows* didn't recognize a DOS program or if you install a DOS program after you install *Windows*, the PIF for a program may be missing. In that case, *Windows* still looks for the program's PIF when it starts the program. However, when *Windows* can't find the PIF for the program, it uses a PIF named _DEFAULT.PIF that's stored in the *Windows* directory. Often, the program may run the way you want it to when this default PIF is used. But if the program has any special system requirements, it may not run properly or it may not run at all. In that case, you need to create a PIF for it.

When you run a program from MS-DOS Prompt, *Windows* uses another PIF named DOSPRMPT.PIF. Because this PIF is general, though, your DOS program may not work the way you want it to. In that case, you need to create a PIF for it so you don't have to run it from MS-DOS Prompt.

When *Windows* recognizes the DOS program   The chances are good that *Windows* will recognize a DOS program that you want to create a PIF for. In fact, you start by assuming that it will. Then, you use the Windows Setup program to create the PIF for the program as illustrated in figure 10-9. Here, the DOS program is Symantec's *Q&A*, a popular database-management and report-generation program.

In part 1 of figure 10-9, you start the Windows Setup program from its icon in the Main program group. In part 2, you issue the Setup Applications command from the Options menu. Then, you work through a series of dialog boxes like those shown in part 3 to identify the program that you want to create the PIF for and the program group that you want its icon to be in. In part 4, you can see that the icon for the DOS program has been placed in the Applications program group.

In the first dialog box in figure 10-9, you tell the Windows Setup program whether you want it to search for all the DOS programs that don't have customized PIFs or whether you want to specify just one DOS program. If you select "Search for applications," the Windows Setup program prompts you for the drive and path you want to have searched. Then, it returns a list of all of the applications it found there and lets you select the ones you want to set up PIFs for. Because this technique involves work that's unnecessary if you're preparing a single PIF, you probably won't want to use it. But if you've added several DOS programs to your system since you set up *Windows* and you want to create PIFs for all of them, you probably will want to use this search technique.

When you want to set up a single program, you can enter its path and file name in the second dialog box shown in part 3 of figure 10-9. Because it's easy to make a mistake when you enter a complicated path and file name, though,

Part 1

Start the Windows
Setup program
from the Main
program group.

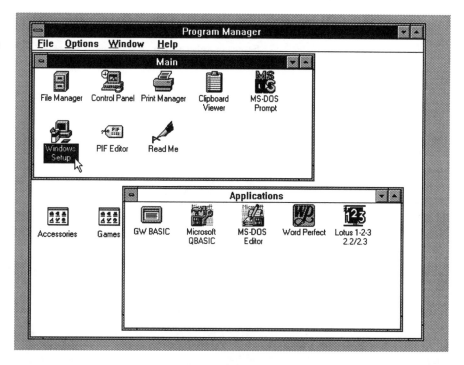

Part 2

Issue the Set Up
Applications
command from
the Options
menu.

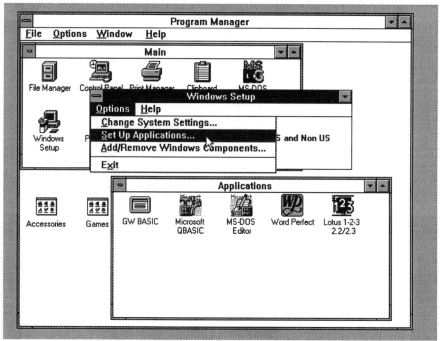

Figure 10-9   How to use the Windows Setup program to create a PIF for a DOS program that
Windows recognizes

Part 3

Reply to each Setup Applications dialog box that appears. When you know which file you want to create a PIF for, select the "Ask you to specify an application" option. If you select "Search for applications," the Setup program searches for all of the DOS programs that don't have a PIF.

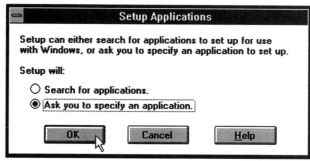

Click on the Browse command button to search for the DOS program file you want to create the PIF for.

In the resulting dialog box, build the path and file name for the program file (EXE or COM) or batch file (BAT).

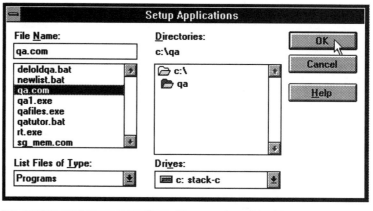

Confirm the command line in the Application Path and Filename box, and use the Add to Program Group box to select the program group that you want the icon for the program added to.

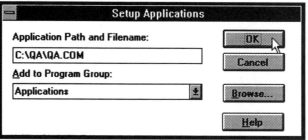

Figure 10-9   How to use the Windows Setup program to create a PIF for a DOS program that *Windows* recognizes (continued)

Part 4

If the procedure works, you can see the new icon in the group window in the Program Manager. Otherwise, the Setup program displays this message in a dialog box: "Setup can't set up this application."

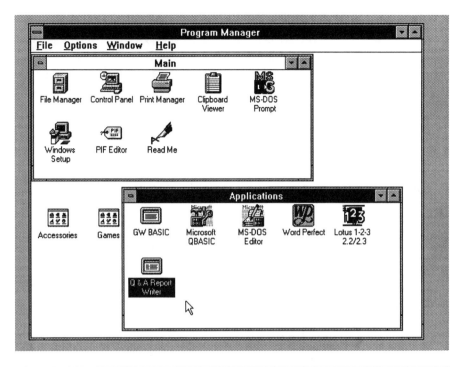

Figure 10-9   How to use the Windows Setup program to create a PIF for a DOS program that *Windows* recognizes (continued)

you may want to use the Browse command button and its resulting dialog box to build the file specification for the program as shown in the third dialog box in part 3. Once you've got the path and file name for the program right, you can use the Add to Program Group drop-down list box in the fourth dialog box in part 3 to specify the program group that you want the DOS program added to. Then, when you click on the OK button, the Windows Setup program creates a PIF for the program, stores it in the *Windows* directory, and adds the icon to the group you specified.

When *Windows* doesn't recognize the DOS program   If *Windows* doesn't recognize a DOS program when you try to create a PIF for it, the Windows Setup program displays a dialog box that says, "Setup can't set up this application...." Unfortunately, it doesn't display this message until the last step in the process that's illustrated in figure 10-9. Only then do you discover that you have to use the PIF Editor to create a PIF for the program.

Figure 10-10 illustrates the procedure for creating a PIF and icon for a popular DOS program named PKUNZIP.EXE. This program is a shareware application that lets you extract files from a compressed archive created by its companion program, PKZIP. It is typical of the type of DOS program that *Windows* doesn't recognize.

After you start the PIF Editor as shown in part 1 of 10-10, you get the screen shown in part 2. Here, the options are for a DOS program running in 386 enhanced mode, but the options in standard mode are similar, though fewer in number. If you want to see all of the options for both modes, you can refer to figure 10-11. In either mode, you can usually create a PIF that works properly by supplying information for just the first four options, and these options are the same for either mode.

In the Program Filename text box, you must supply the file name for the program you want to run. If the program doesn't reside in a directory that's on your system's path, you need enter a complete file specification for it. Most of the time, you specify a program file with the extension EXE or COM, but you can also specify a batch file with the extension BAT. As a result, you can use the same batch files that you used under DOS for starting your DOS programs under *Windows*. In this case, though, you need to make sure that the settings for the other PIF options are appropriate for the commands that the batch file executes.

In the Window Title text box, you can supply the title that you want to appear in the title bar of the application's window and under its minimized icon. This is an optional setting, though. If you don't specify a title, *Windows* uses the name of the program file that you specified in the Program Filename box.

In the Optional Parameters text box, you can supply up to 62 characters of parameters that specify how the DOS program should operate. These parameters are specific to the DOS program, not to *Windows*. If you don't usually use any parameters, you can leave this blank. Or, if you use different parameters each time you run the program, you can type a question mark (?) in this box, as shown in part 2 of figure 10-10. That directs *Windows* to prompt you with a dialog box for the parameters whenever you start the DOS program. For PKUNZIP, you supply a different archive file name on the command line each time you run the program, so this option is useful.

Finally, in the Start-up Directory text box, you can specify the directory that you want used as the current directory when *Windows* starts the DOS program. Because PKUNZIP doesn't require this option, the Start-Up Directory text box is empty in part 2 of figure 10-10.

Part 1

Start the PIF Editor
program from the
Main program
group.

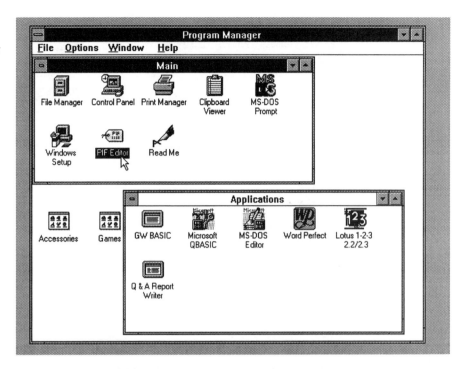

Part 2

Complete the
entries for the first
four text boxes.
Then, issue the
Save As command
from the File
menu.

Figure 10-10   How to use the PIF Editor program to create a PIF for a DOS program that *Windows*
doesn't recognize and how to create a program icon for the PIF

Part 3

In the resulting dialog box, enter a file name for the PIF. This should have the same name as the program file, but with PIF as the extension.

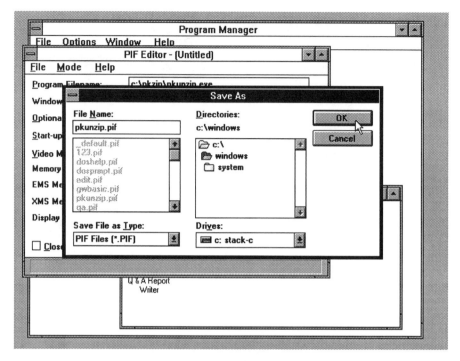

Part 4

To create a program icon for the new PIF, drag the icon for the PIF from the File Manager to the appropriate group window in the Program Manager.

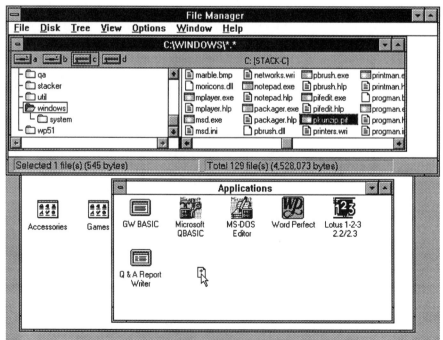

Figure 10-10   How to use the PIF Editor program to create a PIF for a DOS program that *Windows* doesn't recognize and how to create a program icon for the PIF (continued)

Part 5

When you release the mouse button, *Windows* creates the program icon.

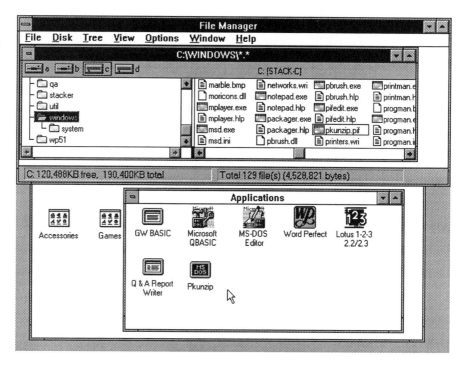

Figure 10-10   How to use the PIF Editor program to create a PIF for a DOS program that *Windows* doesn't recognize and how to create a program icon for the PIF (continued)

As you can see by studying figure 10-11, most of the other options for the PIF Editor are technical, so you shouldn't change them unless you know what you're doing. However, a few of the other options can be used by anyone. For instance, the Close Window on Exit check box determines whether the application window is closed when the DOS program ends. The Display Usage buttons determine whether the program starts on a full screen or in a window. And the Reserve Shortcut Keys check boxes let you reserve keys for use by your DOS program instead of *Windows*. If, for example, your DOS program uses the Alt+Enter key combination, you can reserve it by checking that box. Otherwise, this key combination will switch from full screen to a window or vice versa instead of doing what it's supposed to do in the application program.

In part 2 of figure 10-10, you can see that all of the other options are unchanged except for two. First, the Display Usage option is set to Windowed instead of Full Screen. That means the program will run in a window instead of a full-screen display. Second, the Close Window on Exit option is disabled so the window for the program will stay open when PKUNZIP ends. Because this program displays progress messages as it runs, the messages would disappear along with the application window if the window closed when the program finished. For most programs, though, you will want the window to close when the program ends.

After you set the necessary options, you use the Save As command under the File menu to save the PIF as shown in part 3 of figure 10-10. Since the default location for PIFs is in the *Windows* directory, that's where you should save yours.

At this point, the PIF has been created, but you still don't have a Program Manager icon for the program. To create one, just drag the icon for the new PIF from the File Manager to the right program group in the Program Manager as illustrated in part 4 of figure 10-10. The trick in doing that is arranging the File Manager and Program Manager windows so you can see the source and destination locations at the same time. In part 5 of figure 10-10, you see the icon that results from the drag operation.

Once you complete the procedure in figure 10-10, you can start PKUNZIP by double-clicking on this icon. Then, *Windows* retrieves its PIF, prompts you for the PKUNZIP parameters, and starts PKUNZIP in a window. When PKUNZIP ends, its window remains on the screen because the Close Window on Exit option is disabled. After you've finished reading the messages that PKUNZIP has put in the window, you can close the window by accessing its control menu and issuing the Close command.

How to modify a PIF

If you have problems with a DOS application under *Windows*, you may want to modify its PIF. To do that, you use the procedure in figure 10-12. First, you start the PIF Editor. Second, you retrieve the PIF that you want to change by issuing the Open command under the File menu. Third, you make the changes to the options that are shown in figure 10-11. Fourth, you issue either the Save or Save As command under the File menu to save your changes.

If you want to change one of the less technical options like reserving a shortcut key for your DOS program, you should be able to do so easily. To change one of the technical options, though, you need to be thoroughly familiar with the requirements of your DOS program, such as how much and what kind of memory it needs and how it interacts with the display and other devices. You also need to have a complete understanding of your PC's hardware configuration. For most PC users, that means you need to get technical help if one of your DOS programs isn't working right under *Windows*.

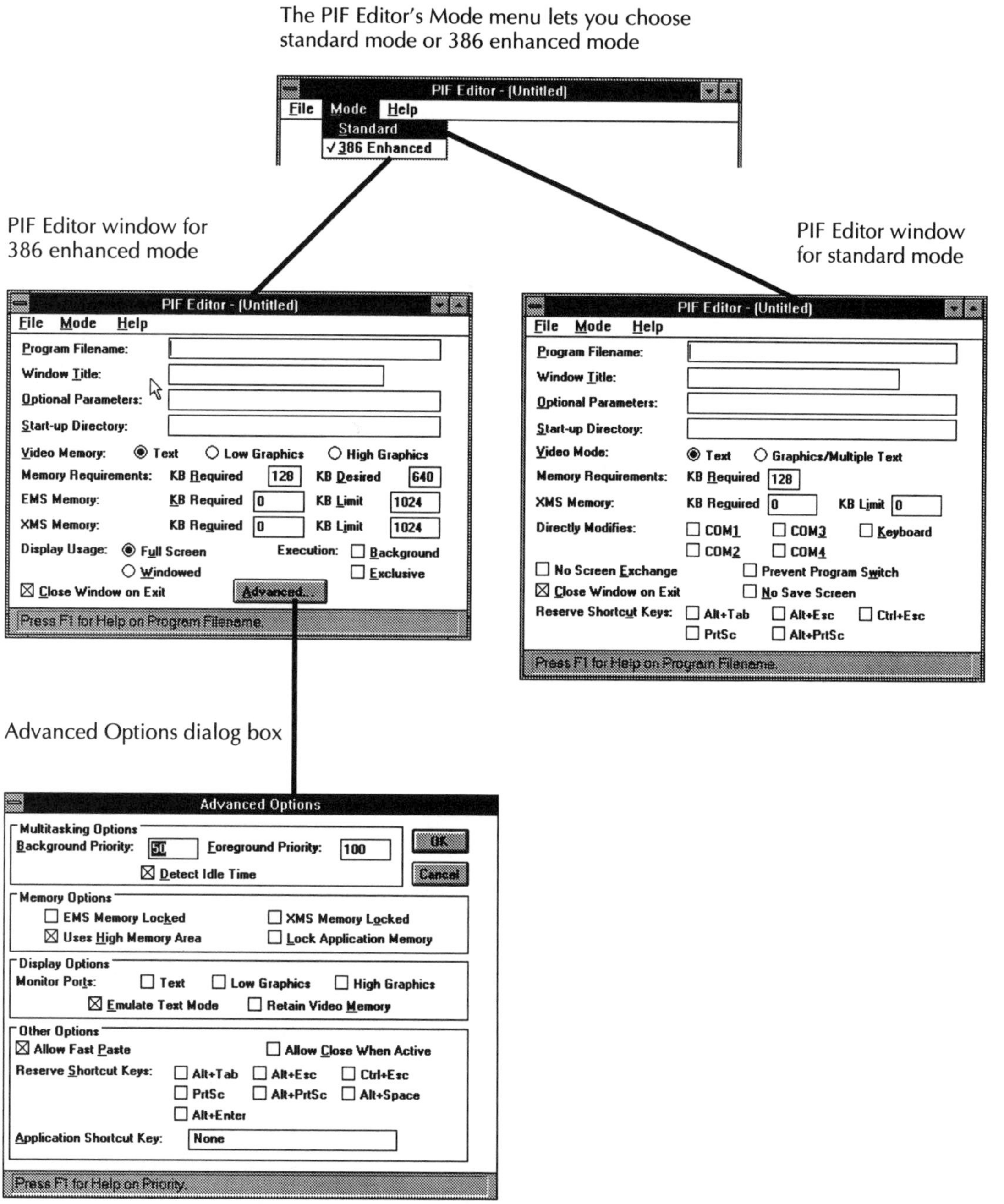

The PIF Editor's Mode menu lets you choose
standard mode or 386 enhanced mode

PIF Editor window for
386 enhanced mode

PIF Editor window
for standard mode

Advanced Options dialog box

Figure 10-11   The PIF options that are available for 386 enhanced mode are more extensive than
those for standard mode

1. Start the PIF Editor from the Main group.
2. Use the Open command in the File menu to open the PIF that you want to modify.
3. Make the changes to the options shown in figure 10-11.
4. Use the Save command to save the changes to the file.

Figure 10-12   How to modify a PIF

Perspective

Although it's reasonable to keep using your old DOS programs under *Windows*, it's just as sensible to learn how to use the *Windows* applications that replace them. Today, most PC software developers are focusing on *Windows* programs, while DOS products are on the "back burner." As a result, *Windows* programs are going to get better and better, while the improvements to DOS programs are going to come slowly. In addition, good *Windows* applications take advantage of all the features of the *Windows* environment, while even the best DOS applications can't.

Summary

- You can start a DOS program under *Windows* by using any of the techniques that you can use for starting *Windows* programs. You can also start a DOS program by using the MS-DOS Prompt program that's in the Main group. When *Windows* is installed, it creates icons for the DOS programs that it recognizes, so the easiest way to start a DOS program is to double-click on its icon.

- If your PC has a 286 processor, the program runs in *standard mode*. If your PC has a 386 processor or higher, it can run in *386 enhanced mode*. In this mode, a DOS program can run on a full screen or in a window.

- You can switch from a DOS program to another application by using any of the techniques for switching from a *Windows* program. Because DOS programs often run in full-screen display instead of in windows, Fast Alt+Tab Switching is one of the best ways to switch between programs.

- You end a DOS program under *Windows* just as you do when you're using it under DOS. Sometimes, though, its application window doesn't close. If you're at the DOS prompt, you can enter *exit* to close the window. If you're at a window, you can double-click on the window's control-menu box.

- You can use the clipboard to copy and paste data between DOS applications and between DOS and *Windows* applications. The techniques you use depend on whether you're operating in standard or 386 enhanced mode and whether or not you're operating in a window.

- *Windows* gets the information it needs for running a DOS program through a *Program Information File*, or *PIF*. When *Windows* is installed, it creates PIFs for common DOS programs that are already on your system. As a result, you probably won't have to set up your own PIFs.

- If you've installed a new DOS program since you installed *Windows* and you want to prepare a PIF for it, you can use the Windows Setup program to do so. For this to be successful, though, *Windows* must recognize the DOS program.

- If Windows Setup doesn't recognize your DOS application or if you want change an existing PIF, you need to use the PIF Editor. Its program icon is in the Main group.

Additional perspective

If you master all of the skills presented in the first ten chapters of this book, you will be able to use *Windows* with confidence and efficiency. However, there are other *Windows* programs and features that you ought to at least be aware of. The two chapters in this section present these programs and features, and you can read either chapter any time after you've finished section 2 of this book.

In chapter 11, you'll get a survey of the other programs that are included with *Windows*. These include programs in the Accessories group like Cardfile and Calculator; programs in the Main group like Clipboard Viewer; and the *Windows* utilities that come with DOS 6.0. For some programs, like the Write accessory, you'll get all the information you need for using the program.

Then, in chapter 12, you'll learn about the Object Linking and Embedding feature. This is an advanced *Windows* feature that offers much promise, but frequently doesn't work the way you want it to in this release of *Windows*.

Chapter 11

A survey of the other programs that come with *Windows*

The programs in the Accessories group
    Write
    Notepad
    Paintbrush
    Cardfile
    Terminal
    Recorder
    Clock
    Calendar
    Calculator
    Character Map
    Sound Recorder
    Media Player
    Object Packager

The other programs in the Main group
    Clipboard Viewer
    Windows Setup

The *Windows* utility programs that come with DOS 6.0
    Microsoft Anti-Virus
    Microsoft Backup
    Microsoft Undelete

Perspective
Summary

$\mathbf{Y}$ou'll be able to use *Windows* with confidence and efficiency if you master the skills presented in chapters 3 through 10. However, *Windows* comes with other programs that you may want to know about, even if you won't use them regularly. So, to give you a complete picture of the *Windows* package, this chapter introduces you to those programs.

First, this chapter introduces you to the 13 accessory programs that come with *Windows*. Of these, the one you're most likely to use is the Write accessory, so this chapter gives you the information you need for using it. Second, this chapter gives you information about the two programs in the Main group that haven't been covered completely in the other chapters in this book: Clipboard Viewer and Windows Setup. Last, this chapter introduces you to the three *Windows* utilities that come with DOS 6.0: Anti-Virus, Backup, and Undelete.

The programs in the Accessories group

Figure 11-1 shows all of the icons in the Accessories group of the Program Manager. Here, I've arranged them to reflect the likelihood that you'll want to use them. In this chapter, these programs are presented in the sequence shown in this figure.

All of these programs come with *Windows*. So if they meet your needs, it makes sense to use them instead of purchasing other programs that do the same things. As you will see, however, most of these programs have limitations that restrict their usefulness.

If an accessory does sound useful, the best way to learn more about it is through its Help information. After you've read this information, you'll find that most of the accessories are easy to understand and use.

Write   Because the Write accessory is a useful word processing program, it makes sense to use it if your word processing requirements are limited. If, for example, you work primarily with spreadsheets so you have only occasional word processing needs, Write may be just the program that you need. Because it is much simpler than a full-featured program like *Word* or *WordPerfect*, Write is an easy program to master. In fact, the next few pages present most of the information that you need for using Write, and you can pick up the rest with little trouble from its Help information.

Figure 11-2 presents the six functional menus of the Write accessory. You should already know how to use most of the commands of the File menu because they're presented in chapter 4. You should also know how to enter and

A simple word processing
program

Other accessory programs you
may want to use

Accessory programs for advanced
Windows features

Figure 11-1   The icons for the *Windows* 3.1 accessory programs

edit text using the techniques presented in chapter 4 including the use of the
Cut, Copy, and Paste commands in the Edit menu.

The only command under the File menu that may not be familiar to you is
the Repaginate command. You use it to insert *soft page breaks* into your
document to show where each page in the document ends based on the page
layout that you've used. These breaks are indicated by double-headed arrows
(>>) in the left margin of the document on the screen, but these marks aren't
printed. If you want to insert a *hard page break* that isn't affected by this
command into a document, you use the Ctrl+Enter keystroke combination.
This type of break is indicated on the screen as a row of dots that spans the width
of the window.

After the Cut, Copy, and Paste commands, the most useful command in the
Edit menu is the Undo Editing command because it lets you reverse the last
editing change that you made. In contrast, the Paste Special, Paste Link, Links,
Object, and Insert Object commands are related to the Object Linking and
Embedding feature that is presented in the next chapter, so you may never need
these commands. Similarly, if you use Write for processing text only, you
won't ever need the Move Picture or Size Picture commands.

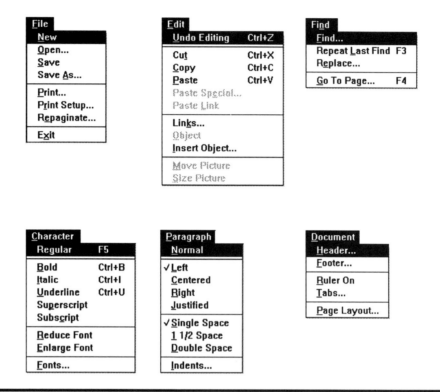

Figure 11-2   The menus for the Write accessory program

The commands in the Find menu let you find and replace strings of characters in a document. If, for example, you want to search an entire document for the word *Don* and replace each occurrence of it with the word *Donald*, that's easily done with the Replace command.

The commands in Character, Paragraph, and Document menus let you format characters, paragraphs, and the entire document. To start, you'll often want to use the Page Layout command of the Document menu to format the pages in a document. If the document is going to be more than one page long, you'll probably want to use the Header command to establish a heading that will print on each page of the document. And if the document is going to include tabular data, you may want to use the Tabs command to set tab stops. Then, as you enter a document, you can use the commands of the Paragraph and Character menus to give paragraphs and characters the proper formatting. Or, if you want to apply formatting after you've entered text, you can select the block of text that you want to format before you issue a command from the Paragraph or Character menu.

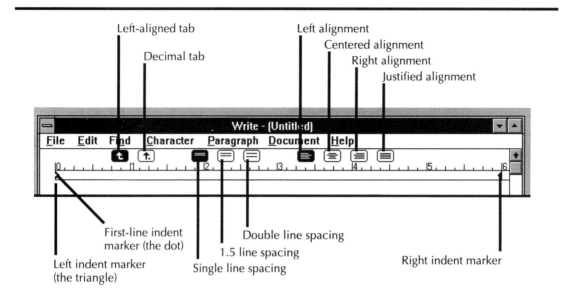

Figure 11-3   The ruler and its controls

To make it easier for you to do some of the formatting, Write provides a *ruler* that you can turn on by issuing the Ruler On command from the Document menu. This ruler is shown in figure 11-3. To use this ruler to set a tab stop, you click on the type of tab stop you want to set (left-aligned or decimal). Then, you point to the spot below the ruler that indicates where you want the tab stop and click again. This function is illustrated in figure 11-4.

To use the ruler for formatting, you first select the block of text that you want to format. Then, you can drag the left and right indent markers to change the margins for the block of text. You can drag the first-line indent marker to change the indentation for the first lines in the paragraphs in the block. You can click on one of the spacing icons to change the line spacing in the block. And you can click on one of the alignment icons to change the alignment of the text in the block. Because you can easily master these functions by experimenting with them, I won't illustrate them in this chapter.

With just this as background, you should be able to use the Write accessory for simple word processing jobs. But if you've ever used a full-featured word processing program, you'll quickly realize how limited Write is. One of its major limitations is that it doesn't include a spelling checker. But it also lacks a thesaurus, a macro feature, and even a way to insert the current date into a

Part 1

To set a tab stop, click on the appropriate tab control. Then, move the mouse to the position in the ruler for the tab stop and click. Here, a left aligned tab will be set at 1/4 inch from the left margin.

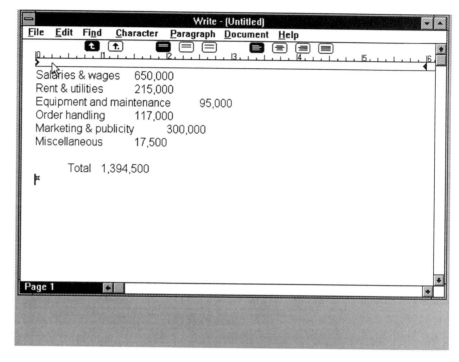

Part 2

Next, a decimal tab was added at 3 inches from the left margin. Write applies the tab setting to the document as soon as you click on the 3-inch mark.

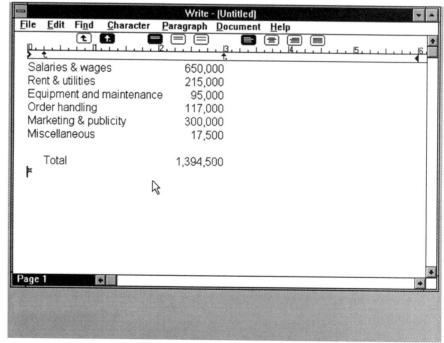

Figure 11-4   How to use the ruler to set tab stops

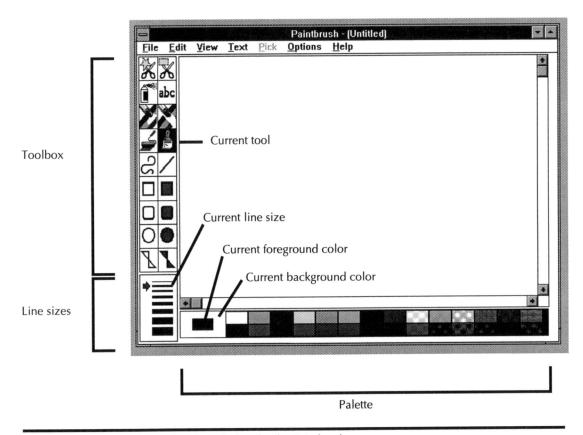

Figure 11-5   The application window for the Paintbrush accessory

document. Beyond that, it only lets you work on one document at a time. If you can live with these limitations, though, Write can be a useful program.

Notepad   The Notepad accessory program is a simple text editor (not a full-featured word processor) that you can use for editing *plain text files* (also known as *ASCII files*). These are files that have no formatting codes within them like the AUTOEXEC.BAT, CONFIG.SYS, and *Windows* initialization files. Because Notepad doesn't offer formatting, it can't damage files like these. In chapter 4, you've seen examples of how Notepad can be used for editing a text file so I won't illustrate it again in this chapter.

Paintbrush   Figure 11-5 shows the application window for Paintbrush. This program lets you create, edit, and save graphics files. Even though Paintbrush has seven menus with numerous commands, most of the work you

Scissors	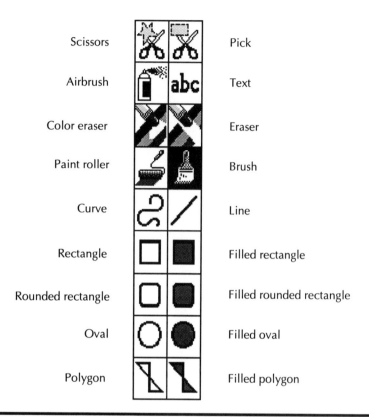	Pick
Airbrush		Text
Color eraser		Eraser
Paint roller		Brush
Curve		Line
Rectangle		Filled rectangle
Rounded rectangle		Filled rounded rectangle
Oval		Filled oval
Polygon		Filled polygon

Figure 11-6   The tools you use in Paintbrush

do with it involves the tools that are available in the *toolbox* on the left side of the window. To draw, you click on one of the tools to select it. If the tool lets you specify line thickness, you click on a line width in the line sizes section of the window. To select colors, you click on color tiles in the *palette* at the bottom of the window.

Most of the tools in the toolbox simulate drawing tools. The default tool is the brush. As you drag the brush across the workspace, Paintbrush leaves a trail of paint in the color you've selected. In contrast, the airbrush tool works like a can of spray paint: the longer you hold it over the same spot, the denser the coating of paint becomes. The paint roller lets you fill a closed area with the selected color. And the geometric tools, like the rectangle and oval, let you paint regular shapes as you drag the mouse pointer. If you make a mistake, the eraser lets you remove the paint that you put down with other tools. And if you want to move, copy, or delete a portion of an image, you can use the scissors and pick to make a selection.

Although Paintbrush can be an entertaining program if you haven't worked much with graphics programs, its usefulness is limited for several reasons. First, the kind of *bit-mapped* images you can create with Paintbrush aren't the sort of images you're likely to use in business documents. Second, the quality of these images when they're printed usually isn't acceptable because the resolution of the bit map isn't high enough. Third, if you try to overlay one part of an image with a new part, the new part replaces whatever it overlays. That limits what you can do with Paintbrush.

Because of those limitations, you'll probably want to use an *object-oriented graphics program* for serious graphics work. With this type of program, the images you draw are separate objects, so it's easy to select an object when you want to change its attributes, move it, copy it, or delete it. And these programs are designed so their images print with the highest resolution. In contrast to bit mapped programs like Paintbrush, which are usually called *painting programs*, object-oriented programs are usually called *drawing programs*. Some of the best are *CorelDRAW!*, Adobe *Illustrator*, Micrografx *Designer*, and Aldus *Freehand*. Even Microsoft *Word for Windows* comes with a basic object-oriented graphics program called Microsoft *Draw*.

Cardfile   The Cardfile accessory lets you store data that includes both text and pictures. As its name suggests, it simulates a file of index cards so you can create a Cardfile document for name and address information, sales leads, recipes, or any other kind of information that you can record manually on index cards. To illustrate, figure 11-7 shows a Cardfile window with data from a document that contains names and addresses. To bring a card to the top of the stack, you can click on a visible card, or you can use commands under the Search menu. Although Cardfile can be useful for simple file handling jobs, it is extremely limited when compared with a database program like *Access* or *Paradox*.

Terminal   The Terminal accessory lets you do telecommunications if your PC is equipped with a modem. With telecommunications, you can connect your PC to other PCs, *bulletin board systems* (*BBSes*), and commercial *information utilities* like CompuServe and Prodigy. To use Terminal, your PC has to have the right hardware, you need to understand telecommunications concepts, and you have to have another system to communicate with. If the other system is a commercial service, you also need to establish an account and arrange for billing.

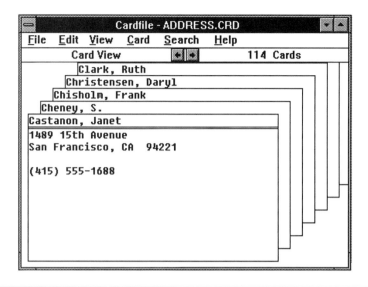

Figure 11-7   The application window for the Cardfile accessory with an open document

Figure 11-8 shows the Terminal window at the start of a telecommunications session. Here, Terminal has dialed the telephone number for another computer, and it's waiting to establish a connection. After the two computers establish the connection, you interact with the other system through Terminal's workspace where messages from the remote system appear and where you type commands to the remote system.

The Transfer menu includes commands that let you transfer files from one computer to another. You use the Send commands to move a file from your PC to the remote system (called *uploading* a file). You use the Receive commands to get a copy of a file that's available on the remote system (called *downloading* a file). Thousands of files (usually programs) are available for downloading from information utilities like CompuServe and from many BBSes, and many files are free or inexpensive. In addition, many software vendors make upgrades and bug fixes for their products available through telecommunications.

If you do telecommunications infrequently, Terminal may be the right program for your needs. But if you need a more advanced set of features than Terminal provides, you'll want to get a dedicated telecommunications program like *ProComm for Windows* or *Microphone II for Windows*.

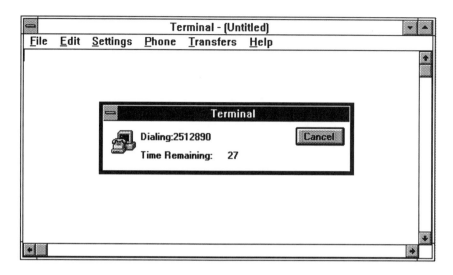

Figure 11-8   The application window for the Terminal accessory as the program attempts to establish a telecommunications connection

Recorder   The Recorder accessory program lets you create and use *Windows* macros. A *macro* is a recorded sequence of keystrokes or mouse actions that you can play back with a single key combination. The most practical use of macros is for inserting blocks of text that you type over and over again like address and signature blocks in word processing documents. You can also use macros to automate procedures that you perform repeatedly.

Because most application programs have their own macro capabilities, you probably won't ever need Recorder. Instead, you'll want to use the macro capabilities of your application programs. But if you think a *Windows* macro or two may come in handy, you should be aware from the start that you can't use Recorder macros in DOS programs. Also, once you create a macro, you can't make any changes to it short of deleting it and starting over.

When you record or play back a macro, the Recorder program must be active. Then, to record a macro, you issue the Record command from the Macro menu. When you do, a dialog box like the one in figure 11-9 appears. Here, you assign a name to the macro and specify the keyboard shortcut that will activate it. By default, Recorder creates a macro that will work only with the program that's active when you do the recording, but you can change that default so the macro will work with any *Windows* application. After you enter all of the information necessary to define the macro, you click on the Start button. At that

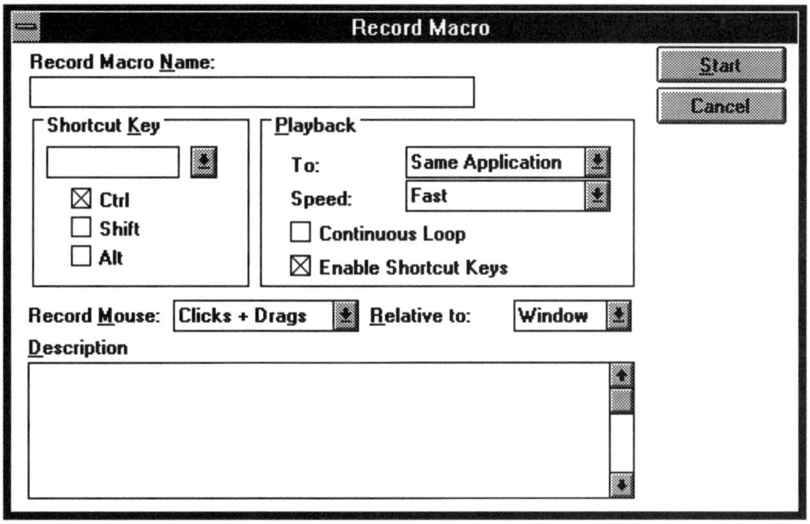

Figure 11-9   The Record Macro dialog box from the Recorder accessory

point, *Windows* automatically minimizes Recorder, but Recorder remains active and records the mouse actions you perform and the keystrokes you type. As it records, its minimized icon flashes at the bottom of the desktop. When you finish with the actions you want to record, you double-click on the Recorder icon, and Recorder displays a dialog box that lets you save the macro, continue recording, or cancel the operation.

After you create a macro file, you can create a program icon for it in the Program Manager's StartUp group. Then, when *Windows* starts, it automatically starts Recorder and opens your macro file. As a result, the macros in the file will be available to you immediately. Whenever you want to use one, you can press its shortcut keys.

Clock   In chapter 3, you've seen examples of the Clock accessory program so I won't illustrate it in this chapter. You can use the commands in its Setting menu to display the clock in either analog or digital form, to change the font the Clock uses in digital view, to specify whether the date appears, and to specify whether seconds appear. However, you don't use the Clock accessory to set the date or time. To do that, you must use the Date/Time option of the Control Panel in the Main program group.

Calendar   As you can see in figure 11-10, the Calendar program simulates an appointment book that lets you record information about your schedule. To switch from day view to month view, you can issue the Month command from the View menu or double-click on the text line that shows the date above the time entries. In month view, the current date is highlighted. If you want to see more detail for a specific day, you can double-click on it in the calendar to jump directly to it in day view.

In day view, you can make entries for appointments at specific hours. By default, Calendar shows information for each day divided into one-hour intervals between 7 a.m. and 8 p.m. However, you can use the Options menu to change the starting time and the interval. To record an appointment, you just click on a time and type a description of the appointment. If you want to attach an alarm to an appointment, you can click on the time and issue the Set command under the Alarm menu. If you want the alarm to sound before the appointment time, you can specify an interval of up to 10 minutes with the Options command under the Alarm menu. To save your entries, you must issue the Save or Save As command under Calendar's File menu.

If you always work at your desk, you may find the Calendar accessory useful. But otherwise, an appointment book is likely to be more useful than the Calendar program. If you start recording information about appointments in both your appointment book and Calendar, you not only have to do double work, but you risk getting the two out of sync. Then, you won't be able to depend on either.

Calculator   Figure 11-11 shows the two views Calculator offers. The standard view, which is the default view, offers the basic functions most people use. The scientific view offers statistical, logarithmic, trigonometric, and logical operations. To switch to this view, you can use the View menu. To make entries into the calculator, you can click on the keys you would press if you were using a real calculator. For basic operations, though, it's easier to use the numeric keypad on your keyboard.

Character Map   You may be surprised to learn that most *Windows* fonts offer many characters other than the familiar letters, numbers, and special characters that appear on the keys of your keyboard. To see the complete character set for a font and to find out how to access any of its characters, you can use the Character Map accessory program.

Figure 11-12 shows you examples of the character sets for two TrueType fonts. The first example shows the Arial font; the second shows Wingdings. To select a font, you use the drop-list box in the upper left corner of the window.

Day view

Month view

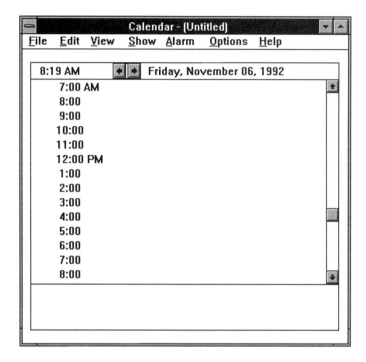

Figure 11-10   The application window for the Calendar accessory in day and month view

Standard view

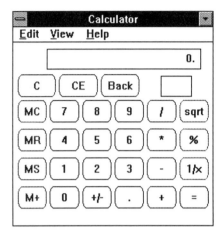

Scientific view

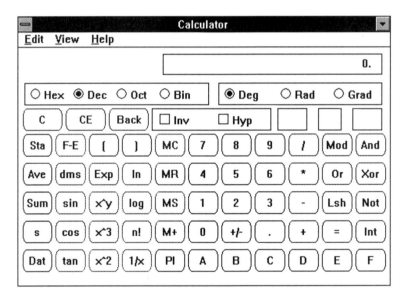

Figure 11-11   The application window for the Calculator accessory in standard and scientific view

Then, you can click on any of the characters in the font to see what keystroke combination you need to type if you want to insert the special character into your document. This keystroke combination is displayed at the lower right corner of the window. To insert the bullet character in Arial, for example, you use Alt+0149. This means you hold down the Alt key while you use the numeric keypad to enter the number. To insert a bullet when you're working with the symbol font Wingdings, you simply type the letter *l*.

To type a bullet character in the Arial font, hold down the Alt key and type *0149* on the numeric pad

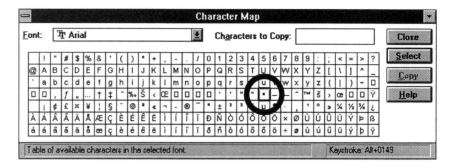

To type a bullet character in the Wingdings font, type the letter *l*

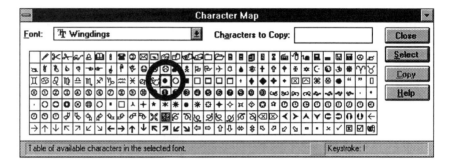

Figure 11-12   How to use the Character Map accessory to access special characters in your fonts

The Character Map program makes it easy for you to use characters that have difficult codes like the bullet character in Arial because it lets you copy one or more characters to the clipboard. Then, you can use the clipboard to paste them into your document. To use this feature, you click first on the special character, then on the Select command button. This adds the marked character to the Characters to Copy text box. To add more characters to the string, you can repeat this process. When you're ready to copy your selection to the clipboard, you highlight your selection in the Characters to Copy text box and click on the Copy command button. Then, you can switch to your application program and paste them into place without having to remember the key combinations for the special characters.

Sound Recorder   The Sound Recorder accessory lets you take advantage of the *multimedia extensions* that are part of *Windows* 3.1. As you can tell from figure 11-13, the Sound Recorder window simulates a tape recorder. It lets you record and save digitized sounds in *waveform* files. Then, it lets you play them back through a set of headphones or external speakers.

Figure 11-13   The application window for the Sound Recorder accessory

Unfortunately, the Sound Recorder is useful only if your PC is equipped with a special sound card like *SoundBlaster* or the Microsoft *Sound System for Windows*. Today, few PCs have these cards. Moreover, most users who have PCs with sound cards use sound for games and entertainment, not for business applications. In fact, except for special applications like training or presentation, the business value of sound is questionable. In addition, waveform files use large amounts of disk space. Even a relatively low-quality recording, comparable to AM-radio sound, requires about 1MB of disk space for a minute of sound. For these reasons, many businesses are reluctant to use audio as part of their daily applications.

Even so, sound can add a dimension to applications that makes them seem to come alive. That's why many software publishers are working to integrate sound capabilities into their programs. For example, the Microsoft *Sound System for Windows* includes a component that can "read aloud" the contents of a spreadsheet to make it easier to proofread. In five years, you may find that nearly all new PCs support sound.

Media Player   The Media Player accessory lets you play back *MIDI* (*Musical Instrument Digital Interface*) files or other files that follow the *MCI* (*Media Control Interface*) standard. Most CD-ROM drives, many of which can play music CDs, follow the MCI standard. However, because Media Player requires hardware that few PCs have and, more importantly, because it offers features with limited practical application even if you have the required hardware, you probably won't want to use this program.

Object Packager   The Object Packager accessory lets you prepare icons that represent data from one program that you can embed in a document created with another program. Figure 11-14 shows an example of its application

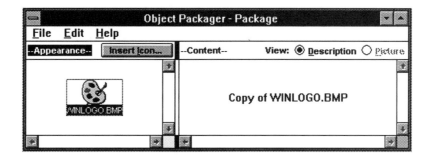

Figure 11-14   The application window for the Object Packager accessory

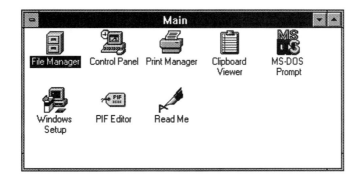

Figure 11-15   The icons for the Main program group

window. The Object Packager is one component of the *Windows* feature that's known as *Object Linking and Embedding*, or *OLE*. To learn about OLE and the Object Packager accessory, please read the next chapter.

The other programs in the Main group

The Main program group of the Program Manager is shown in figure 11-15. With just two exceptions, these programs are presented in detail in other chapters in this book as summarized by figure 11-16. The exceptions are the Clipboard Viewer and Windows Setup accessories.

Clipboard Viewer   The Clipboard Viewer lets you view the current contents of the clipboard, save the contents of the clipboard to a file with the extension CLP, or retrieve the contents of a CLP file back onto the clipboard.

File Manager	Chapters 5 and 7
Control Panel	Chapter 9
Print Manager	Chapter 8
Clipboard Viewer	Chapter 11
MS-DOS Prompt	Chapter 10
Windows Setup	Chapters 10 and 11
PIF Editor	Chapter 10
Read Me	Chapter 6

Figure 11-16   Where you can find more information about the programs in the Main group

Its application window is illustrated in figure 11-17. In this example, the clipboard contains a graphic that shows an outline map of the state of California.

Normally, though, you don't need the Clipboard Viewer because you can remember what you last put on the clipboard. And if you can't remember, it probably doesn't matter what's there. Beyond that, you usually don't need to save or retrieve data with CLP files because you can do so more efficiently by using the functions of your application programs.

Windows Setup   The Windows Setup accessory lets you configure *Windows* for your PC. Normally, you don't need to use this program because the installation program automatically configures *Windows* to work with your system's hardware. In case you do need to change a setting, though, figure 11-18 shows the application window for Windows Setup, and figure 11-19 shows its Options menu and the resulting dialog boxes,

If you install new hardware on your PC, you can use the Change System Settings dialog box to tell *Windows* about the changes. When you request a change to your system's setup, you may need to provide a diskette that contains the correct device driver for the new piece of hardware. This may be one of your original *Windows* installation diskettes or a diskette supplied by the hardware manufacturer.

If you've read chapter 10, you're already familiar with the Setup Applications dialog box. You can use this dialog box to create a Program Information File (PIF) for a DOS application. The only time you're likely to need to do this is if you install a new DOS program after *Windows* is already running on your PC.

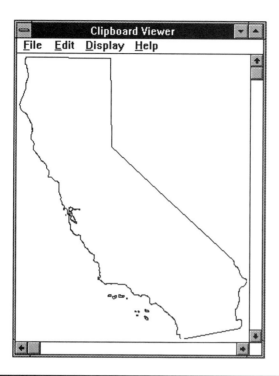

Figure 11-17   The application window for the Clipboard Viewer program

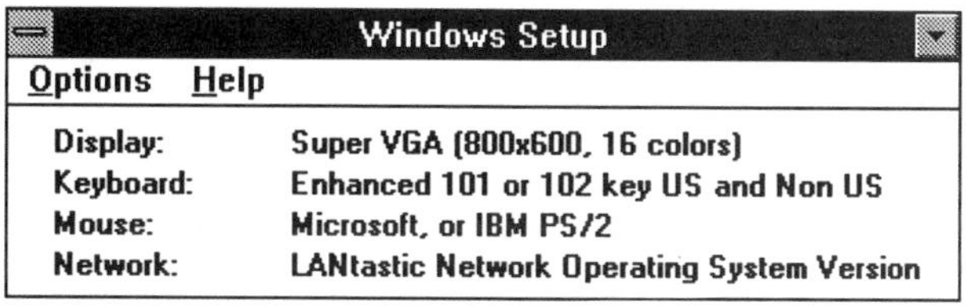

Figure 11-18   The application window for the Windows Setup program

The last dialog box in figure 11-19 is for the Add/Remove Windows Components command. It tells you what *Windows* components are on your hard drive and how much disk space each one takes. Then, if your hard drive is nearly full, you can select the components you don't use and delete them. If,

The Options menu of the Windows Setup program

The first three commands lead to dialog boxes that prompt you for more information

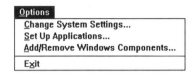

Change Systems Settings

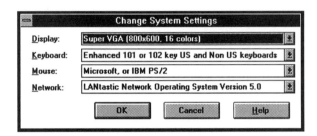

Setup Applications

Add/Remove Windows Components

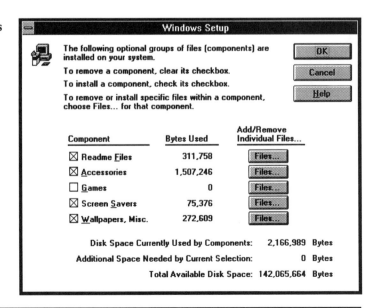

Figure 11-19   The dialog boxes from the Options menu of the Windows Setup program

Figure 11-20 The icons for the Microsoft Tools program group

for example, you don't use the accessory programs, you can reclaim about 1.5MB of disk space by deleting them. Normally, though, the disk space that you recover is relatively small so it's probably not worth deleting a component that someone else may want to use later on.

The *Windows* utility programs that come with DOS 6.0

When Microsoft introduced DOS 6.0, it included three new utility programs that work in *Windows*: Microsoft Anti-Virus, Microsoft Backup, and Microsoft Undelete. When you install these programs, they appear in a new program group called Microsoft Tools, as shown in figure 11-20.

Microsoft Anti-Virus A computer *virus* is a program that can secretly "infect" a computer system, then lie in wait for a specific event to occur or for a specific date to come around. At that time, the virus does something. What it does can be as benign as displaying an amusing message or as serious as destroying the data on your hard drive. To make matters worse, a virus's action can be completely covert. In other words, a virus can damage your system without you knowing that it's doing so.

Viruses can be spread in several different ways. One way is through infected diskettes. Another is through network use. So unless your PC is completely isolated from other systems, it's at some risk of being infected. To make sure that it isn't, you can use the Microsoft Anti-Virus program to scan your hard disk and diskettes for viruses and remove them.

Figure 11-21 shows the window for the Anti-Virus utility along with its Options dialog box. After you select the drive you want scanned, the program examines the disk according to the options you specified. The Prompt While Detect option directs the program to display a dialog box when it finds a suspicious file. Then, it asks you whether to: (1) ignore the file, (2) delete the file with the standard DOS delete, or (3) "wipe" the file. When you wipe a file, it's deleted and the disk areas where it resided are overwritten to obliterate any trace of it.

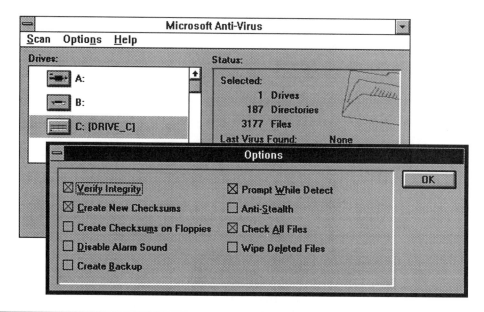

Figure 11-21   The application window for the Microsoft Anti-Virus program and its Options dialog box

Although Anti-Virus does a good job of clearing your system of viruses. it doesn't prevent a virus from infecting your system to begin with. To do that, you need to use another program that comes with DOS 6.0 called VSAFE. This program constantly monitors your system for signs of virus infection and displays a warning message at the first sign of virus activity. However, because this is a DOS program, not a *Windows* program, it is covered in detail in our DOS book, *The Only DOS Book You'll Ever Need*.

Microsoft Backup   Computers fail sometimes, and so do people. When a hard drive fails, you can lose all of the data on it. When you fail, you can accidentally delete important files or directories or mistakenly overwrite important files with information you didn't intend to. Because mechanical and human failures do happen, you need to be able to turn to a backup of your system's data to restore lost files.

One of the major additions to DOS 6.0 is Microsoft Backup, a full-function backup program that replaces the DOS Backup command. Figure 11-22 shows the application window for this program. This figure shows the controls that let you select the source and destination drives for a backup, the files you want to back up, and the type of backup you want to perform (full, incremental, or

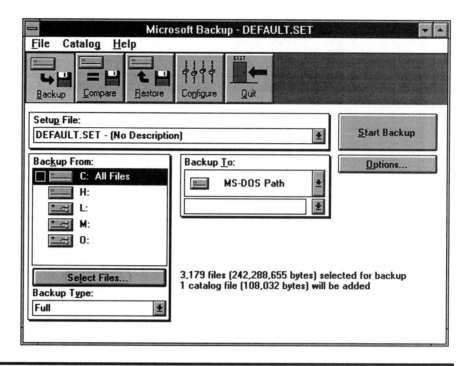

Figure 11-22   The application window for the Microsoft Backup program

differential). As you perform a backup, the program displays a dialog box that reports on the progress of the backup. The program also prompts you for the next diskette or tape that's needed.

The control buttons at the top of the window let you select other program functions. The Compare function verifies a backup by comparing the files on the backup media to the originals on disk. Although this function can give you extra peace of mind, it's rarely necessary, and it doubles the amount of time it takes to complete a backup. So this is a function that you may want to run occasionally, but not for each backup. In contrast, the Restore function lets you recover some or all of the files from a backup. This is the function you'll use at that critical time in the future when you need your backup to restore lost files.

Microsoft Undelete   When you delete a file, DOS doesn't erase it. Instead, DOS changes the directory entry for the file to show that the file is deleted. Then, DOS makes the disk space where the file resides available for new files. As a result, the contents of the file actually remain on the disk until DOS writes the contents of a new file over them.

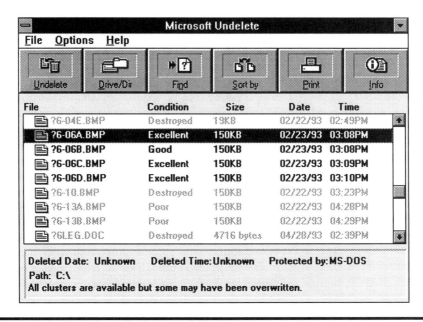

Figure 11-23   The application window for the Microsoft Undelete program

The Undelete utility lets you take advantage of this process to recover deleted files. Figure 11-23 shows its application window. Here, you can navigate through your PC's directory structure and look at entries for files that have been deleted. Then, you can select the ones you want to restore and click on the Undelete command button to recover them.

As you can see from the entries in the Condition column in figure 11-23, some of the files in the selected directory can be recovered completely, others partially, and some not at all. If you try to recover a file immediately after it has been deleted, the chances for success are excellent. But the longer you wait, the more likely it is that the file will be overwritten in whole or in part. Once that happens, the file is damaged, and it loses its value to you.

Perspective

Because the first releases of *Windows* were limited, special applications that ran under it seemed necessary to make *Windows* marketable. As a result, Microsoft included the Accessories programs with each sale of *Windows*. These programs also helped *Windows* compete against Apple and its *Macintosh* computer, which was introduced about a year and a half before the first release of *Windows*. The Macintosh came with a set of simple applications including word processing and painting programs called MacWrite and MacPaint. It also included a suite of what Apple called "desk accessories" that look surprisingly like the *Windows* accessories.

Today, the *Windows* accessories have more historical interest than practical application. In fact, unless you find that some of them meet your needs especially well, you can delete them from the *Windows* directory and remove their program icons from the Program Manager. In contrast, the *Windows* versions of the DOS 6.0 utilities are genuinely useful programs. If you don't already have programs like them on your system, Anti-Virus, Backup, and Undelete by themselves are worth the price of the upgrade to MS-DOS 6.0.

If you want to learn more about DOS 6.0, *The Only DOS Book You'll Ever Need* presents the Anti-Virus, Backup, and Undelete utilities in detail. It also presents complete coverage of all the other utilities and features that come with DOS 6.0. You can find ordering information at the end of this book.

Summary

- The Accessories group includes 13 programs. Write is useful if you need a simple word processor, and Notepad is useful whenever you need to edit *plain text files* like the initialization files for *Windows*.

- Other programs in the Accessories group that you may want to use include: Cardfile for simple data management jobs; Terminal for limited telecommunications; Recorder for creating and using *Windows macros*; Clock to display the date and time; Calendar for recording information about your schedule; Calculator for standard and scientific calculations; and Character Map to provide access to all of the characters that make up a font.

- The Main program group includes icons for two programs that you're not likely to use often: Clipboard Viewer for viewing, saving, and retrieving clipboard data; and Windows Setup for configuring *Windows* so it works properly with your hardware.

- MS-DOS 6.0 includes three utility programs for *Windows*: Microsoft Anti-Virus, Backup, and Undelete. Their program icons appear in a program group called Microsoft Tools.

Chapter 12

Object Linking and Embedding

How OLE works
    An example of an embedded object
    An example of a linked object

Features related to OLE
    Dynamic Data Exchange
    The Object Packager

Perspective
Summary

You're already familiar with the clipboard as a mechanism that lets programs pass data back and forth. Frankly, for most of the work you'll do, the clipboard is what you'll use to let programs work together. However, *Windows* 3.1 supports a more sophisticated mechanism called *Object Linking and Embedding*, or just *OLE* (pronounced *oh-lay*).

OLE can be a confusing subject. Probably the best way to understand it is to see examples of how it works. So to start, I'll show you examples of how you embed an object and how you link an object. Then, I'll present other features of *Windows* 3.1 that are related to OLE: Dynamic Data Exchange (DDE) and the Object Packager accessory program.

After you've finished this chapter, you'll understand OLE well enough to take advantage of it in your OLE-capable application programs. However, you'll have to learn the specific details of how to use OLE in each program from its documentation or its on-line help. That's because OLE is implemented in different ways in different programs. As a result, the consistency you expect for *Windows* functions like using the clipboard, editing text, and managing files just isn't there for OLE.

How OLE works

The purpose of OLE is to enable programs to work together in a way that's tightly integrated. It does that by letting you embed or link an *object* created in one program, the *server application*, into another document, the *destination document,* that's created in a *client application*. An object might be a block of text from a word processing program, a chart from a spreadsheet program, a sound, a graphic from a drawing program, or something else. You can access the object with the server application directly through the client application.

The difference between an *embedded object* and a *linked object* is subtle. When you embed an object in a destination document, the object becomes a part of the destination document although it still maintains a relationship with the program that created it. In contrast, when you link an object to a destination document, the object doesn't become a part of the destination document. Instead, it exists as a separate file that you can access independently of the client application.

If, for example, you embed a graphic that requires 100KB of storage in a word processing document that requires 20KB, the size of the word processing document will jump to 120KB because the graphic becomes part of the word processing document. When you embed an object in a client document, you can be sure that the object will always be available when you access the client document. In contrast, if you link the two files, the size of the word processing document increases only a small amount because the graphic remains in a file separate from the word processing document. In this case, you see some representation of the linked document in the word processing document, but the relationship between the two documents is in the form of a pointer that connects them.

Not all *Windows* programs support OLE. And those that do vary in their capabilities and the OLE-related commands they include. Some applications can participate in an OLE relationship only as a server, others can participate only as a client, and still others can participate as both. Among the accessory programs that come with *Windows*, four are OLE-capable. Write and Cardfile can be OLE clients, and Paintbrush and Sound Recorder can be OLE servers. However, none of the accessories can be both a client and a server.

A good example of an OLE-capable application is Microsoft *Word for Windows*. It can accept objects from other OLE-capable server programs, and it can work as a server. In addition, it comes with simple OLE server applications that provide special functions. One of these servers is a charting program (Chart), another is an object-oriented graphics program (Draw), and a third is an application that lets you create complicated formulas (Equation Editor).

An example of an embedded object   Figure 12-1 illustrates how embedding an object works with *Word for Windows* and the Equation Editor. Part 1 shows a *Word* document that contains a financial formula. Here, the formula was created not with *Word for Windows* itself, but with Equation Editor. As you can see, the characters that make up the formula are arranged in a way that even a powerful word processing like *Word for Windows* can't do easily, if at all.

To add an Equation Editor formula like the one in part 1 to a document, you issue the Object command from *Word*'s Insert menu. Then, you select Equation from the list of possible object types that appears in a dialog box the program displays. At that point, *Word for Windows* starts Equation Editor in a new application window.

In this example, the formula is already in place, but it contains an error. The exponent should be *kn* instead of *in*. If the formula had been created in a program that didn't support OLE and the clipboard was used to insert the formula, fixing the mistake would require several steps First, you'd probably cut the formula from the *Word for Windows* document. Then, you'd have to leave *Word,* start the server application, paste the formula back into that program, fix the formula, select it, copy it, and return to *Word for Windows*. Then, you would have to paste the corrected formula back in its original position.

But in this example, the error is easy to fix because the formula is an Equation Editor object. To access an embedded object in *Word for Windows*,

Part 1

The formula in this destination document is actually an embedded object that was created with Microsoft's Equation Editor, the server application.

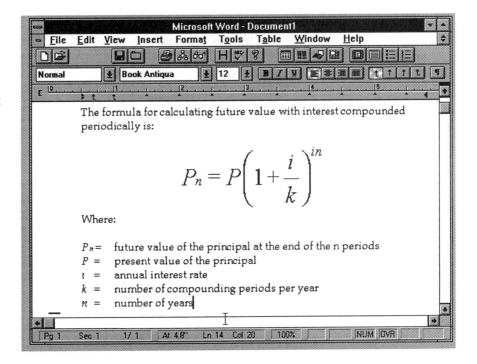

Part 2

You can access an embedded object to edit it. When you click on the object in *Word*, a selection rectangle appears around it. Then, you can open the object for editing through the Edit menu.

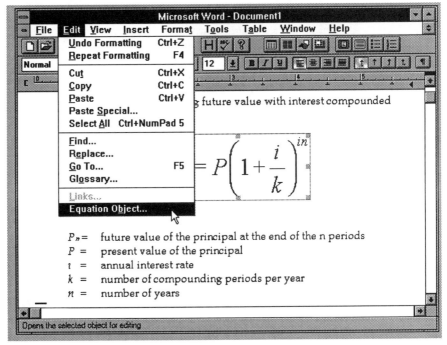

Figure 12-1 *Word for Windows* uses OLE to provide equation-editing capabilities

Part 3

Now, the Equation Editor program is running. Notice that the data from the embedded object automatically appeared in its workspace.

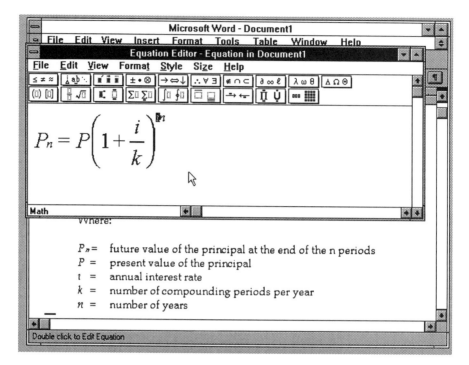

Part 4

After you make a change to an embedded object, issue the appropriate command to save your work and return to the destination document in the client program.

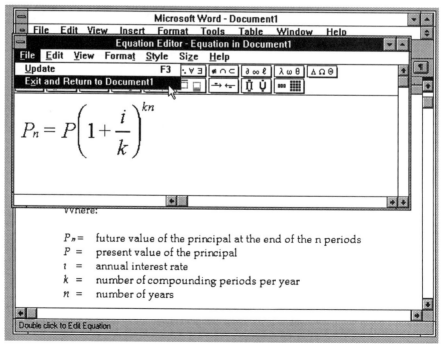

Figure 12-1   *Word for Windows* uses OLE to provide equation-editing capabilities (continued)

Part 5

The embedded object in the destination document was updated automatically.

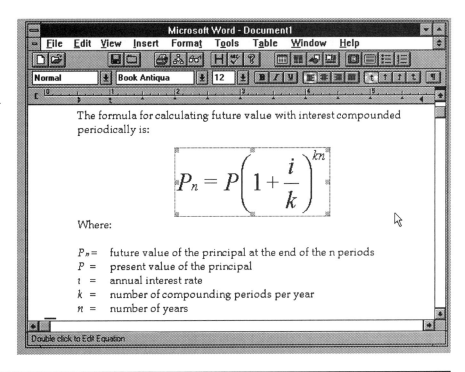

The formula for calculating future value with interest compounded periodically is:

$$P_n = P\left(1 + \frac{i}{k}\right)^{kn}$$

Where:

$P_n =$ future value of the principal at the end of the n periods
$P\ =$ present value of the principal
$i\ =$ annual interest rate
$k\ =$ number of compounding periods per year
$n\ =$ number of years

Double click to Edit Equation

Figure 12-1   *Word for Windows* uses OLE to provide equation-editing capabilities (continued)

you click on it to select it. Then, you open it with its server program. In part 2 of figure 12-1, you can tell that the formula is selected because it's surrounded by a rectangle that has "handles" on each corner. To open the object, you select Equation Object under the Edit menu, as shown in part 2. Part 3 shows the result. Here, you can see that the application window for the Equation Editor is open, and the formula is in its workspace. You can also see that the incorrect character in the exponent has been selected, and it's about to be edited. After the correction is complete, you save the change by issuing the Exit and Return to Document command, as shown in part 4. Part 5 shows that the embedded formula in the *Word for Windows* document was updated as soon as the correction was saved in the server application.

Not every OLE application handles embedded data in the same way. In this *Word for Windows* example, the OLE data appeared almost as if it had been created in *Word for Windows* to begin with. In contrast, some embedded objects show up in a destination document as icons. Then, you can double-click on the icon to access the object. If, for example, you embed a Sound Recorder source document in a Write document, an icon appears that represents the sound. Then, you can double-click on the icon to invoke Sound Recorder to play the sound. If you want to attach voice annotations to text documents, you can use this technique.

An example of a linked object   Embedded objects can use up large amounts of disk storage because multiple copies of the object are present on your system. In contrast, when you *link* an object into a destination document, the object remains in its original file created by the server application. Nevertheless, you can still access the server program that created the linked object from the destination document. When you access it, though, the object you're working with is the original source file, not an embedded copy of the original. Then, when you change the source file, the linked object can be automatically updated.

Different programs support linking in different ways. Microsoft *Excel*'s charting feature offers an excellent example of linking. *Excel* lets you create and save a linked chart file that's based on the contents of a spreadsheet file. In this case, *Excel* works as both a server (for the data from the spreadsheet) and as a client (when it works with the chart).

Figure 12-2 shows an example of this. Here, two document windows are open in *Excel*'s application window. The active document window contains a chart named PROFIT.XLC. It's based on data from the spreadsheet named PROFORMA.WK1 that's in the second document window. If you look closely, you can see that the values on the chart are from rows 6 and 26 in the spreadsheet. When you change the data in the spreadsheet, *Excel* updates the chart automatically.

Figure 12-3 extends the example in figure 12-2. It shows you how to link an *Excel* chart to a Write document. In part 1, the entire chart has been selected, and it's about to be copied to the clipboard. Because *Excel* can work as an OLE server, all of the information required to build a link to the chart is available on the clipboard. After you copy the data you want to link to the clipboard, you switch to the client application, Write.

Part 2 of figure 12-3 shows the Write window. To insert a link, you can issue the Paste Link command from the Edit menu. You can also use Paste Special, but Paste Link is more direct. In part 3, you can see the Write document after the link is in place.

If changes are made to a source document, like the chart in figure 12-3, the destination documents that are linked to it are affected too. *Windows* keeps track of the links, and the next time you open a destination document that contains a link to a changed object, *Windows* prompts you with a dialog box like the one in figure 12-4. Here, you specify whether you want to update the link.

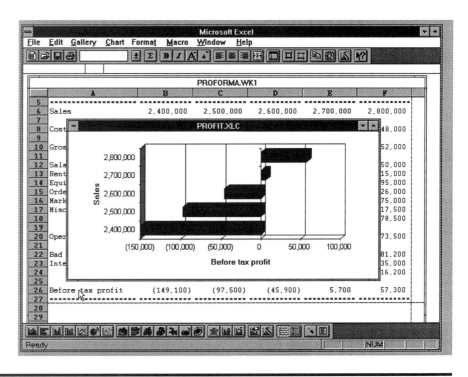

Figure 12-2   *Excel* uses linking to relate a chart to a source spreadsheet

Features related to OLE

As you read about OLE, you may come across two related features of *Windows* 3.1: Dynamic Data Exchange and the Object Packager accessory program. Although both are of limited importance, you may be interested in what they do.

Dynamic Data Exchange   Even though Microsoft introduced OLE with *Windows* 3.1, OLE isn't entirely new. Linking capabilities have been a part of *Windows* since version 2.0. That version of *Windows* introduced a feature called *Dynamic Data Exchange*, or *DDE*, that lets users work with links. DDE is more cumbersome to use than OLE because you have to use cryptic codes in the destination document to define the link.

DDE is still in a part of *Windows*. In fact, OLE is built around DDE. However, Microsoft downplays DDE. It calls OLE a superset of DDE, and it doesn't even include DDE in the index of its primary *Windows* 3.1 manual. As a result, you can forget about DDE and focus instead on OLE's linking features.

Part 1

To create a link to
an *Excel* chart,
you first select the
entire chart.
Then, you copy it
to the clipboard.
Next, you switch
back to the client
application.

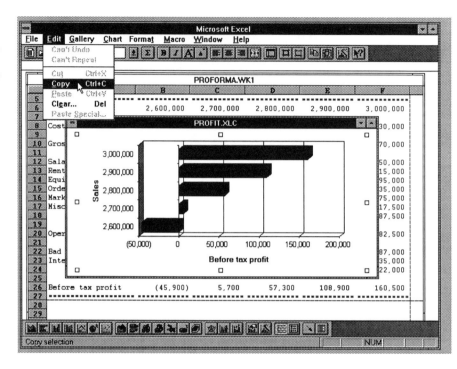

Part 2

Here, the client is
Write. To insert
the link to the
chart, issue the
Paste Link
command from
the Edit menu.

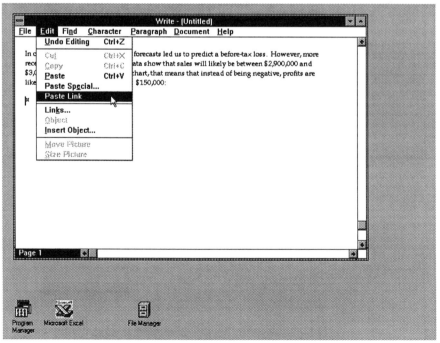

Figure 12-3   How to insert a link to an *Excel* chart into a Write document

Part 3

Now, the linked chart appears in the Write document.

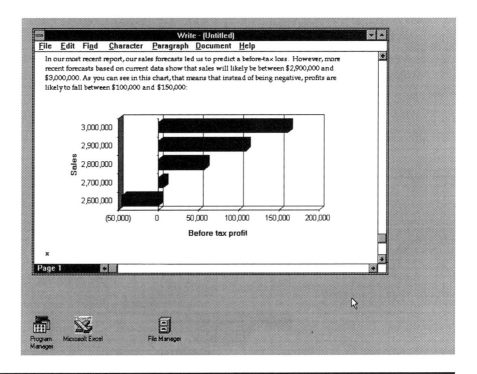

Figure 12-3　　　How to insert a link to an *Excel* chart into a Write document (continued)

The Object Packager　　　The Object Packager is an accessory program that lets you create an icon for an object that you then embed in a document. This may be useful if you don't want a complete representation of a source document in the destination document, but you do want to be able to access the source document directly. The Object Packager lets you specify the contents of a package, select a different icon for it, or change its description.

It's not always necessary to use the Object Packager if you want an icon to represent a linked or embedded object. Some kinds of source documents are automatically represented as icons. For example, when you paste a sound into a document, it shows up as a Sound Recorder icon.

Perspective

In spite of its sophistication, the version of OLE that's a part of *Windows* 3.1 isn't as useful as you might hope. First, not all applications support OLE, and many of those that do support it only partially. For example, you can link to an

Windows keeps track of linked files. When you open a document that contains links to files that have been changed, a dialog box prompts you so you can update the links.

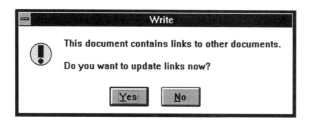

Figure 12-4   How OLE lets you manage references to linked documents

Excel chart from Write, but you can't link to *Excel* from Microsoft's more powerful word processor, *Word for Windows*. Second, because the programs that do support OLE use interfaces that aren't completely consistent, it's harder to work with them than it should be.

Within *Windows* itself, only Paintbrush, Sound Recorder, Write, and Cardfile support OLE. But they do so more as "proofs of concept" than for real application work. As a result, the OLE capabilities of these programs aren't very useful. For instance, how often will you want to embed a Paintbrush graphic in a Cardfile document or a Sound Recorder sound in a Write document?

On the positive side, the OLE that's in *Windows* 3.1 isn't the state of the art. It's really OLE version 1. Microsoft has already released specifications for OLE version 2, which is more powerful, more consistent, and more usable. Because these specifications are already in the hands of developers, they will have enough lead time to integrate OLE version 2 into their applications before it becomes generally available with the next release of *Windows*. OLE version 2 represents a step into the future. With it, you can expect to see more modularity, both in application programs (as with the Graph, Draw, and Equation Editor programs that come with *Word for Windows*) and in the documents they create.

Summary

- *Object Linking and Embedding* provides a sophisticated mechanism that lets programs work together. However, not all programs support OLE, and those that do support it in inconsistent ways.

- OLE lets you *embed* or *link* an object created in a *server application* into a *destination document* created in a *client application*. Some OLE-capable programs can work only as servers, others can work only as clients, and still others can work as both.

- An *embedded object* becomes a part of its destination document, while a *linked object* does not. You can access an embedded object or linked object with the server application that created it directly through the destination document.

- *Dynamic Data Exchange (DDE)* is the predecessor and underlying technology for OLE.

- The *Object Packager* accessory program lets you create icons that represent objects that you can then embed in documents.

- OLE version 2, available in a future release of *Windows*, will solve some of the problems with the current version of OLE.

Keyboard alternatives and shortcuts

General key combinations that apply throughout *Windows*

Alt+Tab	Switch to another program by selecting the one you want as you scan through the names of those that are running.
Alt+Esc	Switch to the next program.
Ctrl+Esc	Access the Task List dialog box.
Alt+F4	Close the current application window and end the program running in it.
Ctrl+F4	Close the current document window.
Ctrl+F6	Switch to the next document window.
Alt+Enter	Switch between full-screen and windowed display for a DOS program (386 enhanced mode only).
Print Screen	Store a bitmap representation of the current screen on the clipboard; for a DOS program in full-screen display, store the text from the screen on the clipboard.
Alt+Print Screen	Store a bitmap representation of the current window on the clipboard.
F1	Start Help for the current program.

Menus

How to access a menu

Alt, *underlined character*	Access the program menu with *underlined character* in its menu name.
Alt, Spacebar	Access the control menu of the current application window.
Alt, Hyphen	Access the control menu of the current document window.

Menus (continued)

Alt, Left or Right arrow keys, Enter

Move the highlight to the menu bar, scroll from one menu to another, and access the menu.

Esc   Remove the highlight from the menu bar and return to the current program's workspace.

How to issue a command from an accessed menu

underlined character   Issue the menu command with *underlined character* in its name.

Up or Down arrow keys, Enter

Move the highlight to the menu command you want, then issue it.

Esc   Dismiss the selected menu and return the highlight to the menu bar so you can choose another menu.

Dialog boxes

How to activate a command button

Enter   Activate the command button that has the focus, or if the focus isn't on a command button, activate the default command button.

Esc   Activate the Cancel command button to dismiss the dialog box.

Alt+*underlined character*

Activate the command button that has *underlined character* in its name.

How to move the focus from one dialog box control to another

Tab   Move the focus forward from one control to another.

Shift+Tab   Move the focus backward from one control to another.

Alt+*underlined character*

Move the focus to the control with *underlined character* in its name.

How to set dialog box controls

Alt+*underlined character*

Set the check box with *underlined character* in its name on or off. (Focus need not be on the check box.)

Select the option button setting with *underlined character* in its name. (Focus need not be on the option button array.)Dialog boxes

Spacebar   Switch a check box setting on or off. (Focus must be on the check box.)

Arrow keys   Select a different option button in the array. (Focus must be on the option button array.)

Move the highlight to the item you want to select in a list. (Focus must be on the list.)

Dialog boxes (continued)

character string   Move the highlight to the first item in the scrolling list box that matches the *character string*. (Focus must be on the list.)

Alt+Down arrow   Access a drop-down list box. (Focus must be on the drop-down list box.)

Editing text

How to move the insertion point and select text

Left arrow	Move the cursor left one character.
Right arrow	Move the cursor right one character.
Up arrow	Move the cursor up one line.
Down arrow	Move the cursor down one line.
Ctrl+Right arrow	Move the cursor right one word.
Ctrl+Left arrow	Move the cursor left one word.
Home	Move the cursor to the beginning of the line.
End	Move the cursor to the last character in the line.
Page Up	Move the cursor up one screen.
Page Down	Move the cursor down one screen.
Ctrl+Home	Move the cursor to the beginning of the document.
Ctrl+End	Move the cursor to the last character in the document.

Shift with any of the above
Extend the selection.

How to copy, cut, and paste text and undo your last editing change

Ctrl+*x* or Shift+Delete
Cut the selection to the clipboard.

Ctrl+*c* or Ctrl+Insert
Copy the selection to the clipboard.

Ctrl+*v* or Shift+Insert
Paste the clipboard's contents at the insertion point.

Ctrl+*z* or Alt+Backspace
Reverse the last editing change.

Program Manager

Enter	When a program group icon is selected, open its window. When a program icon is selected, start the associated application program.
Ctrl+F6	Move the highlight to the icon or group window for the next program group.
Arrow keys	When the highlight is in a group window, move the highlight left, right, up, or down.
Shift+F4	Arrange open group windows with the Tile command.
Shift+F5	Arrange open group windows with the Cascade command.

File Manager

Regardless of where the highlight is located

Tab or F6	Move the highlight forward from the tree pane to the directory pane, from the directory pane to the drive icons, or from the drive icons to the tree pane.
Ctrl+Tab or Ctrl+F6	Switch to the next directory window.
Ctrl+*letter*	Switch the current directory window to drive *letter*.
- (hyphen)	Collapse the current directory in the tree pane.
+	Expand the current directory in the tree pane one level.
*	Expand the current directory in the tree pane completely.
Shift+F4	Arrange open directory windows with the Tile command.
Shift+F5	Arrange open directory windows with the Cascade command.

When the highlight is on one of the drive icons

Left or Right arrow	Move the highlight to the icon to the left or right of its current location.
letter	Move the highlight to drive *letter*.
Spacebar	Switch the current directory window to the highlighted drive.
Enter	Open a new directory window for the highlighted drive.

When the highlight is in the tree pane

Enter	Expand the current directory one level (if it isn't expanded) or collapse it (if it is expanded).
Left arrow or Backspace	Move the highlight to the directory that's superior to the current directory.
Right arrow	Move the highlight to the first directory that's subordinate to the current directory.
Up or Down arrow	Move the highlight to the directory icon immediately above or below the current directory in the tree pane, regardless of its relationship to the current directory.
Home	Move the highlight to the icon for the home directory.

File Manager (continued)

End	Move the highlight to the icon for the last directory in the tree pane.
character	Move the highlight to the next directory in the tree pane whose name starts with *character*.

When the highlight is in the directory pane

Enter	If the selected file is a program file, launch the program. If the selected file is a document associated with a program, launch the program, then open the file with it.
Left or Right arrow	Move the highlight to the icon to the left or right of its current location.
Up or Down arrow	Move the highlight to the icon above or below its current location.
Home	Move the highlight to the first item in the list (the arrow that represents the superior directory).
End	Move the highlight to the icon for the last file in the list.
character	Move the highlight to the icon for the next file whose name starts with that *character*.
Shift+Arrow key	Extend the selection to include adjacent icons.
Shift+F8	Enter and exit non-adjacent selection mode.
Spacebar	Extend the non-adjacent selection to include the currently marked file.
Ctrl+/ or just /	Select all of the files and directories in the directory pane.
**Ctrl+\ or just **	Deselect all of the files and directories in the directory pane except the one at the current location of the highlight.

Index

A

Accessing
    control menu, 67, 69, 75
    Control Panel, 247, 248
    Help, 122-123
    Print Manager, 230, 231
    Task List, 82, 265
Accessories
    groups, 58, 59, 171-172, 287-288
    programs, 58, 171, 172, 287-303
Active
    program, 58
    window, 58, 95
Adapter, 5, 14
Add to Program Group drop-down list box
    (Windows Setup), 274, 275
Add/Remove Windows Components command
    (Windows Setup), 305-307
Advanced Options dialog box (PIF Editor), 281
Advanced printer options, 236, 238
Alarm menu (Calendar), 298
Alert Always command (Print Manager), 234, 235
All File Details command (File Manager), 208, 210
Alt+
    Enter, 264, 279
    Esc, 59, 265
    F4, 42, 75, 77
    Hyphen, 67, 69, 75
    keys to access menus, 66-67
    Spacebar, 67, 69, 75
    Tab, 59, 60, 87, 254, 264, 265
Analog view (Clock), 297
Anti-Virus program (DOS 6.0), 196, 307-308
Applets (accessory programs), 18, 58, 171, 172, 287-303
Application
    menu, 66-68
    program, 18
    window, 39, 43, 47, 75-76, 95
Applications program group, 171-174, 258
Archive attribute, 198, 199
Arrange Icons
    File Manager command, 218, 219
    Program Manager command, 72, 73-75, 176, 177
    Task List button, 81, 84
ASCII text file, 292
Associate command (File Manager), 198, 200, 201-202
Association of file extensions, 28, 134, 187-190, 200, 221-222
Attributes (DOS), 198, 199

B

Back command button (Help), 123
Background processing (Print Manager), 229
Backspace key to delete text, 111
Backup program (DOS 6.0), 196, 308-309
BAT extension, 260, 274, 276
Batch files, 176, 260
BBS, 294
Bit-mapped graphics file (BMP), 294
Blocking text, 111, 113, 114-115
Boot, 19
Border, 48, 50
Browse command button
    Associate dialog box (File Manager), 200, 201
    Change Icon dialog box (Program Manager), 187
    Run dialog box (Program Manager), 189, 191
    Setup Applications dialog box (Windows Setup), 274, 275
Bullet, 300
Bulletin board system, 294
By File Type command (File Manager), 208, 212-214
Byte, 7

C

Calculator accessory program, 298
Calendar accessory program, 298, 299
Canceling your last editing change, 116
Cardfile accessory program, 294, 295
Cartridge drive, 8
Cascade
    File Manager command, 137, 144, 218, 219, 220-221
    Program Manager command, 73, 74, 176, 177, 178
    Task List button, 81, 84
Cathode ray tube, 4
CD command (DOS), 23
CD-ROM drive, 302
Centered alignment (Write), 290
Central processing unit, 11-13, 233, 234
Change Icon dialog box (Program Manager), 188
Change System Settings command (Windows Setup), 304, 306
Change-directory command (DOS), 23

Auto
Auto Arrange command (Program Manager), 72, 73, 75, 176, 177
AUTOEXEC.BAT, 37, 292

Changing
  associations, 200-202
  current directory (File Manager), 136
  current drive (File Manager), 142, 143
  printers, 107
  widths of a directory window's panes, 210
Character Map accessory program, 298-301
Character menu (Write), 289
Check box, 69, 70, 71
Click, 6, 45
Client application, 313
Clipboard, 95, 113, 116-119, 124, 301
  and DOS programs, 265-271
Clipboard Viewer program, 303-304, 305
Clock accessory program, 297
Clock speed, 12-13
Clone (PC), 3
Close command
  application program, 95
  application window, 75-77
  control menu, 77, 265
Close Window on Exit option (PIF Editor), 279
Closing
  document, 103
  DOS program's window, 264-265
CLP file, 303-304
Collapse Branch command (File Manager), 137, 207
Collapsing directories, 134, 137, 139, 141-142, 207
Color (Control Panel option), 249
COM extension, 260, 274, 276
Combo box, 69, 71
Command
  button, 69, 70, 71
  line (for a program item icon), 186
  prompt, 20, 21, 262, 263, 265
Compare function (Microsoft Backup), 309
CONFIG.SYS, 292
Configuration of your system, 37, 304
Confirmation command (File Manager), 214-215
Connect Network Drive command (File Manager), 205, 206
Contents command (Help), 122, 125
Context-sensitive help, 122
Control menu, 42, 43, 66
  application window, 75-76
  box, 42, 43, 69, 77, 265
  commands, 68-69, 75-76
  document window, 75-76
  DOS program icon, 266, 267, 268
  ending an application program, 77
Control Panel program, 247-256
Copy command
  application program, 95, 113, 117
  control menu for DOS application, 266, 267, 268, 270

Copy command (continued)
  DOS, 23
  File Manager, 150, 153-155, 197, 198
  Help, 124
  Program Manager, 174, 176
Copy Disk command (File Manager), 160, 162-164, 205
Copying
  data in a DOS program, 265-271
  files and directories in the File Manager, 148, 150-151
  program item icons, 181-184
  text, 113, 116-119
Corner, 48, 50
CPU, 11-13, 233, 236
  Create Directory command (File Manager), 155, 198, 202
Creating
  program item icon, 174, 176, 184-185, 274 278-279, 280
  program group icon, 174-176, 179, 180
  PIF, 267-282
CRT, 4
Ctrl key
  copying and moving program items in Program Manager, 181-184
  copying and moving file icons in File Manager, 150, 151
  moving the cursor with arrow keys for text editing, 111
  selecting file icons in File Manager, 147, 149, 150
Ctrl+
  c, 116
  Enter (Write), 288
  Esc, 81, 82, 265
  F4 , 75
  v, 116, 271
  x, 116
  z, 116
Current directory
  DOS program, 276, 277
  File Manager, 136, 138, 139
  window, 144
Current drive, 133, 205, 206
Cursor, 110, 111, 112
Customizing program groups, 177-187
Cut command, 95, 113

D
Date/Time option (Control Panel), 249, 250, 297
Day view (Calendar), 298, 299
DDE, 319
Decimal tab (Write), 290, 291
Default
  associations, 190
  command button (dialog box), 70
  PIFs, 272

Default (continued)
    printer, 198, 236, 238
    program groups, 171-174
Delay Before First Repeat option (Keyboard Control
        Panel option), 251, 252
Delete command
    DOS, 23
    File Manager, 197, 198
    Program Manager, 174, 176
Delete key
    File Manager, 148
    text editing, 111, 114-115
Deleted files, 309-310
Deleting
    files and directories (File Manager), 148
    print jobs, 230, 232
    program groups, 179, 181
    program item icons, 181, 184
    text, 111, 114-115
Desktop, 39, 43, 46, 110, 265
    double-click to access Task List, 81, 82
    PC, 3
Desktop (Control Panel option), 249, 254-255
Destination In drop-down list box (Copy Disk com-
        mand, File Manager), 162, 163
Device driver, 23, 249
Dialog box controls, 69-71
Digital view (Clock), 297
Digitized sound, 301
Directories list box (Open dialog box), 96, 98-102
Directory, 23, 26-28, 134, 198, 202
    deleting, 148
    icon (File Manager), 134, 136
    pane, 134, 135, 210
    tree, 134
    window, 133-134, 135, 144, 207-214
    window for diskette drive, 218, 219
Directory command (DOS), 23
Directory Only command (File Manager), 207, 208, 209
Directory window name command (File Manager), 218-
        219
Disabling the Print Manager, 251-252, 253
Disconnect Network Drive command (File Manager),
        205, 206
Disk
    cartridge, 8
    drive identifier, 25-26
Disk menu (File Manager), 160-164, 205-206
Diskette, 9-11
    capacities, 11
    copying, 160, 162-164
    drive, 9-11, 23
    formatting, 160, 161
    specifying in dialog box, 103
Display adapter, 5
Display Usage options (PIF Editor), 279, 280
Document icon (File Manager), 222, 224

Document menu (Write), 289
Document window, 39, 43, 95
    control menu, 75-76
    maximizing, 47
    minimizing, 47
    restoring, 47
DOS (Disk Operating System), 17, 19-25
    application programs, 18, 258-283
    command prompt, 20, 21
    commands, 23, 133
    program icons, 56
    program window, 268, 269-271
    shell, 23, 133
DOS 6.0
    Tools menu (File Manager), 196
    Windows utilities, 307-310
DOSPRMPT.PIF, 272
Dot-matrix printer, 6
Double spacing (Write), 290
DoubleSpace, 196
Double-click, 6, 45
Double-Click Speed option (Mouse Control Panel
        option), 250, 251
Download, 295
Drag, 6, 45
    copying or moving a program item icon, 181-184
    creating a program item icon, 184, 189
    moving a window, 48, 49
    sizing a window, 48, 50-51
    selecting text, 111
Drawing program, 294
Drive
    icon (File Manager), 137, 142, 143, 218
    letter, 25-26
Drivers (Control Panel option), 249
Drives drop-down list box (Open dialog box), 96, 98-
        102, 104
Drop-down
    list box, 69, 71
    menu, 66
Dynamic Data Exchange, 319

E
Edit command (control menu for DOS application
        window or icon), 266, 268, 269
Edit menu, 92-95, 113
    Write, 288, 289
EGA, 5
Electronics unit, 4
Embedded object, 313-318
Emulation, 236
End key, 110
End Task command button of Task List, 81
Enhanced Graphics Adapter, 5
Equation Editor, 314-318
EXE extension, 260, 274, 276

Exit command
    application program, 77, 95, 106
    command line for MS-DOS Prompt, 265
    File Manager, 198, 204
Exit Windows command (Program Manager), 77, 176
Expand All command (File Manager), 137, 207
Expand Branch command (File Manager), 137, 141, 207
Expand One Level command (File Manager), 137, 207
Expandable directories, 136
Expanding directories, 134, 137, 139, 141-142
Extended VGA, 5
Extension, 28-29, 198, 200, 201-202, 212
    association, 187-190, 221-222

F
F1 (to access help), 122
F5 (to refresh a File Manager directory window), 137
Fast Alt+Tab Switching, 59, 60, 87, 254, 264, 265
File, 7, 23
    icon (File Manager), 134
    name, 28-29
    specifications, 25-29, 96-102
File Manager, 21, 23-25, 26, 30, 132-168, 194-226
    and DOS programs, 260, 262
File menu, 77, 92-95, 77
    application program, 96-108
    File Manager, 147-157, 196-204
    Program Manager, 174-176
    Write, 287-288, 289
File Name
    list box (Open dialog box), 98-102
    text box (Open dialog box), 96-102
Find menu (Write program), 289
Fixed disk, 8
Flash If Inactive command (Print Manager), 234, 235
Floppy disk, 9
Focus (dialog box), 69
Font command (File Manager), 214, 215, 216-217
Font dialog box, 238, 239
Font, 298, 300-301
    File Manager, 214, 215, 216-217
    groups, 254
    printing, 238-244
    substitution (PostScript for TrueType), 242, 243, 244
Fonts (Control Panel option), 249, 252-254
Format Disk command (File Manager), 160, 161, 205
Formatting
    codes, 292
    diskettes, 160
    text (Write), 289
Full Screen option of Display Usage (PIF Editor), 279-280
Full-screen display (DOS program), 264, 268, 269-271

G
Games program group, 171-173
Generic PIFs, 272
Group
    font, 254
    icon, 56
    window, 58, 59, 171-174
Group-window name command (Program Manager), 75, 176, 177

H
Hard disk drive, 7-9, 23
    recommended size, 7
Hard page break, 288
Hardware, 3-15
Header command (Write), 289
Help feature, 122-127
Help menu, 92-95, 122, 264
Hercules Monochrome adapter, 5
Hidden attribute, 134, 136, 198, 199
High Priority command (Print Manager), 233, 234
History command button (Help), 123
Home key, 110
Hourglass icon, 37
Hypertext in Help, 123

I
I-beam, 110, 111, 112
Icon
    arranging (Program Manager), 72, 73
    disk drive (File Manager), 133
    document file associated with an application program, 136
    DOS application, 266, 267, 268
    File Manager, 23-25, 134, 136
    fonts types, 239
    minimized directory windows, 144
    Print Manager, 230, 232
    program item, 186, 187, 188
    Program Manager, 20, 22, 39, 73
Ignore If Inactive command (Print Manager), 234, 235
Indent markers (Write), 290
Indicate Expandable Branches command (File Manager), 136, 137, 206, 207
Information utility, 294
Input devices, 4, 5-6, 7
Input/output services, 23
Insert Object command (Write), 288, 289
Inserting
    special characters, 300-301
    text, 111, 112
Insertion point, 95, 110-111, 266, 267, 268
Installing
    fonts, 251
    hardware, 304
    software, 72
    printer driver, 235-236, 237

Intel processors, 12-13
Internal clock, 250
Internal memory, 13-14
    and DOS, 19
    and multitasking, 21-22
International (Control Panel option), 249
I/O services, 23
Issuing menu commands, 66-69

J

Justified alignment (Write), 290

K

Keyboard, 5-6, 23
    shortcuts for Copy, Cut, and Paste, 116
    shortcuts for menu commands, 68
    to move the insertion point, 110-111
    to select text, 111, 113
Keyboard (Control Panel option), 249, 251, 252
Kilobyte (KB), 10-11, 14

L

Label (program item icon), 185, 186
Label Disk command (File Manager), 205-206
Label text box (Format Disk of File Manager), 160, 161
Laptop PC, 3, 251
Laser printer, 6
Left alignment (Write), 290
Left mouse button (swapping with the right button), 250, 251
Left-aligned tab (Write), 290, 291
Limitations of help, 124
Line
    size (Paintbrush), 292, 293
    spacing (Write), 290
Linked object, 313-314, 318-321
Links command (Write), 288, 289
List box, 69
List Files of Type drop-down list box (Open dialog box), 98-102
Local printer, 229
Logical drive, 25-26
Low Priority command (Print Manager), 233, 234

M

Macintosh, 310-311
Macro, 296-297
Main program group, 133, 172, 174, 303
Make System Disk command (File Manager), 205, 206
Make-directory command (DOS), 23
Mark command (control menu for DOS application window or icon), 266, 268, 269
Maximize button, 46, 47, 66
Maximize command, 66
Maximizing
    application windows, 47
    directory windows, 144
    document windows, 47
    help, 122-123

MCI, 302
MD command (DOS), 23
Media Control Interface, 302
Media Player accessory program, 302
Medium Priority command (Print Manager), 233, 234
Megabyte (MB), 7, 10-11, 14
Megahertz (Mhz), 12-13
Menu
    bar, 42, 43, 66
    commands, 66-69
    name, 66
Messages (Print Manager), 234, 235
Microprocessor, 11-13
    time when printing, 233, 234
Microsoft
    Anti-Virus program (DOS 6.0), 307-308
    Backup program (DOS 6.0), 308-309
    Tools program group, 307
    Undelete program (DOS 6.0), 309-310
MIDI, 302
MIDI Mapper (Control Panel option), 249
Minimize button, 46, 47, 66
Minimize command, 66
Minimize on Use command
    File Manager, 214, 215
    Program Manager, 73, 176, 177
Minimized
    application icons, 60-63
    directory window icons, 218, 219
    icon control menu, 75
Minimizing, 39
    application windows, 47
    directory windows, 144
    document windows, 47
    help, 122-123
Minimums to run Windows
    internal memory, 14
    processor, 12-13
Minus sign (on File Manager icons), 134, 136, 138, 139, 140, 207
Modem, 14
Modes
    386 enhanced mode, 266-271
    standard mode, 266-267
Modification date, 208, 210
Modifying
    PIFs, 280-282
    program item icons, 185-187
Monitor, 4-5, 23
Monochrome monitor, 4
Month command (Calendar), 298
MORICONS.DLL, 187, 188
Mouse, 6, 23, 44-45
Mouse (Control Panel option), 249, 250-251
Mouse Tracking Speed option (Mouse Control Panel option), 250, 251
Mouse Trails option (Mouse Control Panel option), 251

Move command
File Manager, 197, 198
Program Manager, 174, 176
Move Picture command (Write), 288, 289
Moving
data through the clipboard (DOS program), 265-271
directory windows, 144
files and directories, 148, 150-151
program item icons, 181, 184
text, 113, 116-119
windows, 48
MS-DOS Prompt, 260, 262-263, 272
Multimedia extensions, 301-302
Multiple documents open at the same time, 102
Multitasking, 21-22, 36, 58
Musical Instrument Digital Interface, 302

N

Name command (File Manager), 208, 210
Navigating
directory tree (File Manager), 207, 209
help information, 123, 125-127
Network, 233, 234, 235
adapter, 14
connections, 205, 206
drive, 26
print queue, 229, 233, 234, 235
printer, 229
Network (Control Panel option), 249
Network Connections command
File Manager, 205, 206
Print Manager, 234, 235
Network Settings command (Print Manager), 234, 235
New command
application program, 95, 102
Program Manager, 174, 176, 184
New Window command (File Manager), 137, 218, 219
Next command (control menu of document window), 76
Notepad accessory program, 56-58, 292
entering text, 112
menus, 92-97
opening a file, 96-102

O

Object, 313
Object command (Write), 288, 289
Object Linking and Embedding, 288, 303, 312-323
version 2, 322
Object Packager accessory program, 302-303, 321
Object-oriented graphics program, 294
OLE, 288, 303, 312-323
version 2, 322
Open command
application programs, 95, 96-102
File Manager, 196-197, 198
PIF Editor, 280
Program Manager, 174, 176

Open dialog box, 96-102
Opening
multiple directory windows, 142, 143, 144
new directory window, 218
new document, 102
Operating modes (standard and 386 enhanced), 264-267, 276, 281
Operating system, 17
functions, 19-25
programs, 17
Option button, 70, 71
Optional Parameters text box (PIF Editor), 276, 277
Options command (Calendar), 298
Options menu
File Manager, 214-218
Program Manager, 72-73, 175-177
Print Manager, 233-235, 236
Windows Setup, 272, 304
Other Net Queue command (Print Manager), 233, 234
Outline font, 239, 242
Output devices, 4-5, 6, 7

P

Page Layout command (Write), 289
Page-Down key, 110
Page-Up key, 110
Paintbrush accessory program, 292-294
Painting program, 294
Pane (directory window), 134, 135, 207, 208, 209
Paper
orientation option, 103, 107
size option, 103, 107
source option, 103, 107
Paragraph menu (Write), 289
Parameters (for a DOS program), 276, 277
Partial Details command (File Manager), 208, 210-211
Password Options (Desktop Control Panel option), 254, 255
Paste command
application program, 95, 113, 116, 118
control menu for icon for minimized DOS program, 266, 267, 268, 271
Paste Link command (Write), 288, 289, 318, 320
Paste Special command (Write), 288, 289, 318
Path, 26-28, 276
Pattern options (Desktop Control Panel option), 254, 255
Pause button (Print Manager), 230, 232
PC (personal computer), 3-15
Picture element, 4-5
PIF, 259, 262, 267-282, 304
extension, 260
PIF Editor, 275-282
Pixel, 4-5
Plain text file, 292
Plus sign
as you drag File Manager icons, 150, 151
on File Manager directory icons, 134, 136, 138, 139, 140, 207

Point (mouse action), 44, 45
Point size (font option), 238, 239, 240-241
Pointer, 6, 44, 45, 48, 50, 110, 111
Port, 14
Ports (Control Panel option), 249
PostScript, 242, 243, 244
Print command
    application program, 95, 103, 106-108
    File Manager, 198, 199-200
Print
    file, 229, 233, 234
    queue, 229-232
Print File Size command (Print Manager), 233, 234
Print Manager, 106, 108, 229-238, 251-252, 253
Print Screen key, 266, 267, 268
Print Setup command, 95, 103, 107
Printer, 6, 23
    driver, 235-236, 237
    emulation, 236
    font, 238-239, 240, 241, 242
    options, 236, 238
Printer Setup command (Print Manager), 234, 235, 236-238
Printers (Control Panel option), 249, 251-252, 253
Printing, 103, 106-108
    from File Manager, 199-200
    help information, 123
    performance, 233, 234, 251-252
    speed and fonts, 240-241, 242
Priority options (Print Manager), 233, 234
Processor, 11-13, 233, 234
Program conventions, 18
Program Filename text box (PIF Editor), 276, 277
Program group, 56, 171-174
Program icon
    Program Manager, see program item icon
    File Manager, 222, 223, 260
Program Information File (PIF), 259, 262, 267-282, 304
Program item icon (Program Manager), 56, 171-174, 187, 191, 260
    creating by dragging from File Manager, 278-279, 280
    for a document, 184-185
    for DOS programs, 258
    properties of, 185-187
Program Item Properties dialog box, 185-187, 188
Program Manager, 20, 21, 22, 37, 39, 170-192
    and DOS programs, 258, 259, 261
    menu commands, 174-177
Properties command
    File Manager, 185, 198, 199
    Program Manager, 176, 199
Pull-down menu, 66

Q
Queue, 233
Quick Format option of Format Disk command, 160, 161

Quitting
    a program, 58, 76-77, 81, 106
    MS-DOS Prompt, 265
    Windows, 42, 44, 77

R
Random Access Memory (RAM), 13-14
    and DOS, 19
    and multitasking, 21-22
RD command (DOS), 23
Read Me program item icon, 189, 190
Read-only attribute, 198, 199
Recorder accessory program, 296-297
Recovering deleted files, 309-310
Refresh command
    File Manager, 137, 218, 219
    Print Manager, 233, 234
Removable hard disk drive, 8
Remove-directory command (DOS), 23
Removing
    fonts, 251-252
    Windows components, 305-307
Rename command
    DOS, 23
    File Manager, 155, 156-157, 197, 198
Renaming a program group, 179
Repaginate command (Write), 288, 289
Repeat Rate option (Keyboard Control Panel option), 251, 252
Replace command (Write), 289
Reserve Shortcut Keys options (PIF Editor), 279
Resolution
    monitor, 5
    printer, 6
    screen and font size, 215
Restore button, 46, 47, 66
Restore command, 66
Restore function (Microsoft Backup), 309
Restoring
    application windows, 47
    document windows, 47
    help windows, 123
    minimized application icons, 60-63
Restricting files in a directory window, 212-214
Retrieving a file (Open command), 96-102
Right alignment (Write), 290
Root directory, 26, 140
    creating, 160
Ruler On/Off command (Write), 290
Run command
    File Manager, 198, 199, 222, 225, 259
    Program Manager, 68, 72, 176, 189-191, 259
Running DOS programs under Windows, 258-283

S
Save command
    application programs, 95, 103, 104-105

Save command (continued)
    Calendar, 298
    PIF Editor, 280
Save As command
    application programs, 95, 103, 104-105
    Calendar, 298
    PIF Editor, 277-279, 280
Save Settings on Exit command
    File Manager, 214, 215, 218
    Program Manager, 72-73, 176, 177
Scalable font, 239, 242
Scientific view (Calculator), 298, 300
Screen saver, 254-255
Scroll
    arrow, 48, 52
    bar, 48, 52
    box, 48, 52
Search command (File Manager), 198, 202, 203
Search button and dialog box (Help), 125-126
Search for Help On command (Help), 122, 123
Search menu (Cardfile accessory), 294
Search Results window (File Manager), 203
Searching for applications (Windows Setup), 272-274
Select Drive command (File Manager), 205, 206
Select Files command (File Manager), 147, 150, 153,
    198, 203-204
Selected Net Queue command (Print Manager), 233,
    234
Selecting
    files and directories (File Manager), 147, 149
    parts of an image (Paintbrush), 293, 294
    program group icons, 178
    text, 111, 113, 114-115
Selection string, 203-204
Server application, 313
Set Up Applications command (Windows Setup), 272-
    275, 304, 306
Setting
    date and time, 250
    default printer, 236, 238
    tab stops and indents (Write), 290, 291
Settings menu
    Clock, 297
    Control Panel, 247, 248
Shell program, 37, 39, 42, 77, 198
    changing, 222-223
Shift key
    copying and moving file icons in File Manager, 147,
    149
    extending a selection, 111, 113
    selecting file icons in File Manager, 147, 149
    with F8 to select noncontiguous files (File Man-
    ager), 150, 151
    with File Manager Tile command, 218, 220-221
Simulated DOS environment, 262-263
Single spacing (Write), 290
Size Picture command (Write), 288, 289

Sizing directory windows, 144
Slider, 71
Soft page break, 288
Sort by Date command (File Manager), 208, 212
Sort by Name command (File Manager), 208, 212
Sort by Size command (File Manager), 208, 212
Sort by Type command (File Manager), 208, 212
Sound (Control Panel option), 249
Sound Recorder accessory program, 301-302
Sound System for Windows, 302
SoundBlaster, 302
Source In drop-down list box (Copy Disk command,
    File Manager), 162, 163
Special characters
    accessing with Character Map, 298-301
    in file names, 29
Spin box, 71
Split bar, 208, 210
Split command (File Manager), 208, 210
Standard
    associations, 200
    density diskette, 11
    menus and commands in Windows programs, 92-95
    mode, 264-267, 276, 281
    TrueType fonts, 240
    view (Calculator), 298, 300
Starting
    DOS program, 259-263
    programs automatically, 191, 297
    programs from the File Manager, 221-222
    programs from the Program Manager, 56-58, 187-
    191
    programs with the Run command of the Program
    Manager, 72
    the File Manager, 135
    the Print Manager, 230, 231
    Windows, 37-39
StartUp program group, 171-173, 191, 297
Start-up Directory text box (PIF Editor), 276, 277
Status Bar command (File Manager), 214, 215
Subdirectory, 26-28, 134, 206
Super VGA (SVGA), 5, 215
Swap Left/Right Buttons option (Mouse Control Panel
    option), 250, 251
Switch To command (control menu), 81, 82, 265
Switching from
    DOS program to another program, 264
    one program to another, 58-63
    one program to another with the Task List, 81, 83
    windowed and full-screen display (DOS program),
    264
SyDOS, 8
Symbol font, 240, 243
System
    attribute, 198, 199
    disk, 206
    files, 134, 136

System (continued)
    formatting, 160
SYSTEM.INI, 222
Systems unit, 4, 5, 6-14

T
Tab
    key to move focus from one dialog box control to
        another, 69
    key to move highlight in the File Manager, 137
    stops (Write), 290, 291
Tabs command (Write), 289
Task List dialog box, 76, 81-84, 265
Task Manager, 81-84
Task switching, 22
Telecommunications, 294-296
Terminal accessory program, 294-296
Text
    box, 69, 70, 71, 96-102
    editor, 292
    entering and editing, 110-119
    tool (Paintbrush), 293
Tile
    button of Task List, 81, 84
    File Manager command, 137, 144, 218, 219, 220-221
    Program Manager command, 73, 74, 176, 177, 178
Time/Date sent command (Print Manager), 233, 234
Title bar, 42, 43, 48
    directory window, 133, 141, 144
Toolbox (Paintbrush), 292, 293
Tools menu (File Manager), 196
Tracks, 160
Tree, 136
    pane, 134, 135, 141
    structure (directories), 26
Tree and Directory command (File Manager), 207, 208
Tree menu (File Manager), 136, 141, 206, 207
Tree Only command (File Manager), 207, 208
TrueType, 238, 239-241, 242
    equivalents of PostScript fonts, 243
TrueType Font Assistant, 253-254
TrueType Font Pack, 242, 243, 244
TrueType Font Pack 2, 253-254
Type
    size, 239, 239
    style, 238, 239, 240

U
Undelete program (DOS 6.0), 309-310
Undo command, 95, 116
Upload, 295
Use Print Manager option (Printers Control Panel
    option), 251-252, 253

V
Variety from one Windows system to another, 37-41
VGA (Video Graphics Array), 5

View menu
    Calculator, 298
    Calendar, 298
    File Manager, 207-214
    Print Manager, 233, 234
Virus, 307-308
Volume label, 205
VSAFE program (DOS 6.0), 308

W
Wallpaper, 254, 255
Warning messages, 214-215
Waveform files, 301
Wildcard, 102, 147, 152, 155, 157, 197, 203-204
Win command to start Windows, 20, 21, 37
WIN.INI, 189, 190, 247
Window menu
    File Manager, 144, 218-221
    Program Manager, 73-75, 175, 176, 177
Window Title text box (PIF Editor), 276, 277
Windowed display (DOS program) 264, 268, 269-271,
    279-280
Windows application program, 18
Windows NT, 19
Windows Printing System, 243
Windows Setup
    create a PIF, 272-275
    general, 304-307
Wipe (a virus-infected file), 307
Word for Windows menus, 92-95
Working directory
    DOS program, 276, 277
    program item icon, 185, 186
Write accessory program, 118, 287-292
    menus, 92-97

X
XVGA, 5

Other
* key (File Manager), 137
+ key (File Manager), 137
- key (File Manager), 137
/key (File Manager), 204
? (for parameters for a DOS program), 276, 277
_DEFAULT.PIF, 272
3.5-inch diskette, 9-11
386 Enhanced (Control Panel option), 249
386 enhanced mode, 264-271, 276, 281
386 enhanced mode PIF options, 281
5.25-inch diskette, 9-11
80286 (286) processor, 12-13, 264
80386 (386) processor, 12-13, 264
80486 (486)processor, 12-13
8088 processor, 12-13

Comment Form

Your opinions count

If you have any comments, criticisms, or suggestions for us, I'm eager to get them. Your opinions today will affect our products of tomorrow. And if you find any errors in this book, typographical or otherwise, please point them out so we can correct them in the next printing.

Thanks for your help.

Mike Murach

Book title: The Least You Need to Know about *Windows 3.1*

Dear Mike: _____

_____

_____

_____

_____

_____

_____

_____

_____

_____

_____

_____

_____

_____

_____

_____

_____

Name _____

Company (if company address)_____

Address _____

City, State, Zip _____

Fold where indicated and tape closed.
No postage necessary if mailed in the U.S.

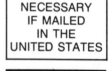

Order Form

Our Ironclad Guarantee

To our customers who order directly from us: You must be satisfied. Our books must work for you, or you can send them back for a full refund...no questions asked.

Name (& Title, if any) _____

Company (if company address)_____

Street address _____

City, State, Zip _____

Phone number (including area code) _____

Fax number (if you fax your order to us) _____

Qty	Product code and title	*Price
Windows		
___LWIN	The Least You Need to Know about *Windows 3.1*	$20.00
Lotus 1-2-3		
___ELTW**	The Essential Guide to *Lotus 1-2-3* for Windows, Release 4	$20.00
___GLOT	The Practical Guide to *Lotus 1-2-3* (for DOS)	25.00
___LLOT	The Least You Need to Know about *Lotus 1-2-3* (for DOS)	20.00
WordPerfect		
___LWP	The Least You Need to Know about *WordPerfect* (for DOS)	$20.00
___WPTU	The *WordPerfect* Tutorial (for DOS)	10.00

Qty	Product code and title	*Price
DOS		
___DOSR	The Only DOS Book You'll Ever Need (2nd Ed.)	$27.50
___LDSR	The Least You Need to Know about DOS (2nd. Ed.)	20.00
___BACK	How to Back Up Your PC	15.00
Multiple Programs		
___DWPL	DOS, *WordPerfect*, and *Lotus* Essentials	$25.00
Business Writing		
___WBPC	Write Better with a PC	$19.95

☐ Bill the appropriate book prices plus UPS shipping and handling (and sales tax in California) to my
    ___VISA ___MasterCard:

Card number _____

Valid thru (month/year) _____

Cardowner's signature _____

☐ Bill me.

☐ Bill my company. P.O.#_____

☐ I want to **save** UPS shipping and handling charges. Here's my check or money order for $_____. California residents, please add sales tax to your total. (Offer valid in the U.S.)

To order more quickly,

Call **toll-free 1-800-221-5528**

(Weekdays, 8 to 5 Pacific Standard Time)

Fax: 1-209-275-9035

Mike Murach & Associates, Inc.

4697 West Jacquelyn Avenue
Fresno, California 93722-6427
(209) 275-3335

* Prices are subject to change. **Please call for current prices.**

** Available September 1993